PRAISE FOR *SOCRATES' CHILDREN*

"When I first began to pursue philosophy, I wanted a single resource to introduce me to all its principal players, to teach me their names, relative importance, and chief works, and to help me think their greatest thoughts. I wanted an introduction that let the philosophers have their say, but at the same time avoided the false impartiality of indifference to truth—one that, moreover, went about the whole daunting business with such brevity, directness, enthusiasm, wonder, storytelling, and humor as would suit my needs as a beginner. That resource did not exist. Now it does. It is *Socrates' Children*."

—**Michael Augros**, Author of *Who Designed the Designer?* and *The Immortal in You*

"The moral, social, and religious problems of our time all ultimately reflect deep philosophical errors and thus, at least in part, require a philosophical solution. Yet philosophy has in recent decades retreated so far within the academy that the average person would not know where to begin to look for instruction. Peter Kreeft has long helped to remedy this problem, and this new work may be his most important yet."

—**Edward Feser**, Professor of Philosophy, Pasadena City College

"Peter Kreeft provides bite-sized snapshots of one hundred of the most famous and influential philosophers who shape, often in unrealized ways, today's world. In his trademark crisp and clear style, he presents ancient, medieval, modern, and contemporary thinkers. While putting each philosopher in historical context, *Socrates' Children* also avoids historical relativism. This book provides both historical context and philosophical summaries of the most important ideas of the most important philosophers. Kreeft focuses on the ideas that make a difference for our lives, as well as on the most influential views of all time."

—**Christopher Kaczor**, Chair of the Department of Philosophy at Loyola Marymount University, St. Thomas Aquinas Fellow for the Renewal of Catholic Intellectual Life for the Word on Fire Institute

I0895679

"Philosophy professors are always seeking ways to reach students with fresh approaches to the wisdom we have found so wonderful. Here is a fine option."

—**Ronda Chervin**, Emerita Professor of Philosophy at Holy Apostles College and Seminary

"True philosophy is a love affair: as Socrates taught long ago, philosophy is born in wonder, and is lived in passionate seeking. In *Socrates' Children*, Peter Kreeft guides the beginner through the history of philosophy with his characteristic wonder, wit, and wisdom. Reading these volumes is like taking a class in philosophy with one of its greatest living teachers. In Kreeft's hands, the history of philosophy becomes a dramatic story, a great conversation punctuated with surprise, humor, and insight. For the beginner curious about philosophy, beware: to pick up *Socrates' Children* is to embark on the great adventure of philosophical thinking, and so to risk falling in love. And when you fall in love, life is changed forever."

—**Paul A. Camacho**, Professor of Philosophy and Associate Director of the Augustinian Institute, Villanova University

SOCRATES' CHILDREN

SOCRATES' CHILDREN

AN INTRODUCTION TO PHILOSOPHY FROM THE 100 GREATEST PHILOSOPHERS

Volume III: Modern Philosophers

Peter Kreeft

Illustrations by Peter Voth

WORD on FIRE INSTITUTE

Published by the Word on Fire Institute, an imprint of
Word on Fire, Elk Grove Village, IL 60007

Printed in the United States of America

Design, typesetting, diagrams, and interior art direction by
Katherine Spitler, Rozann Lee, Cassie Bielak, and Michael Stevens

Cover design and illustrations by Peter Voth

First Edition published 2019 by St. Augustine's Press
Second Edition 2023
26 25 24 23 1 2 3 4

ISBN: 978-1-685780-07-4

Library of Congress Control Number: 2022943791

to William Harry Jellema,
Brand Blanshard,
Balduin Schwarz,
and W. Norris Clarke, SJ,

who taught me how to philosophize

CONTENTS

A Salesman's-Pitch Introduction to This Book xi
A Very Short Introduction to Philosophy xix
A Doable Do-It-Yourself Course in the Classics of Philosophy xxiv
A Personal Bibliography xxvii
A Few Recommended Histories of Philosophy xxx

Introduction to Modern Philosophy xxxii

I. THE EPISTEMOLOGICAL PHILOSOPHERS
55. René Descartes ** 3
56. Blaise Pascal * 26
57. Baruch Spinoza * 38
58. Gottfried Wilhelm Leibniz * 48
59. Francis Bacon 56
60. John Locke * 61
61. George Berkeley * 67
62. David Hume ** 74
63. Thomas Reid 103
64. Immanuel Kant ** 110
65. Johann Gottlieb Fichte 150
66. Friedrich Wilhelm Joseph von Schelling 154
67. Georg Wilhelm Friedrich Hegel ** 156
68. Arthur Schopenhauer 182

II. THE POLITICAL PHILOSOPHERS
Introduction to the Political Philosophers 189
69. Niccolò Machiavelli 190
70. Thomas Hobbes * 202
71. Jean-Jacques Rousseau * 225
72. Karl Marx 241

Conclusion 255

(indicates important philosophers; ** indicates very important philosophers)*

A Salesman's-Pitch Introduction to This Book

Why the History of Philosophy Is the Best Introduction to Philosophy

There have been two very different conceptions of philosophy in the English-speaking world for the last century. Traditionally, philosophy was about life, and it was something to be lived. Philosophers were looked up to as "wise men" rather than "wise guys." Philosophical reason was something computers simply did not have. But ever since (1) Russell and Whitehead's *Principia Mathematica* in 1910, 1912, and 1913; (2) Wittgenstein's *Tractatus* in 1921; and (3) Ayer's *Language, Truth and Logic* in 1936, there has been a new conception of the task of the philosopher: (a) not to tell us what is, but to analyze the language of those who do; (b) in so doing, to imitate scientific and mathematical thinking, which is "digital," rather than ordinary language, which is "analog"; and (c) to that end, to use symbolic, or mathematical, logic (basically, computer logic) rather than traditional, Aristotelian, ordinary-language logic.

Indeed, this has been the mainline conception of philosophy in English-speaking cultures for over half a century. It calls itself "analytic philosophy." It has moved far beyond the early, narrow, and dogmatic claims for it, such as Ayer's, but its *style* of philosophical writing is still easily identifiable: you can spot an analytic philosopher by reading just one paragraph.

Such philosophers are useful as vacuum cleaners and garbage collectors are useful: to identify and dispose of waste. They clean well. But they do not cook very tasty or interesting meals. I think large philosophy departments should have at least one and at most two of them, as restaurants should have cleaning crews.

The best way to teach philosophy is by a story: the dramatic story of the history of philosophy, the narrative of the "great conversation," which you find in the "great books." It's politically incorrect to say it, but there is indeed a canon or list of great books. That's why Plato and Shakespeare never die. Of course, the canon is arguable and not sacrosanct. It's only human. It's not a canon of sacred scriptures.

The most effective way to teach *anything* is by a story, a narrative. All the great teachers used stories, parables, examples, analogies, illustrations. It's really very easy to get ordinary human beings interested in philosophy: just put the picture back into the frame. The frame is the abstract, difficult questions that philosophers ask. The picture is the context of history, where they actually came from: the real, lived human conversations and arguments that passionately divided real individuals like Socrates and the Sophists, and whole cultures like ancient Rome or medieval Christendom and modern, secular, scientific democracies.

The primary reason why the history of philosophy works better than analytic philosophy—the primary reason why most students love it and often become philosophers and philosophy teachers through it—is embarrassingly simple: because the great masters of the past are more *interesting* than present-day philosophers.

But we are too arrogant to admit that. We judge the past by the standards of the present; the opposite idea hardly ever even occurs to us. So we study the past not to learn from them but to teach them, to show how primitive they were compared to ourselves. I refute this "chronological snobbery" by three simple words: Socrates, Plato, Aristotle.

The sciences progress almost automatically; the humanities do not. Philosophy is one of the humanities, not one of the sciences.

Our ancestors made mistakes, just as we do, but different ones. Theirs are now usually obvious to us; our own are not, and therefore are much more harmful. They are the glasses through which we look rather than the things we look at. "To see ourselves as others see us" is to broaden our minds. We wonder how we will we appear to our remote descendants, but we cannot know. We cannot read the books that haven't been written yet. But we can know how we would look to our remote ancestors, for we can read their books.

The only alternative to listening to the many who have already spoken, and died, is listening to the few who are now alive and speaking: ourselves. The first option, often called "tradition," is more democratic. It is what Chesterton called "the democracy of the dead": extending the vote to those who otherwise would be disqualified not by accident of birth but by accident of death.

A scientist studies the history of science as a series of instructive errors and gradual progress to enlightenment. And this is right in science, because in science the past really is inferior to the present, and has been proved to be that. But it is not right to do this in philosophy because philosophy is not science, and past philosophers have *not* been proved to be inferior to present ones. Here is a proof of that fact—or, rather, of the fact that at least unconsciously we *believe* that they were wiser than we are, and not vice versa: we do not speak of "modern wisdom" but of "ancient wisdom." The noun we spontaneously connect with "modern" is not "wisdom" but "knowledge." Knowledge is incremental, like a stairway—it naturally progresses. Wisdom is not. And philosophy is the search for wisdom.

The best way to learn philosophy, then, is through its history. This is true even if your eventual goal is to be an analytic philosopher and analyze the issues logically and not historically (which is a perfectly legitimate and necessary job). For you simply can't find any better teachers to begin with than the ancients, especially Socrates, Plato, and Aristotle, even if you want to move beyond them.

The history of philosophy is not a series of dead facts but living examples. It is not to be studied simply for its own sake. We should apprentice ourselves to the great minds of the past for our sakes, not for theirs; for the sake of the present and the future, not the past.

I have tried just about every possible way to introduce philosophy to beginners (and some impossible ways too), and by far the most effective one I have ever found is the great books, beginning with the dialogues of Plato. (Why anyone would oppose "great books" blows my mind. Do they prefer tiny books, shallow books, or stupid books?) Most of the great books in the history of philosophy are surprisingly short and surprisingly clear, for they were written for intelligent, literate ordinary people, not for other philosophers. (This becomes increasingly rare as we approach the present time.)

If Plato was the first great philosophical *writer*, Socrates, his teacher, was the first great *philosopher*. Plato was to Socrates what Matthew, Mark, Luke, John, and Paul were to Jesus. (Socrates, like Jesus and Buddha, wrote nothing. He was too busy *doing* it to publish it.) And Aristotle, Plato's prime pupil, is to the West what Confucius is to China: the archetype of common sense, the one whom subsequent thinkers either build on as a primary foundation or attack as a primary opponent.

So here is the story of philosophy. It's the story of a long, long series of arguments in a very large and dysfunctional family; and Socrates is its main patriarch, so I've called it *Socrates' Children*. Welcome to the commodious and contentious family of his children.

Something About Passion

Most philosophy textbooks aren't fully human because they deliberately cut out all emotions, such as enthusiasm and wonder—even though Socrates, Plato, and Aristotle all said that wonder was the origin of philosophy! Most textbook authors try to imitate computers. I gladly announce that I am not a computer. I am a person, with both rational and irrational passions and feelings. One of these is the passion for philosophy, and the conviction that philosophy should be exciting—rather, that it is exciting, and therefore should be taught that way.

I am convinced that reason and passion, head and heart, are both very, very valuable and ought to be allies, not enemies.

The purpose of an introduction to philosophy is to introduce philosophy—that is, to lead-*into* (the literal meaning of "introduction") the-love-of-wisdom (the literal meaning of "philosophy"). To lead-into, not merely to see-and-analyze-from-afar. To be a door, not a microscope. And to lead the reader into the-love-of-wisdom, not the-cultivation-of-cleverness.

Love is a passion. Without blood from the heart, the brain does not work well. Without the will to understand, we do not understand. The brain is not merely a computer; it is a *human* brain. My ambition in this book is not just to inform and to summarize historical facts. I want to be your matchmaker. Jack and Jill, come up the hill and meet Plato. Fall in love with him. Struggle, be puzzled, get angry, fight your way out of the cave. This book is not just *data*—this is drama.

Why This Book?

I decided to write this book when the umpteenth person asked me the following question: "Could you recommend just one book that covers the whole history of philosophy that beginners can understand and even get excited about?"

Since I could not answer that question in words, I decided to try to answer it in deeds. I write the books I want to read when nobody else will write them. Sometimes you have to write a book first in order to get the satisfaction of reading it.

Twenty-one features make this book distinctive:

1. *It is "existential," practical, personal.* Philosophy is about human life and thought, so I concentrated on the ideas that *make a difference* to our experience, to our lives. That is William James' "pragmatic criterion of truth." His point is that if you can't specify *what difference it makes* if you believe or disbelieve an idea, then that idea is neither true nor false in any humanly significant sense.
2. *It is selective.* It doesn't try to cover too much. For an "introduction" means, literally, a "leading-into" rather than a summary or survey. It is not the last word but a first word, a beginning, for it is for beginners. Little philosophers get only a page or two; great philosophers get only a dozen; medium-sized philosophers get between three and six.
3. *It concentrates on the "Big Ideas."* (In fact, I thought of entitling it "What's the Big Idea?") This involves minimizing or omitting many "smaller" ideas. I think it is true of ideas, as of friends, that you can have too many of them. Better to have a few that are deeply understood and cherished than to have many that are not.

This book includes only what most students will find valuable. They will find valuable only what they remember years later. They will remember years later only those ideas that make a difference to their lives. And that's usually one Big Idea from each philosopher.

4. *It covers one hundred philosophers.* I chose them by two standards: (a) intrinsic excellence, wisdom, and importance; and (b) extrinsic historical influence and fame.
5. *It gives much more space to the "Big Nine": Socrates, Plato, Aristotle, Augustine, Aquinas, Descartes, Hume, Kant, and Hegel.* These are the most influential philosophers of all time.
6. *It presents the history of philosophy as a story, a "great conversation."* A book about the history of philosophy is not about history but about philosophy; yet, philosophers can be understood best historically, as partners in a dialogue with other philosophers. The whole history of Western philosophy is a very long and complex Socratic dialogue. The dialogue is exciting, for thought-revolutions are more important than political revolutions, and battles between ideas are more important than battles between armies.
7. On the other hand, *its point of view is not historical relativism.* I do not try to explain away any philosophers by reducing them to creatures of their times, as Marxists and Hegelians do. Though humans are rooted in *humus* (earth) like trees, yet like trees we also reach into the sky. Historians read the *Times*, but philosophers try to read the eternities.
8. *It is for beginners, not scholars.* It is not "scholarly" in style. It does not break new ground in content. It does not push any new philosophical theory.
9. *It is not "dumbed down."* Even though it is for beginners, it is for intelligent beginners, not dumb beginners. (It is also appropriate for intelligent high school seniors and for graduate students in departments other than philosophy.)
10. *It is for college courses in the history of philosophy.* But it is also a "do-it-yourself" book that does not require a teacher to interpret it.
11. *Its point of view is traditional rather than fashionable.* It neither assumes nor tries to prove any one particular philosophical position. Though I try to be fair to all philosophers and get "into their heads," I confess at the outset *a sympathy for common sense.* In philosophical terms, this usually (but not always) means, in one word, Aristotle rather than, for example, Nietzsche, Marx, or Derrida.
12. *It tries to be both clear and profound, both logical and existential.* For two or three generations, philosophers have been divided into two camps separated by these two ideals. English-speaking analytic philosophers have sought maximum clarity and logic, while continental philosophers have sought a more synthetic "big picture" that is more profound and existential. The result is that the former sound like chirping birds while the latter sound like muttering witch doctors.

I try to bridge this gap by going back to Socrates, who demanded both clarity and profundity. Many other philosophers today are also trying to bridge that gap by dialoguing with each other across the Channel.

13. *Like Socrates, it takes logic seriously.* Therefore, *it summarizes not just conclusions but arguments*, and evaluates them logically. But it uses ordinary-language logic, commonsense logic, Socratic logic, rather than the artificial language of modern mathematical, symbolic logic.
14. *It uses three kinds of logic*, as Socrates did:
    a. It uses *inductive* logic by grounding and testing its abstract and general ideas in concrete and particular instances.
    b. It uses *deductive* logic in tracing practices back to their principles and principles back to their premises, and in following premises, principles, and practices out to their logical conclusions.
    c. And it uses *seductive* logic as a woman would seduce a man by her beauty. For philosophy can be very beautiful.
15. *It naturally interfaces with religion.* Many of the questions philosophers ask are also questions religion claims to answer, though the methods of these two enterprises are fundamentally different: philosophy uses human reason alone, while religion relies on faith in something that is more than human. Therefore, this book naturally interfaces with religion in its questions, but not in its methods. Neither religious belief nor unbelief is either presupposed or aimed at.
16. *It is so unfashionable as to seek truth, of all things!* Much of contemporary philosophy looks like intellectual navel-gazing. But real philosophy ("the love of wisdom") seeks the fruit of truth, not just fun, play, or displays of cleverness. It is mentally procreative.
17. *It emphasizes the classical philosophers*, for two reasons:
    a. We don't yet know which contemporary philosophers will be acknowledged as great and which will be forgotten. It takes time for history, like a sieve, to sort out the big and little stones. Every era makes mistakes about itself. "Our era is the only one that doesn't" is perhaps the stupidest mistake of all.
    b. The questions contemporary philosophers typically ask are not the questions real people ask. They are questions like whether we can prove that we're not just brains in vats being hypnotized into seeing a world that isn't there. How many people do you know who worry about that question? I suspect even philosophers don't really worry about it if they're sane; they just pretend to. (In other words, they pretend to be insane.) Real people ask questions like: What are we? What should we be? Why were we born? Why must we suffer? Why must we die? Why do we kill? How should we live? Is there a God? An afterlife? Where does morality come from? What is the greatest good? How do you know?

18. *It is full of surprises.* It emphasizes things readers probably do *not* already know, understand, or believe. It does not patronizingly pass off clichés as profundities. It emphasizes wonder, since "philosophy begins in wonder."

    This does not contradict its preference for common sense (point 11 above), for common sense, when explored, turns out to be more wonderful than any cleverly invented ideologies. For real life is much more fantastic than any fantasy; fantasy only imitates life, while life imitates nothing. (You can learn this, and similar things, from the most maverick pick among my one hundred philosophers, G.K. Chesterton.)
19. *It dares to be funny.* It includes humor whenever relevant, because reality does. Reality is in fact amazingly funny.
20. *It includes visual aids.* We both learn and remember more effectively with our eyes than with our ears.
21. The treatment of each of the 100 philosophers usually contains *eleven parts*, as follows:
    1. A *portrait* of the philosopher.
    2. A brief *bio*, including *the seven W's*:
        a. *Who*: his complete name
        b. *Where*: his place of birth and nationality
        c. *When*: his birth and death
        d. *What*: his job or career
        e. *Whimsy*: unusual, dramatic, or humorous facts or legends about him
        f. *Which*: his most famous book
        g. *Why* he asked the questions he did, which is the next point (point 3). Obviously, some philosophers' lives are much more interesting than others. Some philosophers are almost all life and hardly any theory (e.g., Diogenes the Cynic); others are almost all theory and almost no life (e.g., Hegel).
    3. His *historical situation* and problem; his dialogue with previous philosophers.
    4. His *Big Idea* or central insight or most important teaching.
    5. His *most famous quotation(s).* (You will find the following piece of advice unusual but practical, I think. When you come to a quotation from a philosopher in this book, long or short, read it *aloud*. This helps you to remember and also to more deeply understand it, because this not only reinforces one sense [seeing] with another [hearing] but also brings into play your unconscious mind, your intuition and feelings.)
    6. A *diagram* or sketch whenever possible, translating the abstract idea into a visual image.
    7. The *practical difference* the idea makes:
        a. to life—to *your* life;

   b. to thought (the idea's logical implications); and
   c. to history (to subsequent thinkers).
8. The essential *argument(s) for* this idea.
9. The essential *argument(s) against* it.
10. A short, recommended *bibliography*, both primary and secondary sources, but only when readable and helpful. (These bibliographies at the end of some of the chapters in this book—only the important ones—are for beginners, not scholars. They are chosen for readability, for their power to interest and move the reader.)
11. *Probable reading experience*; hints to make the philosopher come clear and alive.

A Very Short Introduction to Philosophy

The best introduction to philosophy is the history of philosophy. The best answer to the question "What is philosophy?" is not an ideal definition of it but real examples of it. If you want to know what philosophy is, read philosophers.

Start with Plato. Whitehead famously summarized the whole history of Western philosophy as "footnotes to Plato." (I thought of using that for the title of this book.) Plato is the first philosopher from whom we have whole books. He is the greatest philosophical writer, for no philosopher has ever improved on his style.

Philosophy Begins in Wonder

Philosophy, according to its three greatest inventors—Socrates, Plato, and Aristotle—begins in wonder and ends in wisdom. It is literally "the love (*philia*, friendship) of wisdom (*sophia*)."

"Wonder" means three things:

1. It starts with *surprise* (e.g., "What a wonder!—that despite my deepest desire to live, I must die!").
2. It leads to *questioning* (e.g., "I wonder *why* I must die").
3. It ends with deepened *appreciation* (e.g., "How wonderful that my life, like a picture, has a frame, a limit! How wonderful that what I so deeply fear—death—I also deeply need!").

The first kind of wonder (surprise) leads to the second (questioning). We question only what we find remarkable. And the second kind of wonder (questioning), when successful, leads to the third kind (appreciation, contemplative wonder): we contemplate, and appreciate, and intellectually "eat" the truths we discover through questioning and investigating and reasoning.

The Divisions of Philosophy

What do philosophers ask questions about? These are the *divisions* of philosophy. They include four main parts:

1. *Metaphysics*, which is the study of the truths, laws, or principles that apply to all reality, not just physics but "beyond" (*meta*) those limits, though including them.
2. *Philosophical anthropology*, or philosophical psychology, which is the philosophical study of human nature, or the self.
3. *Epistemology*, which is the study of knowing and how we know; this can include logic and methodology.
4. *Ethics*, which is the study of what we ought to do and be.

In other words:

1. What is real?
2. What am I?
3. How can I know?
4. What should I do?

But philosophers also apply philosophy to many other areas, such as:

1. social and political philosophy
2. philosophy of religion
3. philosophy of education
4. philosophy of art, or aesthetics
5. philosophy of science

etc.

We can philosophize about anything: sexuality, sports, humor, even soup. E.g., I wrote a philosophy of surfing entitled *I Surf, Therefore I Am.*

The Importance of Philosophy

Why is philosophy important?

1. Because it is distinctively human. Animals do not philosophize because they know too little, and God, gods, or angels do not philosophize because they know too much. To be human is to philosophize, for to be human is to wonder.

2. Because it makes a difference to everything. Sometimes the difference is a matter of life or death. Wars are fought for philosophical reasons. The Civil War was fought over the rightness or wrongness of slavery. World War II was fought over fascism, which was a philosophy. The Cold War was fought over a philosophy: Marxism, or communism. The present "culture wars" are being fought throughout Western civilization over many related philosophical issues: religion, human nature, "natural laws," human sexuality, the meaning of marriage and family, whether human lives have absolute or relative value, just and unjust wars, and the role of the state in human life.

Books of Philosophy

For a short but dramatic introduction to philosophy, I recommend you read four of the dialogues of Plato that center around the death of Socrates, the first great philosopher: *Euthyphro*, *Crito*, *Apology*, and *Phaedo*. Or—a very distant second best—read my *Philosophy 101 by Socrates: An Introduction to Philosophy via Plato's "Apology."*

The best way to learn philosophy is not through books *about* the philosophers—books like this one—but from the books written *by* the philosophers. Fortunately, most great philosophers wrote short, simpler books as well as long, harder ones; and almost always it was the shorter ones that became classics. For instance:

PHILOSOPHER	EASY, SHORT BOOK	HARD, LONG BOOK
Plato	*Apology*	*Republic*
Augustine	*Confessions*	*City of God*
Boethius	*The Consolation of Philosophy*	*On the Trinity*
Anselm	*Proslogion*	*Monologion*
Bonaventure	*Journey of the Mind to God*	(many)
Machiavelli	*The Prince*	*The Discourses*
Pascal	*Pensées*	*Provincial Letters*
Descartes	*Discourse on Method*	*Meditations*
Leibniz	*Monadology*	(many)
Berkeley	*Three Dialogues between Hylas & Philonous*	(many)
Hume	*An Enquiry Concerning Human Understanding*	*A Treatise of Human Nature*

PHILOSOPHER	EASY, SHORT BOOK	HARD, LONG BOOK
Kant	*Foundations of the Metaphysics of Morals*	*Critique of Practical Reason*
Heidegger	*Discourse on Thinking*	*Being and Time*
Sartre	*Existentialism and Human Emotions*	*Being and Nothingness*
Marx	*The Communist Manifesto*	*Capital*
Kierkegaard	*Philosophical Fragments*	*Concluding Unscientific Postscript*
Marcel	*The Philosophy of Existentialism*	*The Mystery of Being*

Unfortunately, four of the most important philosophers—Aristotle, Aquinas, Hegel, and Nietzsche—never wrote a short, clear, and simple book (though Aristotle wrote a long and simple one, the *Nicomachean Ethics*; Nietzsche wrote a few short but not simple ones; and Aquinas wrote a very long and clear but not simple one, the *Summa theologiae*).

Philosophy and Religion

Philosophy is not religion and religion is not philosophy.

All religions, however diverse their content, originate in faith rather than pure reason, and their ultimate appeal is to divine authority, the authority of divinely revealed scriptures (e.g., the Bible, the Quran), or institutions (e.g., the Catholic Church), or mystical experiences (e.g., Buddhist *nirvana*).

Philosophy, classically conceived, originates in and is justified by appeal to reason. Medieval philosophers often use philosophical reason to justify religious faith (e.g., rational proofs for the existence of God). Ironically, modern philosophers, in reaction against medieval philosophy, often begin by questioning the validity of faith and end by questioning the validity of reason and substituting ideology, feeling, or will (e.g., Hobbes, Hume, Rousseau, Kant, Fichte, Schopenhauer, Nietzsche, Dewey, Derrida). Philosophers who make this move usually construe "reason" much more narrowly than classical (premodern) philosophers did. They think of "reason" as *scientific* reasoning. If medieval philosophy is in bed with religion, modern philosophy is in bed with science.

The greatest difference between philosophers and other human beings is probably not philosophy but religion. For everyone has a philosophy, whether well thought out or not, but not everyone believes in a religion. According to the polls, only 5–10 percent of Americans identify themselves as atheists, but 75 percent of philosophers do. That fact explains why most histories of philosophy do not understand religious philosophies very well. Religion, like sex, humor, and music, is something one understands from within much better than from without. Whenever I have my class argue about religion, I make the believers argue for atheism and the doubters, agnostics, and atheists argue for faith, and the result is always the same: the pretend atheists do a far better job than the pretend believers. Then we argue about whether this was because only the believers understood both sides or whether it was because the pretend believers had to argue for unarguable myths and superstitions.

This book is not about religion but about philosophy, but one of the primary questions of philosophy is whether something like God exists; for this idea makes more of a difference to everything else, both in life and in philosophy, than just about any other idea. It makes a difference to personal identity, death, morality, and "the meaning of life." The God-idea is almost certainly either the most important error and illusion or the most important truth in the history of human thought. So a book on philosophy cannot ignore the idea. Most great philosophers did not. However, it treats the idea philosophically (by reason) rather than religiously (by faith). It is no part of this book either to presuppose or to try to prove or disprove religious faith, either overtly or as a hidden agenda. I have tried to be equally fair to all points of view, including philosophies I strongly disagree with such as nihilism, skepticism, Marxism, and even deconstructionism, which I cannot help suspecting is not even serious but just "jerking our chain."

A Doable Do-It-Yourself Course in the Classics of Philosophy

Many people have asked me for a recommended booklist for a teach-yourself philosophy course. Many beginning philosophy teachers have asked me for a similar list for an introductory course in philosophy.

Again, I know of no more effective way to teach philosophy, to yourself or others, than the apprenticeship to the masters that is called the "great books." The canon of great books is certainly not fixed, or stuffy, or irrelevant to today's world. The list is pragmatic: it is a list of what has "worked."

Based on my own experience of what works—that is, what (a) is comprehensible to beginners and (b) inspires them to think and perhaps even to fall in love with philosophy—here is my list.

There is a primary list and a secondary list for each of the four periods in the history of philosophy. For a high school course, one of these eight lists would seem to fit into one semester; for a college course, two; and for a graduate course, three or four. The lists are deliberately short and selective; far better to spend much time with a few great friends than a little time with many little ones.

Ancient Philosophy (Primary)

Solomon, *Ecclesiastes*

Plato, *Meno* and *Apology*

Plato, *Republic*, excerpts. (If you use the Rouse translation, *Great Dialogues of Plato*, and mentally divide each book into three parts—A, B, and C—you could cover Book I, Book IIA, Books VB through VIIA, Book IXC, and Rouse's helpful summary of the rest.)

Aristotle, *Nicomachean Ethics*, excerpts. (Select your own excerpts but be sure to cover Books I and VIII.)

Plotinus, "Beauty"

Ancient Philosophy (Secondary)

Parmenides' poem

The rest of Plato's *Republic*

Plato, *Gorgias*

The rest of the *Nicomachean Ethics*

A secondary source summary of Aristotle, either Adler's *Aristotle for Everybody* (easy) or Ross' *Aristotle* (intermediate).

Medieval Philosophy (Primary)

Augustine, *Confessions* 1–10 (Word on Fire Classics edition, which uses the Sheed translation)

Boethius, *The Consolation of Philosophy*

Anselm, *Proslogion*

Aquinas, *Summa theologiae*, at least 1.2.3 ("On God's Existence") and 1-2.2 ("On Those Things in Which Happiness Consists"). These and more, with explanatory notes, are included in my *A Shorter Summa*.

Medieval Philosophy (Secondary)

Bonaventure, *Journey of the Mind to God*

Aquinas, more of the *Summa*. My *Summa of the Summa* anthology is five hundred pages, with many footnotes.

Nicholas of Cusa, *Of Learned Ignorance*

Modern Philosophy (Primary)

Machiavelli, *The Prince*

Descartes, *Discourse on Method*

Hume, *An Enquiry Concerning Human Understanding*

Kant, *Foundations of the Metaphysics of Morals*

Modern Philosophy (Secondary)

Pascal, *Pensées* (or my *Christianity for Modern Pagans: Pascal's "Pensées"—Edited, Outlined & Explained*)

Descartes, *Meditations*

Leibniz, *Monadology*

Kant, *Critique of Pure Reason*, excerpts

Contemporary Philosophy (Primary)

Sartre, *Existentialism and Human Emotions* (or *Existentialism Is a Humanism*)

James, "What Pragmatism Means" and "The Will to Believe" (short lectures)

Marx, *The Communist Manifesto*

C.S. Lewis, *The Abolition of Man*

Buber, *I and Thou*

Contemporary Philosophy (Secondary)

Mill, *Utilitarianism*

Russell, *The Problems of Philosophy*

Ayer, *Language, Truth and Logic*

Wittgenstein, *Tractatus Logico-Philosophicus*

Chesterton, *Orthodoxy*

Clarke, *Person and Being*

A Personal Bibliography

Please note: this is merely *a* bibliography—one among many possible lists of recommended further reading—of other books I have written about these philosophers. The very best books to read are, of course, the books of the great philosophers themselves.

1. Solomon: *Three Philosophies of Life: Ecclesiastes: Life as Vanity, Job: Life as Suffering, Song of Songs: Life as Love* (chapter 1)
2. Shankara, Buddha, Confucius, and Lao Tzu: "Questions of Faith: The Philosophy of Religion" (recorded lectures)
3. Pre-Socratics, Greeks, and Moderns: *The Journey: A Spiritual Roadmap for Modern Pilgrims*
4. Socrates: *Philosophy 101 by Socrates: An Introduction to Philosophy via Plato's "Apology"*
5. Plato: *The Platonic Tradition*
6. Plato: *A Socratic Introduction to Plato's "Republic"*
7. Aristotelian logic: *Socratic Logic: A Logic Text Using Socratic Method, Platonic Questions, and Aristotelian Principles*
8. Jesus: *The Philosophy of Jesus*
9. Jesus: *Socrates Meets Jesus: History's Greatest Questioner Confronts the Claims of Christ*
10. Jesus: *Jesus Shock*
11. Augustine: *I Burned for Your Peace: Augustine's "Confessions" Unpacked*
12. Muhammad: *Between Allah & Jesus: What Christians Can Learn from Muslims*

13. Aquinas: *Summa of the Summa*
14. Aquinas: *A Shorter Summa: The Essential Philosophical Passages of St. Thomas Aquinas' "Summa Theologica" Edited and Explained*
15. Aquinas: "The Modern Scholar: The Philosophy of Thomas Aquinas" (recorded lectures)
16. Aquinas: *Practical Theology: Spiritual Direction from Saint Thomas Aquinas*
17. Machiavelli: *Socrates Meets Machiavelli: The Father of Philosophy Cross-Examines the Author of "The Prince"*
18. Pascal: *Christianity for Modern Pagans: Pascal's "Pensées"—Edited, Outlined & Explained*
19. Descartes: *Socrates Meets Descartes: The Father of Philosophy Analyzes the Father of Modern Philosophy's "Discourse on Method"*
20. Hume: *Socrates Meets Hume: The Father of Philosophy Meets the Father of Modern Skepticism—A Socratic Cross-Examination of Hume's "An Enquiry Concerning Human Understanding"*
21. Kant: *Socrates Meets Kant: The Father of Philosophy Meets His Most Influential Modern Child—A Socratic Cross-Examination of Kant's "Critique of Pure Reason" and "Foundations of the Metaphysics of Morals"*
22. Marx: *Socrates Meets Marx: The Father of Philosophy Cross-Examines the Founder of Communism—A Socratic Dialogue on "The Communist Manifesto"*
23. Kierkegaard: *Socrates Meets Kierkegaard: The Father of Philosophy Meets the Father of Christian Existentialism*
24. Freud: *Socrates Meets Freud: The Father of Philosophy Meets the Father of Psychology*
25. Sartre: *Socrates Meets Sartre: The Founder of Philosophy Cross-Examines the Founder of Existentialism—A Socratic Dialogue on "Existentialism and Human Emotions"*
26. Tolkien: *The Philosophy of Tolkien: The Worldview Behind "The Lord of the Rings"*
27. Lewis: *C.S. Lewis for the Third Millennium: Six Essays on "The Abolition of Man"*

28. Modern philosophers systematically argued with from a Thomist perspective: *Summa Philosophica*

29. The history of ethics: "What Would Socrates Do? The History of Moral Thought and Ethics" (recorded lectures)

30. Ethical classics: *Ethics for Beginners: Big Ideas from 32 Great Minds*

A Few Recommended Histories of Philosophy

Here are a few selected histories of philosophy that do not duplicate mine but have somewhat different ends.

1. Frederick Copleston, SJ, has written the most clear and complete multi-volume history of Western philosophy available, with increasing detail and attention as it gets more and more contemporary. It is not exciting or dramatic or "existential," but it is very fair, clear, logical, and helpful.
2. Will Durant's *The Story of Philosophy* is charmingly and engagingly written, though very selective and very personally angled toward Enlightenment thinkers.
3. Bertrand Russell, a major philosopher himself, has written a very intelligent, elegant, and witty little history of Western philosophy from the viewpoint of a modern Enlightenment atheist, semi-skeptic, and semi-materialist. Don't expect fair and equal treatment of both sides.
4. Francis Parker's one-volume history of philosophy up to Hegel, *The Story of Western Philosophy*, neatly structures this history by centering on the theme of the one and the many.
5. Mortimer Adler's *Ten Philosophical Mistakes* does not offer a complete history but a diagnostic treatment of key errors in modern philosophy.
6. Étienne Gilson's *The Unity of Philosophical Experience* does the same, finding reductionisms of philosophy to one of the sciences as a nearly universal modern error.
7. William Barrett's *Irrational Man*, though purportedly only an introduction to existentialism, has some very powerfully written and engaging historical chapters on pre-existentialist philosophy from an existentialist viewpoint, as well as the best one-chapter summaries of Kierkegaard, Nietzsche, Heidegger, and Sartre available in print. His *The Illusion of Technique* thoughtfully compares James, Wittgenstein, and Heidegger.

8. Richard Tarnas' *The Passion of the Western Mind* is indeed passionate, and existential, and focuses on the more general surrounding historical and cultural events and influences.
9. Samuel Enoch Stumpf (*Socrates to Sartre*) and Robert Solomon and Kathleen Higgins (*A Short History of Philosophy*) have also produced good one-volume histories of Western philosophy.

Most philosophy texts today are not "great books" histories but anthologies of recent articles written by recent philosophers about recent systematic, logical issues. Most of these are thin, dry, technical, dull, and lacking in existential bite as well as style, though all of them are very intelligent. They have their place, but usually only math and science students, not English or history students, like them. Students, especially in the humanities, will find *histories* of philosophy much more interesting for the same reason they find stories more interesting than formulas, and dialogues more interesting than monologues. That was Plato's genius. His Socratic dialogues remain the single best introduction to philosophy ever written.

Introduction to Modern Philosophy

This is the third volume in a four-volume history of philosophy.

This volume is longer than the previous two, even though its time period is shorter. The two centuries between Descartes and Hegel, between 1637 (the publication of the *Discourse on Method*) and 1831 (Hegel's death), are like a sudden jungle growth of philosophical systems. Comparing modern with medieval philosophy is like comparing New Yorkers with Alaskans. (This is not a value judgment: I personally love them both.)

The Story Line of Modern Philosophy

The story line of ancient and medieval philosophy is fairly straightforward, but the story of modern philosophy is messy, multiple, and complex. The history of modern philosophy presents a challenge to the teacher because the logical developments and the chronological developments do not coincide as they usually did in the ancient and even the medieval era. So if we arrange our philosophers strictly chronologically, we will be jumping from one topic to another and back again. So I have divided this volume into two sections, corresponding to the two main new foci in modern philosophy: epistemology and politics.

Thus, though Machiavelli and Bacon precede Descartes chronologically, we begin with Descartes, who is logically "the father of modern philosophy." Bacon is an early empiricist, and most of modern empiricism is a later reaction against the rationalism that begins in Descartes, so Bacon is put after Descartes even though he lived earlier. Also, Machiavelli and Hobbes, though earlier than Descartes, fit into our second topical category, political philosophers. (Look at the Table of Contents if this confuses you.)

Postmedieval philosophy focuses on five issues. The first two will be covered in Volume III (modern) and the last three in Volume IV (contemporary):

1. The primary modern issue is epistemology (theory of knowledge). Modern philosophers are like teenagers who, instead of thinking first of all about the

world and other people, think about themselves: Who am I? Am I ugly? Am I any good? And above all, how can I be certain of anything? Epistemology is like taking off your glasses and looking at them. Almost all premodern philosophers are first of all metaphysicians; almost all important modern philosophers are epistemologists, either *instead* of being metaphysicians or at least *before* being metaphysicians. All the classical modern philosophers think they have to critique reason, their tool, before they build philosophical buildings with it.

This begins with Descartes, who is called "the father of modern philosophy" because he changed the central topic of "the great conversation" when he published his *Discourse on Method* in 1637. Classical modern philosophy begins there and runs through Hegel (who died in 1831). It has a clearly defined story line of three options, three epistemologies, three answers to the epistemological question: (a) rationalism (Descartes, Spinoza, and Leibniz); (b) empiricism (Bacon, Hobbes, Locke, Berkeley, Hume, and Reid); and (c) German idealism (Kant, Fichte, Schelling, Hegel, and Schopenhauer).

But it is impossible to do epistemology without doing at least an implicit metaphysics, or at least a discussion of the possibility or impossibility of metaphysics. The two always imply each other. For whatever comes under metaphysics (all being that we know) comes under epistemology (the study of knowing). And whatever comes under epistemology (all that knowing is) comes under metaphysics (the study of what-is). This is sometimes called "the gnoseo-ontological circle." Each half presupposes the other.

2. A second issue, and second conversation, is practical and political. It is not new, but it begins anew with Machiavelli, the founder of modern political philosophy, and moves through Hobbes, Locke, Rousseau, and Marx, all of whom offer alternatives to the natural law theory common to all premodern philosophers except the Greek Sophists and the late medieval nominalists.
3. A third issue is "existential" (personal, psychological, ethical, and religious). This, too, is not new, but it begins anew with Pascal, in a much more typically modern way—that is, subjectively—and, after a two-century hiatus, emerges with Kierkegaard, Nietzsche, Heidegger, Sartre, Marcel, and Buber, all of whom are loosely classified as "existential" philosophers, who center on questions of concrete, individual human existence like death, evil, freedom, values, and purpose.
4. A fourth issue, about language, begins later, in the twentieth century. Its main founders are Moore, Ayer, and Russell, and its main figure is Wittgenstein. From it emerges "analytic philosophy," which is the main way of "doing philosophy" today everywhere in the world where English is the primary language.
5. Not neatly fitting into any one of these four conversations but intersecting with all of them are pragmatists, phenomenologists, and postmodernists

(especially deconstructionists), three more twentieth-century developments, all focusing on methodology.

"Ancient" and "Medieval" vs. "Modern"

What is "modern"? What distinguishes "the modern mind" from the ancient and medieval minds?

Answer #1 (the most obvious): They can be distinguished by their relation to Christianity. The ancient mind was pre-Christian, the medieval mind was Christian, and the modern mind is (in varying and increasing degrees) post-Christian.

Answer #2: They can be distinguished by their center, which gives them their perspective on everything else. All minds think about three levels of things: things subhuman (the cosmos), things human, and things superhuman (God or gods or absolutes). But any one of the three can be taken as the assumed center, the perspective, the context, or the frame for the other two. So the ancient mind was *cosmocentric* (gods and men found their place in the cosmos, the ordered whole); the medieval mind was *theocentric* ("nature" was re-christened "the creation" and man was defined by his divine origin and destiny); and the modern mind is *anthropocentric* (philosophers think about God and the cosmos more for their relation to us than for themselves, philosophy becomes increasingly distinct from theology, and natural science becomes increasingly distinct from philosophy).

Answer #3: The model for philosophy in the Middle Ages was theology. Philosophy was labeled "the handmaid to theology." The model for philosophy in modern times is modern science. Philosophy usually both seeks to imitate the method and certainty of science and responds to the issues raised by science.

Answer #4: The ancient mind was objective. Human and divine *subjects* (persons) were viewed *objectively*. With the exception of the mystics, the same was true of the medieval mind. But the modern mind becomes more and more subjective. Even *objects* are viewed *subjectively*, and solipsism (look it up!) appears as a real problem and danger, as it never did in premodern thought.

Answer #5: They can be classified according to their fears. The cosmocentric ancient mind feared death. The theocentric medieval mind feared guilt, sin, and hell. The anthropocentric modern mind fears uncertainty, unfreedom, and powerlessness.

Answer #6: They can be classified by their answer to the classic, obviously primary question of the *summum bonum* or "greatest good," the ultimate meaning and end and purpose of human life. The *summum bonum* for the ancients was *eudaimonia*, "blessedness," an objectively perfect and therefore subjectively happy human life ("perfect" especially intellectually and morally). For the medievals it was union with God. For moderns it is the scientific and technological power over nature.

Answer #7: They can be classified as three kinds of women. Ancient philosophy was like a virgin; medieval philosophy was like a married woman (married to religion); modern philosophy is like a separated, divorced, and remarried woman. It gradually separates from its old husband (Jewish, Christian, or Muslim religion) and marries another (science).

Answer #8: They can be classified according to their place on a kind of intellectual road map. Imagine two rivers, independently sourced but joined at one point, then separated again. Medieval philosophy is a synthesis or marriage of the two rivers of Greek reason and Christian faith; it ends in a divorce, and modern philosophy moves in two opposite streams from the divorce. One stream tightens "reason" to something more scientific; the other stream loosens it to something more personal (Romanticism, existentialism, subjectivism).

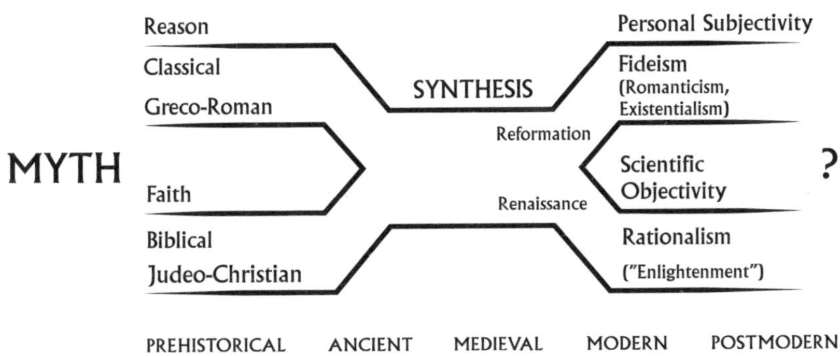

These are all analogies. Analogies prove nothing, but they illumine and suggest much. Good analogies do not contradict, but complement, each other.

Modern vs. Medieval

One of the best short answers to how modern philosophy differs from medieval is given by Frank Parker in *The Story of Western Philosophy* (numbering added):

> 1. The most basic and general feature of the transition from medieval to modern philosophy is a new, deeper, and more enduring separation of reason from faith.
>
> This new freedom of man's mind from its medieval tie to a revealed transcendent God who establishes nature and man's bond with nature will be seen to grow gradually into . . . the isolation of the human subject from nature, which develops out of reason's isolation from a transcendent author of nature. . . . Subjectivity, the freedom of the

subject from the objective world, therefore will emerge as the defining essence of modern philosophy as a whole.

2. Secondarily and less fundamentally modern philosophy will be marked by a struggle to achieve the correct definition of this freed human reason in terms of a proper balance between its conceptual and its sensory powers, between sensation and reason in the narrow sense of intellection and conceptualization. . . . Continental Rationalism (Descartes, Spinoza, Leibniz) will emphasize deductive, conceptual reason; British Empiricism (Bacon, Locke, Berkeley, Hume) will emphasize inductive, sensory experience; and the final movement, usually called German Idealism (Kant, Fichte, Schelling, Hegel . . .) will seek a synthesis of rationalism and empiricism in a . . . dynamic conception of mind. . . .

   To understand better this interplay of faith and reason and reason and sensation, and also to grasp the mediating position of Thomas Aquinas as a background of the development of modern philosophy, let us use the image of man as created lower than angels and higher than the brutes. Man is the highest being in the natural order but the lowest being in the supernatural order. Caught in between these two orders of existence, he shares something with both and also possesses a unique in-betweenness, his own peculiar difference. The supernatural factor in man, that which he shares with the angelic and the divine, is his participation in God's vision by means of divine revelation. The purely animal factor in man, that which he shares with the brutes, is his sense experience, an awareness of the particular and fluctuating features of the things in nature. And his peculiar in-betweenness, his distinctively human characteristic, which marks him off both from the brutes below and the angels above, is his reason . . . his native power of discerning the unchanging and universal characteristics of things through his sense experience. . . . Thus did Thomas Aquinas try to hold sensation, reason, and revelation all together in a harmony in which each is necessary and none is reducible to any other. What basically distinguishes late medieval and early modern philosophy is the gradual breaking down of this union.

We could summarize the five typical new features of modern philosophy as follows:

1. Its relation to religion: not a marriage but a divorce or a separation.
2. Man's adversarial relationship with nature; the subject (the "conqueror") versus the object (the "conquered").
3. The crisis of reason; the priority of epistemology; the problem of skepticism and solipsism.

4. The turn to self-consciousness and subjectivity.
5. Dropping two key concepts of premodern ethics and politics: the natural moral law and the *summum bonum*.

Introduction to Epistemology

The following is a very oversimplified introduction to a difficult subject.

"Epistemology" means "the science of knowing." It is the division of philosophy that studies how human knowledge works or ought to work. This is a typically modern question. Premodern philosophers usually began with (1) metaphysics and (2) philosophical anthropology, and deduced their (3) epistemology from this, since they thought that (3) how man knows depends on (2) what man is, and that (2) what man is depends on (1) what is.

But modern philosophers, beginning with Bacon and Descartes, typically begin with epistemology, since they think that a builder should examine his tools before he builds buildings. For them, the justification of reason comes before the use of it.

Like all of philosophy, epistemology is distinctively human, for even if animals have consciousness, only humans have self-consciousness, and therefore think about thinking.

Three main questions emerge here: (1) the origin, (2) the nature, and (3) the extent of human knowledge. Three main answers, or schools of thought, emerge, each of which answers all three of these questions: rationalism, empiricism, and German idealism.

Their differences concern the relationship between the two parts or poles of human knowing: sensation and reason (or intellection). They differ on: (a) Which of the two do we begin with? (b) Which is closer to the essence of knowledge? and (c) Which gives us more certainty? Rationalism answers "reason" and empiricism "sensation" to all three of these questions.

A third epistemological answer, an alternative to both rationalism and empiricism that Kant calls "the Copernican revolution in philosophy," joins reason and sensation. It does this, however, not as Aristotle and Aquinas did, by abstracting rational concepts from sense images, but in the opposite way, by reason imposing its structures on experience so that objects conform to mind rather than mind conforming to objects. (This will become clearer when we get to Kant.)

We can distinguish five possible answers to question (c) above, the question of certainty, arranged in a hierarchy from less certainty to more:

1. *Skepticism*: we know nothing with certainty at all.
2. *Kantianism*: we cannot know "things-in-themselves" (objective reality) but only phenomena (appearances, how things appear to human minds).

3. *Empiricism*: we can know only what is given in sense experience (and reflection, or inner experience), and (usually) only with probability.
4. *Epistemological realism* (Aristotle): we can know the nature of real things by intellectually abstracting their forms (natures) from sense images of material things, and we can know what we can deduce from these things (e.g., a First Cause).
5. *Rationalism*: we can know beyond experience by direct intellectual intuition into essences (Plato) or deduction from innate "clear and distinct ideas" (Descartes).

If you find this section too confusing at this point, just ignore it and read the philosophers instead; then come back to it and it will look simple—probably much too simple.

Four Epistemologies

Classical modern philosophy is neatly divided. Its main interest is epistemology, and the three positions that emerge are all geographically located.

1. First there is continental (European) rationalism, with Descartes (French), Spinoza (Portuguese and Dutch), and Leibniz (German). This has roots in Plato and Augustine.
2. Then there is British empiricism, with Bacon, Hobbes, Locke, Berkeley, and Hume, who were respectively English, English, English, Irish, and Scottish. This epistemology has roots among the medievals in William of Ockham and Roger Bacon, who were also British. Most empiricists are British and most British philosophers are empiricists. (Don't ask me why; maybe it's in the tea.)
3. Then there is German idealism, Kantianism, or voluntarism, including Kant, Fichte, Schelling, Hegel, and Schopenhauer. This position is a new one, in fact so new that Kant called it "the Copernican revolution in philosophy." All five of these philosophers are German. (Don't ask me why; maybe it's in the sausages.)
4. A fourth epistemology, that of Aristotle and Aquinas, is surprisingly absent from the list of modern options, especially since it is the most popular and most commonsensical option in the opinion of most non-philosophers.

These four epistemologies, or theories of how human knowledge works, can be visualized by the following diagram:

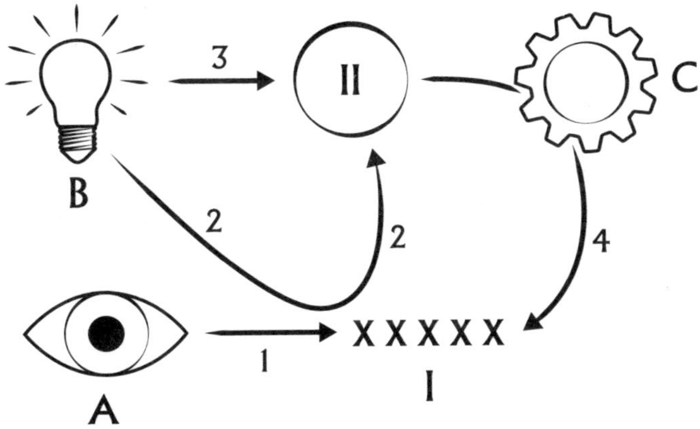

Key to the symbols:
Subjective Human Faculties of Knowing: A. Senses; B. Intuitive Reason; C. Calculating Reason.
Objects Known: I. Concrete Particular Substances; II. Universal Forms.
Operations in Knowing: 1. Sensation; 2. Abstraction; 3. Understanding; 4. Deduction.

This is a picture of how human knowledge works according to Aristotle, in four steps. (1) First, the senses perceive particular concrete substances (e.g., human beings), which are made up of form and matter. (2) Then, the intellect abstracts the essence or essential nature from the accidents (body-and-soul from height, weight, gender, etc.). (3) This essence is understood by intellectual intuition. (4) On the basis of this understanding, the reason deduces consequences (e.g., that all human beings, even those we do not see or those yet to be born, can think [because they have minds] and die [because they have bodies]).

Step 2 is the connector between steps 1 and 3 to explain where we get universals, and step 3 is the connector between steps 2 and 4 to explain the mutual dependence of induction, or "inductive abstraction," and deduction.

The other three epistemologies can be plotted on this graph. They all lack the distinctive Aristotelian step of abstraction (step 2). Cartesian rationalism begins with step 3 as innate ideas, then deduces from them (step 4). Humean empiricism begins and ends with step 1. Descartes affirms only the top half of the circle, Hume the bottom. Both lack the link between them (step 2). Kant, like Aristotle, synthesizes top and bottom, reason and sensation, but "backward," with form imposed on matter instead of abstracted from it.

(If this strange-looking picture hinders you more than it helps you to understand the four epistemologies, just ignore this subsection. Diagrams are sometimes almost as hard to explain as jokes.)

Rationalism is essentially steps 3 and 4 without 1 and 2. It begins not with sense experience (1), but with innate ideas (3), and emphasizes deduction (4) rather than induction or abstraction (2).

Empiricism is essentially steps 1 and sometimes 2, but without 3 and 4; but step 2 signifies only induction, not abstraction, for all empiricists are suspicious of abstract, universal ideas. They are nominalists.

Rationalism is essentially the affirmation of the top part of the circle, and empiricism the bottom part.

Kantian epistemology, like Aristotelianism, joins the two halves of the circle, but it reverses the direction of it (the movement goes from the top down rather than from the bottom up), since it has the mind actively imposing three kinds of innate structures, (a) sensory, (b) logical, and (c) metaphysical, on the objects known rather than abstracting them from the objects. (If you don't understand this yet, don't worry; we'll get to Kant soon. If you *do* understand it, perhaps you ought to worry.)

The four epistemologies fit with four metaphysics, four answers to the classical "problem of universals."

Rationalism fits extreme realism, for if universals *exist* separately from particular things, they can be *known* separately, as "innate ideas."

Aristotelian "soft empiricism" fits moderate realism, for if universals exist but only in particular, concrete, sensible things, they can be known by abstraction from those things.

Kantian epistemology fits Abelard's "conceptualism" or "moderate nominalism": universals are needed, but they are only mental concepts, not existing realities.

Humean "hard empiricism" fits extreme nominalism: there are no universals, period. There are not even concepts, only words. Hard empiricists mercilessly attack "abstract ideas."

Metaphysics and epistemology always go together. Which one comes first, which is the source of the other, is a "chicken/egg" question. But empiricism in epistemology always corresponds to an empiricist metaphysics, as rationalism in epistemology always corresponds to a rationalist metaphysics. For the objects of empirical knowledge, such as Zeus, Socrates, Lassie, the apple you just ate, and Uranus, are always

1. concrete and individual, not abstract and universal;
2. temporal and changing, not timeless; and
3. contingent (they could be different), not necessary.

Thus, our knowledge of them is only probable, not certain. For the empiricist's world is full of a plurality of concrete, changing, contingent particulars.

But the objects of rational, intellectual knowledge, such as *the essential nature of* a god, a man, a dog, an apple, or a planet, are

1. abstract and universal,
2. timeless, and
3. necessary.

Thus, the rationalist's world is full of Ideas, Forms, truths, laws, and principles that are general (universal), changeless, necessary, and known with certainty.

If all this continues to be confusing, re-read the short paragraph just before the subsection entitled "Four Epistemologies" again.

I have not included recommended bibliographies for modern or contemporary philosophers because the relatively few primary sources that are accessibly clear and short are mentioned in the text. I have written secondary sources on Descartes, Pascal, Hume, Kant, Machiavelli, Marx, Sartre, and Kierkegaard.

I

THE EPISTEMOLOGICAL PHILOSOPHERS

55

RENÉ DESCARTES

AD 1596–1650

Descartes' *Discourse on Method* (1637) changed the philosophical landscape. It made more of a difference to how philosophy was done than any other book ever written, except perhaps Plato's dialogues. Every major philosopher for the next two hundred years, except Pascal, followed Descartes in attempting to apply some aspects of the scientific method to philosophy, though they all produced different philosophical systems than Descartes'.

Descartes' revolution was similar to that of Socrates': both changed the meaning of "reason" itself by tightening it, so to speak. Socrates was the first person in history who clearly understood and practiced the art of deductive reasoning, while Descartes was the first to deliberately apply to philosophy the new scientific method. Or perhaps he was the second: Bacon had done this too, before Descartes. But where Bacon emphasized the empirical and inductive aspect of the scientific method, Descartes emphasized the mathematical and deductive aspect of it.

Why did Descartes try to do philosophy by a new method? Because he noticed two things: that every one of the sciences had progressed remarkably in his age, and that philosophy had not.

He asked the simple question "Why?" What made the difference? And his answer was the scientific method. That was the common factor in the progress of all the sciences. Yet no one had applied it to philosophy.

He then asked: What was in this new method that gave it the power to progress to a point where disagreements were actually settled conclusively for the first time in history? And he answered: The method of mathematics. He wrote:

> I took especially great pleasure in mathematics because of the certainty and the evidence of its arguments. But I did not yet notice its true usefulness and, thinking that it seemed useful only to the mechanical arts, I was astonished that, because its foundations were so solid and firm, no one had built anything more noble upon them. On the other hand, I compared the writings of the ancient pagans who discuss morals to very proud and magnificent palaces that are built on nothing but sand and mud. They place virtues on a high plateau and make them appear to be valued more than anything else in the world, but they do not sufficiently instruct us about how to know them.

If we imagine a great palace on a foundation of sand next to a little shed on a foundation of rock, we can see why Descartes wanted to rebuild the old palace on the new foundation.

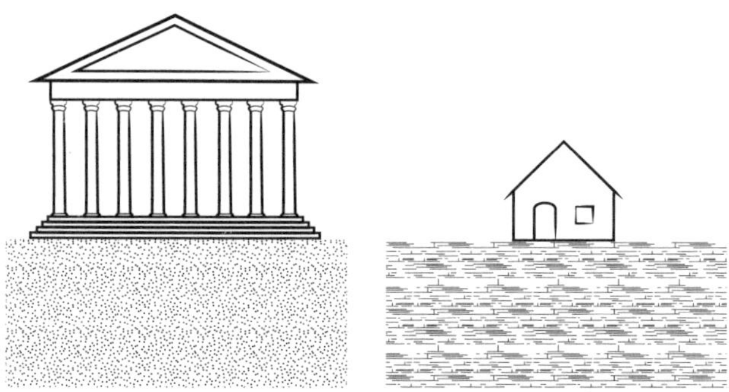

Descartes' "buildings," i.e., his essential conclusions (that God and the world, mind and matter, soul and body, all exist), are quite traditional, but his method of proving them (the new "foundation") is radically new. (Socrates, too, was also both traditional and radical in the same way.)

Descartes' revolution can best be defined by comparing Plato's "divided line" in the *Republic*. Plato distinguishes four levels of reason and, thus, of education:

1. seeing secondhand images of real things;
2. firsthand sense perception of real things;
3. logical and mathematical reasoning; and
4. intellectual intuition, wisdom, or understanding of the eternal Forms.

The scientific method essentially omits (1) and (4), for opposite reasons (because (1) is too low and (4) is too high). It combines (2) observation of empirical data with (3) exact reasoning.

Descartes' method demands mathematical exactness, what he calls "clear and distinct ideas"—like numbers. His ideal is a universal mathematical science.

Aristotle had taught that *method* depends on *object* (subject matter), and that there are different sciences and different methods because there are different objects, or subject matters, dealt with by the different sciences. He distinguished the methods of practical science from the methods of theoretical sciences and, within the latter, three different levels of abstraction and thus three different kinds and methods of theoretical sciences: physical, mathematical, and metaphysical. Descartes' contrary idea is that there is one and only one best method for every subject. (Thus, his title is literally "Discourse on *the* Method," *Discours de la méthode*.)

It is probably not possible to decide whether Descartes' attempt to do philosophy by the method of science can work until we see how he does it. But even if his attempt proves to be a confusion and a failure, the attempt was inevitable. Philosophy was in a sorry state in 1637, divided between (1) verbal quibbles and partisan battles among unoriginal late medieval Scholastics who used highly technical language and multiplied abstract verbal distinctions, (2) flaky nature-mystics and occultists like Paracelsus, and (3) smart but cynical skeptics like Montaigne. Every other science had made more progress in the previous two hundred years than in the previous two thousand, but not philosophy. Why? Descartes' answer seemed obvious. The scientific method was the fuel that sent all the other rockets (sciences) up. Why not use it for philosophy too?

Descartes' Life

Descartes was the man to do it. He was one of the most intelligent men who ever lived. He thought of himself primarily as a scientist rather than a philosopher. He personally knew all the great scientists of his day, many of whom congregated around a circle of friends in Paris of which Descartes was the center. He made essential contributions in geometry (he invented analytic geometry), optics, astronomy, physiology, and other sciences. He was one of the last of the universal geniuses, before the age of specialization.

He summarized his intellectual biography briefly and charmingly in *Discourse on Method*. Trained in the best Jesuit schools in the world, interacting with all the greatest minds of his age, he sought certainty rather than probability or arguments from "fittingness" or from authority; and he found certainty nowhere except in mathematics. He wondered why this exact reasoning had been confined to quantity (number) alone, and not applied to the great questions of philosophy such as the nature of knowledge, truth, human nature, God, and the soul.

One day, returning from the battlefields of the Thirty Years' War (which terribly traumatized Europe and tarnished the religion(s) that caused it), while snowbound in a little heated room, he conceived the essential idea for a whole new philosophy, which was (1) to come from his own individual mind alone rather than relying on the great philosophers of the past, (2) to begin with his own experience, and (3) to use only logical reasoning and the scientific method.

This was the beginning of the career of the most famous philosopher in the world. The end came when the Queen of Sweden, a would-be intellectual herself, persuaded Descartes to come to Sweden to instruct her. Descartes accepted, but died of pneumonia, brought on by the Swedish winter and the queen's demand to rise at 4:30 a.m. to give her philosophy lessons.

Reading the *Discourse on Method*

The *Discourse on Method* (DM) is one of the easiest and clearest philosophy books ever written.

Section I is a brief and charming intellectual autobiography.

Section II sets forth the four rules of the method.

Section III gives four temporary and pragmatic rules of practice to live by in an untroubled way until a more scientific ethics is formulated.

Section IV summarizes, in five pages, the application of the method to philosophy. Descartes expanded this to a whole book in *Meditations on First Philosophy*. These two books should be read together.

Section V is about some applications of the method to physics.

Section VI forecasts that the application of the method would result in a utopia; the conquest of nature; and the cure of "an infinity of maladies, both of body and mind, and even perhaps the enfeeblement brought on by old age." Despite the contrast between Descartes' rationalism and deductivism and Bacon's empiricism and inductivism, these opposite methods, or opposite emphases within the scientific method, were used by both philosophers as means to the same end: a utopian heaven on earth brought about by what Bacon called "man's conquest of nature" by science and technology, the new *summum bonum* of modernity.

The Starting Point

DM begins with a revolutionary claim—the claim that reason (which Descartes calls "good sense" or "common sense") is by nature equal in all men. This amounts to a redefinition of "reason." For this is obviously *not* true of *wisdom*, the ultimate meaning of "reason" for the ancients and the fourth level of Plato's "divided line"; but it is true of levels 2 and 3 of Plato's line, which together make up the scientific method. This method, unlike wisdom, is impersonal and public; anyone can do it. It does not require superior personal gifts of wisdom.

Thus, Descartes democratizes reason, and implies that if everyone used the same method, everyone would discover the same truths and come to the same conclusions. The implication is that if this were done, then the terrible ideological and religious wars that were destroying Europe could end. A bold and idealistic hope indeed! But Descartes had to conceal this radical political implication of his philosophy from the censors, and only hint at it for the few more perspicacious readers who would pick up the hints—thus in practice treating reason as not so democratic after all.

> Good sense is the most evenly distributed commodity in the world, for each of us considers himself to be so well endowed with it that even those who are the most difficult to please in all other matters are not likely to desire more of it than they have. It is not likely that anyone is mistaken about this, but it provides evidence that the power of judging rightly and of distinguishing the true from the false (which, properly speaking, is what people call good sense or reason) is naturally equal in all men.*

If "reason" means "wisdom," it is obviously *not* equal in all men. But if it means only what we call "science," it is. Wisdom is personal; science is impersonal. Because of this difference, philosophers and ordinary people who seek wisdom have always disagreed, while scientists, who have lowered their aims from "wisdom" to "testable empirical knowledge," have always eventually come to consensus and agreement. Descartes' revolution here is to seek universal agreement in philosophy by using the methods of science. This would overcome "diversity of opinions"—*if*, as Descartes goes on to say, this diversity is based not on innate differences in wisdom but only differences in (1) method and (2) data, which can easily be overcome by (1) using the scientific method and (2) sharing data.

> Thus the diversity of our opinions does not arise from the fact that some people are [innately] more reasonable than others, but merely from the fact that we conduct our thoughts along different lines [methods] and do not consider the same things [data].

Machiavelli (see chap. 69) had divided all causes of human achievement into two categories: *virtù* (internal strength of mind and will) and *fortuna* (external chance). Descartes claims that everyone has equal rational *virtù*, or strength of

* Can you detect the logical fallacy of "begging the question" (look it up!) in Descartes' argument in this very first paragraph?

mind, so it must have been mere chance (*fortuna*), and not his innate genius and superiority, that caused him to discover this new method:

> I have never presumed that my mind was in any respect more perfect than anyone else's. [Can he really mean this?] But . . . I have been fortunate; I have, since my youth, found myself on paths that have led me to certain considerations and maxims from which I have formed a method.

The old method for philosophy had always begun by humbly learning from past philosophers before entering "the great conversation" at the present point in its history. Philosophy was a historical and communal activity, not a purely individual and private one. Descartes is the first to repudiate this method and to claim to begin all over again, all alone, like Adam in Eden, as if there were nothing to learn from his predecessors except their mistakes:

> I thought that book learning . . . having been built up from and enlarged gradually by the opinions of many different people, does not draw as near to the truth as the simple reasonings that can be made naturally by a man of good sense concerning what he encounters. . . . For I have already reaped from it [this method] such a harvest that . . . I take immense satisfaction in the progress that I think I have made in the search for truth.

(What would Socrates say about this "satisfaction"?)

The Method

In Part II, Descartes gives us the four rules of his new method (numbering added):

1. The first was never to accept anything as true that I did not know evidently to be so; that is, carefully to avoid precipitous judgment and prejudice; and to include nothing more in my judgments than what presented itself to my mind with such clarity and distinctness that I would have no occasion to doubt it.
2. The second, to divide each of the difficulties I was examining into as many parts as possible and as is required to solve them best.
3. The third, to conduct my thoughts in an orderly fashion, commencing with the simplest and easiest to know objects, to rise gradually, as by degrees, to the knowledge of the most composite things, and even supposing an order among those things that do not naturally precede one another.
4. And last, everywhere to make enumerations so complete and reviews so general that I would be sure of having omitted nothing.

On the one hand, these rules seem commonsensical, useful, practical, and open-minded. On the other hand, they have hidden assumptions:

1. a. Can we in fact doubt *everything*? How can we begin with nothing at all?
   b. Is clarity and distinctness the criterion for either certainty or truth? Aren't some truths unclear and confusing, and aren't some falsehoods quite clear and distinct?
2. Is all truth reached by analysis ("division") and not synthesis?
3. Is all truth reached by moving from oneness to manyness, from simple to complex, rather than vice versa?
4. If we are not infallible and omniscient, can we ever be sure our enumerations and reviews have been total?

Descartes then makes an amazing claim for this method:

> These long chains of reasoning, each of them simple and easy, that geometricians commonly use to attain their most difficult demonstrations, have given me occasion for hoping that all the things that can fall within human knowledge follow one another in the same way and that, provided only that one abstain from accepting anything as true that is not true [rule 1] and that one always maintain the order to be followed in deducing the one from the other [rule 3], there is nothing so far distant that one cannot finally reach nor so hidden that one cannot discover.

This is the typical "Enlightenment" optimism: the hope of answering *all* questions and solving *all* problems, theoretical and practical, by scientific reason. (Has it in fact been fulfilled? Can it be? Why or why not?)

Universal Methodic Doubt

Rule 1 is the most important and radical one. It consists of (a) universal methodic doubt and (b) the clarity and distinctness of an idea as the test of its truth.

Descartes, far from embracing doubt as his *conclusion*, like the skeptics, wants to overcome it more definitively than ever before. He demands not just *truth* but *certainty*. But to do that, he begins, as his premise, with a more total doubt than ever before. He climbs down to the depth of the doubter's pit because he is convinced he has a ladder strong enough to escape into total sunlight. The doubt is only methodic, not lived. He is not a skeptic; in fact, he is the opposite of a skeptic: he demands absolute certainty. But to get there, he begins with skepticism, with universal doubt, as his method.

In the scientific method, doubt is indeed essential. Ideas must be treated as guilty (doubtful) until proven innocent (certain). But in real life, persons, in their words, and even things, in their appearances, should be treated as innocent (truthful) until proven guilty (deceptive). Which of these two methods should philosophy use?

Socrates, Plato, and Aristotle all said that philosophy should begin with *wonder*, which is not the same thing as doubt. Rabbi Abraham Heschel says that "wonder rather than doubt is the root of all knowledge." And Augustine said, in his *Confessions*, "I began to realize that I had believed countless things which I had never seen or which had taken place when I was not there to see, so many events in the history of the world, so many facts about places and towns which I had never seen; and so much that I believed on the word of friends or teachers or various other people. Unless we took these things on trust, we should accomplish absolutely nothing in life." Descartes does not disagree with this rule for practical everyday life. The question that divides Descartes from these thinkers is whether philosophy should more resemble science or life. For Descartes, it is science; and that is the essence of the Enlightenment.

Socrates, too, began by doubting others' ideas, but he gave the believer the default position, so to speak, taking upon himself the onus of disproof. It was a kind of methodic faith. ("Let's assume you are right . . . *but* . . .") Descartes puts the onus of proof on the believer, no matter what idea is believed. And this is indeed the strict scientific method. But he does not pretend to live this way. There is a disconnect between philosophy and life in Descartes because philosophy is now conceived as a science in the modern sense. No one can live as a skeptic, but a scientist should think as a skeptic.

Descartes mentions four levels of doubt, each one more radical and universal than the one before:

1. "Thus, since our senses sometimes deceive us, I decided to suppose that nothing was exactly as our senses would have us imagine."
2. "And since there are men who err in reasoning, even in the simplest matters of geometry . . . judging that I was just as prone to error as the next man, I rejected as false all the reasonings that I had previously taken for proofs."
3. "And finally, taking into account the fact that the same thoughts we have when we are awake can also come to us when we are asleep, without any of the latter thoughts being true, I resolved to pretend that everything that had ever entered my mind was no more true than the illusions of my dreams." ("All that we see or seem / Is but a dream within a dream." —Edgar Allen Poe)
4. In the *Meditations* he adds: "I will suppose not a supremely good God, the source of truth, but rather an evil genius, as clever and deceitful as he is powerful, who has directed his entire effort to misleading me. I will regard the heavens, the air, the earth, colors, shapes, sounds, and all external things as nothing but the deceptive games of my dreams, with which he lays snares for my credulity.

I will regard myself as having no hands, no eyes, no flesh, no blood, no senses, but as nevertheless falsely believing that I possess all these things."

How can you be certain that all your consciousness is not hypnosis and mental telepathy from the devil? This is, of course, a mere methodic thought experiment, a puzzle to be solved by a philosopher, not a real doubt to be lived. That would be paranoia in need of psychoanalysis.

Pascal argued, against Descartes, that this doubt will not lead us to certainty; that we *cannot* be certain by reason alone; that we must make an initial leap of faith in reason itself, since our reason cannot, without begging the question, decide whether or not to trust our reason (i.e., to trust that it comes from a trustable mind [God] rather than an untrustable mind [the devil] or from no mind at all but only blind chance [which is just as untrustable]). So faith in reason must precede reason. But must there not also be *reasons* for any faith or trust? Is this a "which comes first, the chicken or the egg?" problem?

The most distinctively Cartesian aspect of the method is the demand for "clear and distinct ideas" as the criterion for truth, or rather for certainty about truth. Descartes demands not just *truth*, like any honest philosopher, but *certainty*. This also is distinctively Cartesian.

By the "clarity" of an idea Descartes means its power to irresistibly impress itself upon the mind. By the "distinctiveness" of an idea Descartes means its being so sharply separated from all other ideas (like whole numbers) that there is no overlapping, nothing in common between the two ideas to allow them to be confused with each other.*

This "atomistic" conception of ideas corresponds to an atomistic conception of reality, especially the clear and total distinction between mind and matter, which will lead to Descartes' most famous and problematic heritage, the "mind-body problem." *Mind = thought without spatial extension, matter = spatial extension without thought*; therefore, it seems that the two cannot meet or touch, any more than two positive integers can.

Descartes' Provisional Ethics

Part III of DM is a purely pragmatic, temporary moral code to live by "conveniently" while working on a serious philosophy, which eventually would produce a more scientific, rationally certain ethics. Descartes never produced this ethics.

---

* Many questions arise here: (1) Is time atomistic, like numbers? Are its moments separate? (2) Is space? (3) Are events? Is one historical event related to another one as numbers are? (4) On the other hand, doesn't quantum physics reduce all physical reality to atomistic quanta? Yet light is both continuous waves and discontinuous particles (photons).

He is one of the very few major philosophers who never wrote an ethics. Perhaps he just died too early. But more likely, he was not really all that interested in ethics. For ethics consists in conforming the soul and its desires to objective reality in the form of spiritual moral principles; but from DM Part VI it is clear that what interested Descartes most was the opposite: the Baconian program of conforming objective reality in the form of the material world to the desires of the soul, and among these desires not so much the desire for moral virtue but for material pleasure, long life, and contentment.*

The four rules of the provisional ethics (DM Part III) parallel the four rules of the method (DM Part II) in *form*. The first is about what to doubt. The second is about procedural success. The third is about order and priorities. The fourth is about a universal review. But the *content* of the first three of these four rules is just the opposite of the content of the first three rules of the method.

1. The method tells us to doubt everything in thinking; the ethics tells us to doubt nothing in practice. "The first [rule] is to obey the laws and customs of my country." It is not profitable, in a conservative society, to appear to be a revolutionary, even (especially) if you really are one.
2. "The second maxim was to be as firm and resolute in my actions as I could be, and to follow with no less constancy the most doubtful opinions, once I have decided on them, than if they were very certain." This works best in practice, even though its opposite works best in scientific theorizing.
3. "The third maxim was always to try to conquer myself rather than fortune, to change my desires rather than the order of the world." This is the exact opposite of the Baconian program of conquering nature by applied science. Descartes advises us to be humble, conservative, and traditional in ethics, but radical, progressive, and demanding in science. His successors would change his ethical advice but not his scientific advice.
4. "Finally . . . to review the various occupations that men take up in this life so as to try to choose the best one."

Descartes applied his new scientific method to every other division of philosophy—metaphysics, cosmology, natural theology, anthropology, and epistemology—but not ethics. Kant, who took ethics much more seriously and centrally, tried to do just that 150 years later—to construct a purely rational,

* This perhaps defines the difference between premodern and modern man more primordially than anything else. C.S. Lewis puts it simply and strikingly in *The Abolition of Man*: "There is something which unites magic and applied science [technology] while separating both from the 'wisdom' of earlier ages. For the wise men of old, the cardinal problem had been how to conform the soul to reality, and the solution had been knowledge, self-discipline, and virtue. For magic and applied science alike the problem is how to subdue reality to the wishes of men: the solution is a technique."

logical, almost geometrical ethics (though with a different epistemology than either Bacon's empiricism or Descartes' rationalism)—thus filling in this blank space in Descartes' "Enlightenment" program.

Descartes' Door to Certainty: "Cogito Ergo Sum"

"Cogito ergo sum" (I think, therefore I am) is probably the single most famous sentence in the history of philosophy. It is Descartes' first and foundational certainty, the first rung on his escape ladder from skepticism. It is his "Archimedean point." Archimedes, the Greek scientist who discovered that the power of the lever to move heavy objects was proportionate to the length of the lever, reputedly said, "Give me only a lever long enough and a fulcrum to rest it on, and I can move the whole world." A philosopher's "Archimedean point" is his first premise, starting point, or foundation for the rest of his philosophy.

> I resolved to pretend that everything that had ever entered my mind was no more true than the illusions of my dreams. But immediately afterward I noticed that, during the time I wanted thus to think that everything was false, it was necessary that I, who thought thus, be something. And noticing that this truth—*I think, therefore I am*—was so firm and so certain that the most extravagant suppositions of the skeptics were unable to shake it, I judged that I could accept it without scruple as the first principle of the philosophy I was seeking.

This even answers the *Meditations*' extreme skepticism in which he asks how he can be sure he is not being hypnotized by a demon: "But there is a deceiver (I know not who he is) powerful and sly in the highest degree, who is always purposely deceiving me. Then there is no doubt that I exist, if he deceives me. And deceive me as he will, he can never bring it about that I am nothing so long as I shall think that I am something. Thus . . . the statement 'I am, I exist' is necessarily true every time it is uttered by me or conceived in my mind."

Augustine had used the same argument long ago, in his *Contra academicos* (Against the Academics). His version was "Dubito ergo sum" (I doubt, therefore I am). But he had not based his whole subsequent philosophy on it, as Descartes is about to do. Descartes had studied Augustine and clearly borrowed this argument from him (but without crediting him with it, for Descartes is claiming to begin philosophy anew).

There is an obvious strength to this argument against skepticism. Even if a demon is deceiving me, I must exist in order for him to deceive me. So my own existence is the one thing I cannot doubt. But there are also weaknesses to Descartes' "Cogito ergo sum" refutation of skepticism.

The most obvious weakness is that it is a deductive argument, and thus presupposes unproved premises. It is an enthymeme, a syllogism with an implied premise:

Implied premise: Whatever thinks, exists.
Expressed premise: I think.
Conclusion: I exist.

This argument is logically valid (the conclusion follows with logical necessity from its premises), both its premises are true, and all its terms are unambiguous and clear. So there is nothing logically wrong with it. But it is a syllogism (i.e., an argument with two premises). A total skeptic would doubt each premise and demand proof for them. And that would require two more arguments with four more premises. This process would never end: the skeptic would demand premises for the premises of the premises, et cetera ad infinitum. As one skeptic said, Descartes should have written, "I think I think, therefore I think I am—I think."

In *Meditations*, published four years later, Descartes avoids this difficulty, because there he calls "I am, I exist" *not* the conclusion of an argument but a self-evident *proposition*. He says, "The *statement* 'I think, I exist' is necessarily true."

A necessary truth or self-evident proposition like "*a=a*" or "*x* is not non-*x*" or "black birds are birds" needs no proof and no premises; it proves itself. It is literally indubitable. Its denial is self-contradictory, self-refuting, because its predicate merely repeats all or part of its subject. Its predicate is essential, not accidental, to its subject. "Birds" is part of the essence of "black birds," as "small" is not.

Will this refutation of skepticism work? If the proposition "I exist" is necessarily true, as Descartes claims, then his whole philosophy is founded on a certainty; if not, it's not. Everything in his philosophy depends on this, since everything else in his system is deduced from this. The system is like an upside-down pyramid, standing on its point.

But "I exist" is *not* logically self-evident, or "necessarily true," as Descartes claims it is. For its predicate, "exist," is not essential but accidental to its subject, which is Descartes. Descartes exists contingently, not necessarily. He is *given* existence at birth (or conception) and *no longer* exists in this world after death. Only God's existence is essential, is his essence. Descartes is implicitly confusing himself with God. (He was, after all, a bit arrogant, like most geniuses!)

"I exist" is, however, *psychologically* self-evident even though it is not logically self-evident. The individual who utters it can be absolutely certain that it is true, even though no one else can. That is why Descartes added the last phrase to the sentence in *Meditations*: "'I exist' is necessarily true *every time it is uttered by me or conceived in my mind.*" It is certain to *him* but only to him. It is a private certainty. "I do not exist" is personally, practically, subjectively, or existentially self-contradictory. The proposition does not contradict itself; it contradicts the person proposing it while he is in the very act of proposing it.

But that is not science. What Descartes needs is a public certainty, not just a private one. His "cogito" is not the logical foundation for an objective, scientific philosophy, as he thinks it is; but it can be the personal foundation for a subjective, experiential philosophy, i.e., for what later would be called existentialism. Sartre, the inventor of the term "existentialism," explicitly credits Descartes for this subjectively certain starting point. But that was far from Descartes' intention. He wanted to found a scientific philosophy, not an "existential" one.

Another logical problem with the "cogito" is that thinking does not necessarily logically imply an individual human thinker as its cause. The cause of thinking might be God (as it is for the pantheist Spinoza, the next great rationalist philosopher after Descartes), or a single impersonal, universal Mind (as it is for some forms of Hinduism and Buddhism).

Descartes' Anthropology

Now that he has his first certainty, that he exists, Descartes' next step is to investigate what he can know with certainty about *what* he is. He has not yet proved his senses to be trustworthy, or the material world to be real, so all he knows about himself so far is that he thinks. And this proves to him that thinking is his essence:

> Then, examining with attention what I was, and seeing that I could pretend that I had no body and that there was no world nor any place where I was, but that I could not pretend, on that account, that I did not exist; and that, on the contrary, from the very fact that I thought about doubting the truth of other things, it followed very evidently and very certainly that I existed. On the other hand, had I simply stopped thinking, even if all the rest of what I have ever imagined were true, I would have no reason to believe that I existed. From this I knew that I was a thing which in order to exist, needed no place and depended on no material thing. Thus this "I," that is, the soul through which I am what I am, is [1] entirely distinct from the body, [2] and is even easier to know than the body, [3] and even if there were no body, the soul would not cease to be all that it is.

(Why does Descartes believe these three conclusions logically follow? Is he right or wrong? Why?)

Descartes' anthropology centers on these four theses:

1. The essence of the self is simply the soul, or at least its power of thinking (i.e., the mind). Descartes often identifies self with soul, soul with mind, mind with reason, and reason with his new, narrowed, mathematically clear scientific reasoning.
2. The soul and body are two distinct substances. His criterion of truth, "clear and distinct ideas," proves this; mind and body are two clear and distinct ideas and therefore two clear and distinct realities. They are two clear and distinct ideas because a mind can think and is not extended in space (it has no physical size), while a body is extended in space but cannot think. The atoms of your brain are not the thinker. The second after you die, they are all there, yet thinking is no longer possible.

   Descartes is not a materialist but a dualist. A materialist believes that only matter exists; a dualist believes that both matter and mind, or soul, or thought, exist. A brain is not a mind; a brain is an organ of the body. Brains do not think; persons, souls, or minds think, using brains. When the soul (the source of life) leaves the body at death, all brain activity stops. Brains, of themselves, can no more think than typewriters can type. *People* do both.
3. The soul (mind) is known not empirically, from sensory experience of what it does (e.g., art, speech, technology), but is known directly, easily, and with certainty by immediate self-consciousness ("I think").

   This, Descartes believes, is our essence, because it cannot be thought away. Descartes argues that we can be certain only of essences, not accidents. He shows this by the famous example of a piece of wax. The wax changes all its visible, bodily accidents when melted or reshaped, but not its (chemical) essence. It becomes hotter, smaller, or rounder, but not more or less waxy. Thus, we can be certain of our minds, which are our essence, but not our bodies, which change like the wax. Our minds can know unchanging truths by reason, which can give us certainty, while sensation can only know changing material things, which do not give us certainty.
4. Souls are immortal. The soul has an essence distinct from the body, for it thinks, while bodies don't; meanwhile, bodies have size (spatial extension), while souls don't. Therefore, the soul must be a separate substance, for (Descartes assumes) what is essentially distinct in thought must be essentially distinct in reality. And since the soul is a separate substance, a separately existing entity, it follows that it is not dependent on the body for its existence. And therefore it does not die when the body dies, since each substance has its own existence. (This is similar to Plato's argument in Book 10 of his *Republic*.)

It is instructive to contrast Descartes with Aquinas here. Aquinas, using Aristotle's hylomorphism (matter-form theory), saw man as one substance, not two, with the soul as the form of the body (and, implicitly, the body as the matter of the soul). This is essentially what psychologists call "psychosomatic unity": body and soul are two dimensions of one person, like the words and the meaning of a book. So Aquinas would disagree with the first three of these theses of Descartes—though he also affirmed the substantiality and immortality of the soul, as Plato did and Aristotle did not. For him the soul is both a substance *and* a form (of the body). The body is neither.

The relation between these two substances constitutes the "mind-body problem" that Descartes left to his successors. We will see how difficult it is to solve that problem at the end of this chapter.

Descartes' Epistemology: the Criterion of Truth

If man is essentially mind, then knowledge is essentially reason, not sensation. (Descartes is a rationalist, not an empiricist.) This means essentially two things:

1. that reason, not sensation, is to be *trusted*, and
2. that reason, not sensation, is the *origin* of true and certain knowledge.

The criterion for truth, then, is the indubitability of a rational idea. The second half of the first rule of the method tells us that this certainty comes from two qualities of the idea. The first is positive: its clarity (as the open eye cannot avoid seeing light, the mind cannot avoid "seeing" the essence or meaning of an idea like "two" or "mind" or "size"). The second is negative: the idea's distinctness (absence of any confusion with any other idea).

Descartes offers this argument for clear and distinct ideas as the universal criterion for truth:

> After this, I considered in a general way what is needed for a proposition to be true and certain; for since I had just found one proposition that I knew was true ["I exist"], I thought I ought also to know in what this certitude consists. And having noticed that there is nothing in all of this—I think, therefore I am—that assures me that I am uttering the truth, except that I see very clearly that, in order to think, one must exist, I judged that I could take as a general rule that the things we conceive very clearly and very distinctly are all true.

This is a merely inductive argument, from a particular example to a universal principle, and therefore only probable. (In fact, it is from only *one* example, so it is a very weak induction.) Later, Descartes will strengthen his case by a deductive argument from God's perfection (a perfect God would not deceive us). But he has not yet proved God's existence. If he uses his criterion of truth to prove

God's existence and also uses God to prove his criterion of truth, he is arguing in a circle. This criticism is so famous it has come to be called "the Cartesian circle." His contemporary Arnauld put it this way: "I have . . . an uncertainty about how a circular reasoning is to be avoided in saying: the only secure reason we have for believing that what we clearly and distinctly perceive is true, is the fact that God exists. But we can be sure that God exists only because we clearly and evidently perceive that."

If clear and distinct ideas do not deceive us, what is the cause of error? Descartes' answer is that the cause of error is not the mind itself but its improper use by the will, when the will runs ahead of the evidence presented by the mind and makes judgments precipitously. There is no error in simple concepts like "Socrates" and "angel," but only in hasty judgments like "Socrates is an angel." For judgment is an act made (or at least caused) by the will, which actively chooses to combine two concepts that had been passively received by the mind as subject and predicate of a proposition; while the mind is limited to the essences it knows, the will is unlimited in its ability to choose how to combine these essences in judgments, so that the will can easily run ahead of the mind in making judgments.

Descartes' Arguments for God's Existence

Descartes has now

1. doubted everything,
2. proved his own existence,
3. deduced that the self is essentially a soul (mind), and
4. arrived at clear and distinct ideas as the criterion for truth.

Where can he go from here? He is still confined to his ideas and has not yet proved that anything in the external world exists, including his own body. He cannot use sense experience to prove anything without abandoning his universal doubt. All he knows are ideas. Are there any ideas that, simply by being the ideas they are, prove the existence of anything else, anything outside the ideas?

Descartes finds one and only one such idea: the idea of God. God will be his only logical bridge between the knowledge of himself and the knowledge of the world, between subject and object, mind and matter.

Of course, he cannot prove God's existence from any external data such as the existence of things or design or causal order in the universe, because thus far he has only doubted, and not proved, the universe. But two unique aspects of the idea of God, he thinks, give Descartes two ways to prove God's existence.

1. "God" means "a wholly perfect being." Descartes knows that his mind is imperfect, for it is full of doubts and ignorance. Where could the idea of a perfect being have come from? Not from his own imperfect self, nor from anything else in an imperfect world, but only from God himself. Why? Because the cause of something perfect cannot be less than perfect. The effect cannot be greater than the cause.

   Descartes takes this principle of causality as a logically self-evident truth:

   > It is evident by the light of nature [natural reason] that at the very least there must be as much in the total efficient cause as there is in the effect of that same cause. For, I ask, where can an effect get its reality unless it be from its cause? And how can the cause give that reality to the effect unless the cause also has that reality? Hence it follows that something cannot come into existence from nothing, nor even can what is more perfect, that is, that contains in itself more reality, come into existence from what contains less.

   And the idea of God as a wholly perfect being does exist, at least in his mind. Why does Descartes think that this proves that it must exist in reality? Because by the principle of causality, *something* that exists must cause the existence of the idea of God, and the cause cannot have less perfection or less reality than its effect. How could the imperfect mind of Descartes be the adequate cause of something as infinitely perfect as the idea of God?
2. Descartes also uses St. Anselm's "ontological argument," which likewise argues not from any external data in the world but from the perfect *idea* of God to the reality of God; but it does so without using the principle of causality. Instead, Anselm deduces God's existence from his essence (definition). The shortest way to put his argument is:
   a. "God" means "the being that lacks no conceivable perfection."
   b. Real, objective existence, independent of a mind, is a conceivable perfection: it is more perfect than merely subjective, mental existence, dependent on a human mind.
   c. Therefore, God cannot lack real, independent, objective existence.

   If you say that he does lack real, independent, objective existence, you contradict yourself: you say that the being that by definition has all conceivable perfections lacks this conceivable perfection.

   Descartes realizes that this argument "feels" wrong because we are deducing the real existence of something from its mere idea. It feels like a magician pulling a live rabbit out of nothing but a paper hat. But he explains why he thinks it is logically legitimate to deduce God's existence merely from his essence, or definition, or concept, even though he cannot do this validly for anything else:

> I saw very well that by supposing, for example, a triangle, it is necessary for its three angles to be equal to two right angles, but I did not see anything in all this which would assure me that any triangle existed. On the other hand, returning to an examination of the idea I had of a perfect being, I found that existence was contained in it, in the same way as the fact that its three angles are equal to two right angles is contained in the idea of a triangle. . . . Consequently it is at least as certain that God [a being so perfect] exists as any demonstration in geometry can possibly be.

(See Aquinas and Kant for critiques of this argument.)

3. There is also a third, and most commentators think weaker, argument for the existence of God in Descartes: that God must exist as the ultimate cause of the origin of Descartes' thinking self, because if he had been his own cause and creator, he would not have made himself with any imperfections, which he evidently has (e.g., ignorance and doubt).

The World

But all Descartes has proved so far is his own mind and God. Among the countless ideas in his mind, they are the only two that prove themselves. How can he build a bridge from self (mind) to world? How can he escape solipsism? How can he be sure that even if he perfectly obeys the rules of his method, his conclusions will be true not just in the realm of ideas but also in the realm of objective reality that these ideas claim to reveal?

An assurance that thinking according to the method will correspond to the world cannot come from the method itself. Nor can it come from the world, for that has not yet been proved to exist. It must therefore come from God. God is Descartes' "bridge" from self to world. For a perfect God would neither deceive nor be deceived. And if God is the author of my mind and my senses, he would "program" these powers in me correctly, so to speak, so that so long as I used these instruments properly, I would not err.

> Since God is no deceiver, it is very manifest that He does not communicate to me these ideas [of material things] immediately and by Himself. . . . For since He has given me no faculty to recognize that this is the case, but on the other hand a very great inclination to believe that they are conveyed to me by corporeal objects, I do not see how He could be defended from the accusation of deceit if these ideas were produced by causes other than corporeal objects. Hence we must allow that corporeal things exist.

Thus, the validity of sense experience and the existence of the material world they reveal, all of which Descartes began by doubting, are now proved.

Notice that the idea of matter thus "proves itself," in a sense, as the idea of self and God did:

> If any one of my ideas [viz., the idea of the material world] is of such a nature as clearly to make me recognize that it is not in me . . . and that . . . I cannot be the cause of it, it follows of necessity . . . that there is another being . . . which is the cause of this idea.

Descartes also argues that the material world often influences me against my will (e.g., pain and death), so that I could not have been its author.

Is it true that we cannot help but believe that material things exist? Yes, answers Descartes, and that is his premise for concluding that they do exist. Berkeley would answer no and say that we not only can but should believe that matter does not exist, but only mind (see chap. 61).

Pascal criticized Descartes here not logically but psychologically, by pointing out that once Descartes proved God's existence and deduced from it the reliability of our mind and senses, and thus the reality of the world, he was no longer interested in God at all but only in our scientific and technological conquest of that world. God was merely the necessary foundation for science and, like the foundation for a building, remained underground, invisible and forgotten. He was used as a means rather than as the End (though Descartes, as a Catholic, does not *deny* that he is our final end).

Thus, Descartes claims to prove the existence of (1) his own mind, (2) God, and (3) bodies (the material world), in that order. But he never attempts to prove a fourth thing: the existence of other minds (although he does believe they exist).

Descartes' *Summum Bonum*

Pascal's criticism may be unfair, but it is certainly true that the rest of Descartes' life, and the rest of the *Discourse on Method*, is entirely concerned with "the conquest of nature." In Part V he predicts the triumphs in physics that the use of his method would bring. The method is a means to a better (more certain) philosophy, which in turn is a means to a better (more certain) foundation for physical science, which in turn is a means to the technological "conquest of nature" that is Descartes' *summum bonum* or final end as much as it is Bacon's. As at least a nominal Catholic, Descartes would believe, or say he believed, that our *summum bonum* is God's conquest of man (salvation), but in his philosophical practice his *summum bonum* was "man's conquest of nature" (technology).

In Part VI he gives us his "salesman's pitch" and prophecy of the utopia that the new technology would give to humanity. I quote it at length because this is for Descartes the ultimate goal of his whole philosophy.

> As soon as I had acquired some general notions in the area of physics, and, beginning to test them on various specific difficulties, I had noticed just how far they can lead and how much they differ from the principles that people have used up until the present, I believed I could not keep them hidden away without greatly sinning against the law that obliges us to procure as best we can the common good of all men. [This is the only time Descartes gets serious enough to use the word "sinning."]
>
> For these general notions show me that it is possible to arrive at knowledge that is very useful in life and that in place of the speculative philosophy taught in the Schools, one can find a practical one, by which, knowing the force and the actions of fire, water, air, stars, the heavens, and all the other bodies that surround us, just as we understand the various skills of our craftsmen, we could, in the same way, use these objects for all the purposes for which they are appropriate, and thus make ourselves, as it were, masters and possessors of nature. ["Speculative" means not "uncertain" but "seeking truth for its own sake as an end rather than as a means to use"; see vol. 1, chap. 25, "The Ordering of All Knowledge," for Aristotle's defense of this "speculative" or "theoretical" knowledge.]
>
> This is desirable not only for the invention of an infinity of devices that would enable us to enjoy without pain [back to Eden!] the fruits of the earth and all the goods one finds in it, but principally for the maintenance of health, which unquestionably [sic!] is the first good and the foundation of all the other goods in this life. [Nearly all philosophers offer candidates for the *summum bonum*; has any other one ever offered *health*? Is this the philosophy of the young or of the old?]
>
> For even the mind depends so greatly upon the temperament and on the disposition of the organs of the body that, were it possible to find some means to make men generally more wise and competent than they have been up until now, I believe that one should look to medicine to find this means.

Descartes may be obscurely thinking of something like the fruits of genetic engineering here, though of course he did not know about genetics, for he continues:

> It is true that the medicine currently practiced contains little of such usefulness; but without trying to ridicule it, I am sure that there is no one, not even among those in the medical profession, who would not admit that

> everything we know is almost nothing in comparison to what remains to be known, and that we might rid ourselves of an infinity of maladies, both of body and mind, and perhaps also of the enfeeblement brought on by old age, were one to have a sufficient knowledge of their cause and of all the remedies that nature has provided for us.

"Man's conquest of nature" is not complete until he has conquered pain, disease, old age, and perhaps even death itself, nature's trump card. Descartes wrote, in a letter to Burnham, "It should not be doubted that human life could be indefinitely prolonged if we knew the appropriate art." If that is what Descartes had in mind, this raises the ghost of the serpent-tempter in Genesis 3 ("You shall be as gods"). It is the dream of Faust, and of Prometheus, and of the Tower of Babel.

This is typical "Enlightenment" optimism, not only concerning how far science and technology can progress but also concerning the social consequences of this progress, which the Enlightenment took to be wholly benign. Because of what we have seen of the use of technology in the twentieth century, "the century of genocide," the century of Auschwitz and Hiroshima, most people are much less optimistic today. Descartes may be "the father of modern philosophy," but it is Pascal (chap. 56), Descartes' less famous, less rationalistic, less optimistic, and more existential critic, who seems much more prophetic for our present and future.

The Mind-Body Problem

This is the loose thread Descartes left hanging in his system. Mind and body are two clear and distinct ideas, for *mind = thought without spatial extension* and *body = extension without thought*. Since clear and distinct ideas are the criterion of truth, it must be true that mind and body really are distinct.

This produces the problematic anthropology of "the ghost in the machine." A mere ghost cannot change a machine; it has no physical fingers to press buttons. Nor can a machine change a ghost (e.g., you can't kill a ghost with a gun).

But our constant experience seems to show that the "ghost" and "machine" constantly interact causally, or, even more intimately, always act together like two blades of a pair of scissors, or rather like two *dimensions* of one thing rather than two things. If they are indeed two substances, they must meet somewhere in order to interact. Where? Why does my arm actually move when my mind commands it to move?

Descartes' only answer was the pineal gland, a newly discovered ductless gland at the base of the brain. Of course, this is no answer at all, for it is wholly on the material side and not a bridge to spirit. If the mind has no size, it cannot be a gland, or in a gland; for a gland, no matter how small, has size. And if the mind has no size, how can it influence things that do have size? And how can things that do have size influence thought, which has no size?

This dualism also seems to entail a very strange view of animals, which Descartes views as merely complex machines, so that there is no *essential* difference between breaking a lever off a machine and breaking a leg off a dog.

The mind-body dualism also seems to invalidate Descartes' argument for the real existence of the corporeal world (bodily things); in fact, it seems to make it impossible for the mind to know (and thus be influenced by) bodies at all. If bodies (the universe) cannot act on minds, they cannot produce ideas of themselves in minds.

Occasionalism: Geulincx and Malebranche

None of Descartes' successors solved the mind-body problem that he left to them. His immediate disciples, Geulincx and Malebranche, offered "occasionalism" as the solution: since mind and matter, as two clear and distinct ideas and therefore two clear and distinct substances, have nothing in common, they cannot touch or cause or act on each other. Therefore, the apparent causal interaction between our minds and bodies must be brought about not by mind on body or by body on mind but by God, who authored both and can change both. On the occasion of God knowing an event happening in one of these two worlds, he, and he alone, causes a corresponding event in the other world.

Geulincx (1624–1669) affirmed only God-to-body causality, not God-to-mind causality: when I will my arm to move, God moves it, but when my eye sees a tree, God does not put the idea of the tree into my mind. Matter, not God, moves my mind, through my senses; but my mind does not move my body—God does.

Malebranche (1638–1715), more consistently, said that God was the cause of mental events as well as bodily events. On the occasion of his knowing that a knife cuts our flesh, he causes our pain-awareness. There are no natural, finite causes at all. God does everything. He is not only the first cause but the sole cause. This is possible, Malebranche said, because all finite minds are "in" God's mind as bodies are in space. (This is a kind of semi-pantheism, which Spinoza would extend into a full pantheism.)

This occasionalism is similar to that of the Muslim Ash'arite philosophers of the Middle Ages: creatures are nothing, God is everything. Augustine flirted with this sort of explanation just a little bit, but only in the area of explaining sensation, since as a Platonist he also believed, like Descartes, that matter could not act on mind.

The Mind-Body Problem and Man's Alienation

The mind-body problem is not just a conceptual problem for philosophers but a social and psychological problem for modern man as a whole: our felt alienation from nature—our reduction of nature to a passive, lifeless object for physical science and the reduction of ourselves to mental, detached scientific observers of it—has spilled out of the laboratory into life, and has produced a deep longing to "return to nature." Such a longing was unknown in premodern societies because they did not feel the modern problem of alienation. That problem comes more from Descartes than from any other philosopher.

But this alienation seems inseparable from science itself, for science succeeds only when it reduces the world to manageable dimensions, ignoring any that do not fit its method.

The only difference between Descartes and a materialist is that he affirms mind as well as body. But he reduces the bodily half of his mind-body dualism to a machine. This includes our own bodies, as well as animals. They are only complex machines. His own body is thus depersonalized into an "it" rather than a "him." It is not part of his soul and thus not part of him but only the most intimate part of the external world.

This is deeply problematic psychologically: to see a human body, even your own, not as a dimension of a person, a subject, "in here," but as an object, as part of the "out there." One cannot help wondering how many distinctively modern psychological problems, especially in the area of sexuality, are rooted in this Cartesian dualism.

56

BLAISE PASCAL

AD 1623–1662

Pascal versus Descartes—this is not only a personal contrast and a contrast in philosophical styles but a cultural contrast that will characterize modern Western civilization as a whole. It is the contrast between "Enlightenment" scientific rationalism and anti-rationalism. Pascal is really the founder of modern existentialism. One can find his influence on almost every page of Kierkegaard.

The term "existentialism" was invented by Sartre in the early 1940s, but he defined it so narrowly that only his own position fit it: that "existence precedes essence" (i.e., that we have no essence, nature, meaning, or purpose but must invent our own). The term is now used by philosophers more broadly—indeed, so broadly that it applies to very diverse philosophers: atheists and theists, optimists and pessimists, humanists and anti-humanists. It has a definite meaning, but it points not to a set of answers but to a set of questions; it is not a doctrine or teaching but a method or approach or point of view, which is typically modern rather than ancient in being subjective and personal rather than objective and impersonal. It tends to be individualistic and suspicious of universals and abstractions. It sees our essence or our center as the heart rather than the mind. If philosophy is "the love of wisdom," existentialists interpret this love as a passionate personal romance rather than a cerebral scientific curiosity.

What distinguishes the modern mind the most is "the turn to the subject." In this sense, Augustine's *Confessions* is a historical anomaly, a uniquely modern book from premodern times. It is significant that when he knew he was dying, Pascal gave away his entire large library except for the Bible and the *Confessions*. Pascal's *Pensées*, like the *Confessions*, is a dramatic journey. It is a quest for the two things he says we all want most and get least: truth and happiness. More attention is paid to the journey and its troubles than to the outcome. As in the early Socratic dialogues, we are shown the thought *process* and its failures and problems as well as the solution. And when we get the solution, Pascal proposes it as a "wager" or gamble (what later existentialists will call a "leap of faith") rather than a proof.

Pascal is rightly classified as an existentialist because the questions he deals with are the typically "existential" questions, which intrigue not just professional philosophers but all sensitive human beings—questions such as personal identity, unhappiness, uncertainty, alienation from nature, death, evil, human vanity, passion, love, suffering, freedom, immortality, and God. (Many existentialists are atheists, but none are indifferent to the question.)

Pascal was also a scientific genius who invented the world's first working computer (a simple mechanical calculating machine that he designed for his accountant father to relieve his arthritic fingers), vacuum cleaner, and urban public transportation system (in Paris), as well as making important discoveries in physics. Descartes tried to use the scientific mind and method for philosophy, but Pascal did not; he contrasted the scientific "geometrical" mind with the "intuitive" mind, and famously said that "the heart has its reasons, of which [scientific] reason knows nothing."

The *Pensées*

Because his style is so clear and "punchy," I have used his own words to summarize him, adding only topical headings to make clear the logical outline and order of his thoughts. His masterpiece, the *Pensées* (*Thoughts*), is not a *book* but almost one thousand short *notes* for one. The book was cut short by that inconvenient visitor, death.

Outline

First Part: Wretchedness of man without God.
Second Part: Happiness of man with God.

Method

We think playing upon man is like playing upon an ordinary organ. It is indeed an organ, but strange, shifting and changeable. Those who only know how to play an ordinary organ would never be in tune on this one. You have to know where the keys are.

Our Fundamental Fourfold Data

We desire truth, and find in ourselves nothing but uncertainty. We desire happiness, and find only wretchedness and death. We are incapable of not desiring truth and happiness and incapable of [attaining] either certainty or happiness.

The Greatness and Wretchedness of Man

Man is neither angel nor beast, and it is unfortunately the case that anyone trying to act the angel acts the beast. . . .

It is dangerous to explain too clearly to man how like he is to the animals without pointing out his greatness. It is also dangerous to make too much of his greatness without his vileness. It is still more dangerous to leave him in ignorance of both. . . .

If he exalts himself, I humble him. If he humbles himself, I exalt him. And I go on contradicting him until he understands that he is a monster that passes all understanding. . . .

Man is only a reed, the weakest in nature, but he is a thinking reed. There is no need for the whole universe to take up arms to crush him: a vapour, a drop of water is enough to kill him. But even if the universe were to crush him, man would still be nobler than his slayer, because he knows that he is dying and the advantage the universe has over him. The universe knows none of this. Thus all our dignity consists in thought. It is on thought that we must depend for our recovery, not on space and time, which we could never fill. Let us then strive to think well; that is the basic principle of morality. . . .

It is not in space that I must seek my human dignity, but in the ordering of my thought. It will do me no good to own land. Through space the universe grasps me and swallows me up like a speck; through thought I grasp it.

Man's greatness comes from knowing he is wretched: a tree does not know it is wretched. Thus it is wretched to know that one is wretched, but there is greatness in knowing one is wretched. . . .

All these examples of wretchedness prove his greatness. It is the wretchedness of a great lord, the wretchedness of a dispossessed king. Who indeed would think himself unhappy not to be king except one who had been dispossessed? . . . Who would think himself unhappy if he had only one mouth and who would not if he had only one eye? It has probably never occurred to anyone to be distressed at not having three eyes, but those who have none are inconsolable. . . .

Vanity

How vain painting is, exciting admiration by its resemblance to things of which we do not admire the originals! . . .

Let each of us examine his thoughts; he will find them wholly concerned with the past or the future. We almost never think of the present, and if we do think of it, it is only to see what light it throws on our plans for the future. . . . Thus we never actually live, but hope to live, and since we are always planning how to be happy, it is inevitable that we should never be so. . . .

A trifle consoles us because a trifle upsets us. . . .

Anyone who wants to know the full extent of man's vanity has only to consider the causes and effects of love. The cause is a *je ne sais quoi*. And its effects are terrifying. . . . Cleopatra's nose: if it had been shorter the whole face of the earth would have been different.

The Vanity of Human Justice

"Why are you killing me for your own benefit? I am unarmed." "Why, do you not live on the other side of the water? My friend, if you lived on this side, I should be a murderer, but since you live on the other side, I am a brave man and it is right." . . .

There no doubt exist natural laws, but once this fine reason of ours was corrupted, it corrupted everything. . . .

As men could not make might obey right, they have made right obey might. As they could not fortify justice they have justified force. Right is open to dispute, might is easily recognized. . . . Being thus unable to make right into might, we have made might into right. . . .

When everything is moving at once, nothing appears to be moving, as on board ship. When everyone is moving towards depravity, no one seems to be moving, but if someone stops he shows up the others who are rushing on, by acting as a fixed point.

The Weakness of Human Reason

This internal war of reason against the passions has made those who wanted peace split into two sects. Some wanted to renounce passions and become gods, others wanted to renounce reason and become brute beasts. But neither side has succeeded, and reason always remains to denounce the baseness and injustice of the passions and to disturb the peace of those who surrender to them. And the passions are always alive in those who want to renounce them.

Imagination: it is the dominant faculty in man. . . . Would you not say that this magistrate, whose venerable age commands universal respect, is ruled by pure reason? . . . See him go to hear a sermon in a spirit of pious zeal, the soundness of his judgment strengthened by the ardour of his charity. . . . If, when the preacher appears, it turns out that nature has given him a hoarse voice and an odd sort of face . . . then whatever great truths he may announce, I wager that our senator will not be able to keep a straight face. Put the world's greatest philosopher on a plank that is wider than need be: if there is a precipice below, although his reason may convince him that he is safe, his imagination will prevail. . . . If physicians did not have long gowns and mules, if learned doctors did not wear square caps and robes four times too large, they would never have deceived the world. . . . If they possessed true justice, and if physicians possessed the true art of healing, they would not need square caps. . . .

The Refutation of Both Dogmatism and Skepticism

What amazes me most is to see that everyone is not amazed at his own weakness. . . . Nothing strengthens the case for skepticism more than the fact that there are people who are not skeptics. . . .

The strongest of the skeptics' arguments . . . is that we cannot be sure that these [self-evident first] principles are true, faith and revelation apart, except through some natural intuition. Now this natural intuition affords no convincing proof that they are true. [For] there is no certainty, apart from faith, as to whether man was created by a good God, an evil demon, or just by chance, and so it is a matter of doubt, depending on our origin, whether these innate principles are true, false or uncertain. . . . I pause at the dogmatists' only strong point, which is that we cannot doubt natural principles if we speak sincerely and in all good faith. To which the skeptics reply, in a word, that uncertainty as to our origin entails uncertainty as to our nature. The dogmatists have been trying to answer that ever since the world began. . . . You cannot be a skeptic without stifling nature, you cannot be a dogmatist without turning your back on reason.

Alienation; Relativity; Lostness

Nature is an infinite sphere whose centre is everywhere and circumference is nowhere. . . . For after all, what is man in nature? A nothing compared to the infinite, a whole compared to the nothing, a middle point between all and nothing, infinitely remote from an understanding of the extremes; the end of things and their principles [origins] are unattainably hidden from him in impenetrable secrecy. Equally incapable of seeing the nothingness from which he emerges and the infinity in which he is engulfed. . . . We are floating in a medium of vast extent, always drifting uncertainly, blown to and fro; whenever we think we have a fixed point to which we can cling and make fast, it shifts and leaves us behind; if we follow it, it eludes our grasp, slips away, and flees eternally before us. Nothing stands still for us. This is our natural state and yet the state most contrary to our inclinations. We burn with desire to find a firm footing, an ultimate, lasting base on which to build a tower rising up to infinity, but our whole foundation cracks and the earth opens up into the depth of the abyss. . . .

When I consider the brief span of my life absorbed into the eternity which comes before and after—"as the remembrance of a guest that tarrieth but a day"—the small space I occupy and which I see swallowed up in the infinite immensity of spaces of which I know nothing and which know nothing of me, I take fright and am amazed to see myself here rather than there: there is no reason for me to be here rather than there, now rather than then. Who put me here? By whose command and act were this time and place allotted to me?

Death

Anyone with only a week to live will not find it in his interest to believe that all this is just a matter of chance. . . .

Between us and heaven or hell there is only life half-way, the most fragile thing in the world. . . .

Imagine a number of men in chains, all under sentence of death, some of whom are each day butchered in the sight of the others; those remaining see their own condition in that of their fellows, and looking at each other with grief and despair await their turn. This is an image of the human condition. . . .

The last act is bloody, however fine the rest of the play. They throw a little earth over your head and it is finished forever. . . .

We run heedlessly into the abyss after putting something in front of us to stop us seeing it. . . .

Selfishness

The bias towards self is the beginning of all disorder, in war, politics, economics. . . . We are born unfair. . . .

Anyone who does not hate the self-love within him and the instinct which leads him to make himself into a God must be really blind. Who can fail to see that there is nothing so contrary to justice and truth? For it is false that we deserve this position and unjust and impossible to attain it, because everyone demands the same thing. We are thus born into an obviously unjust situation from which we cannot escape but from which we must escape.

The predicament in which [the self] thus finds itself arouses in it the most unjust and criminal passion that could possibly be imagined, for it conceives a deadly hatred for the truth which rebukes it and convinces it of its faults. It would like to do away with this truth, and not being able to destroy it as such, it destroys it as best it can, in the consciousness of itself and others; that is, it takes every care to hide its faults both from itself and others, and cannot bear to have them pointed out or noticed. It is no doubt an evil to be full of faults, but it is a still greater evil to be full of them and be unwilling to recognize them, since this entails the further evil of deliberate self-delusion. . . .

There are only two kinds of men: the righteous who think they are sinners and the sinners who think they are righteous.

The Pseudo-Solution of Diversion

If our condition were truly happy, we should not need to divert ourselves from thinking about it. . . .

Sometimes, when I set to thinking about the various activities of men, the dangers and troubles which they face at Court or in war, giving rise to so many quarrels and passions, daring and often wicked enterprises and so on, I have often said that the sole cause of man's unhappiness is that he does not know how to stay quietly in his room. . . .

That is why we prefer the hunt to the capture. That is why men are so fond of hustle and bustle. That is why prison is such a fearful punishment. That is why the pleasures of solitude are so incomprehensible. . . .

All our life passes in this way: we seek rest by struggling against certain obstacles, and once they are overcome, rest proves intolerable because of the boredom it produces. We must get away from it and crave excitement. . . .

A given man lives a life free from boredom by gambling a small sum every day. Give him every morning the money he might win that day, but on condition that he does not gamble, and you will make him unhappy. It might be argued that what he wants is the entertainment of gaming and not the winnings. Make him play then for nothing; his interest will not be fired and he will become bored. So it is not just entertainment he wants. A half-hearted entertainment without excitement will bore him. He must have excitement, he must delude himself into imagining that he would be happy to win what he would not want as a gift if it meant giving up gambling. He must create some target for his passions and then arouse his desire, anger, fear, for this object he has created, just like children taking fright at a mask they have made themselves.

The Pseudo-Solution of Indifference

Copernicus' opinion need not be more closely examined. But this: It affects our whole life to know whether the soul is mortal or immortal. . . .

The immortality of the soul is something of such vital importance to us, affecting us so deeply, that one must have lost all feeling not to care about knowing the facts of the matter. All our actions and thoughts must follow such different paths, according to whether there is hope of eternal blessings or not, that the only possible way of acting with sense and judgment is to decide our course in the light of this point, which ought to be our ultimate objective. And that is why, amongst those who are not convinced, I make an absolute distinction between those who strive with all their might to learn and those who live without troubling themselves or thinking about it. I can feel nothing but compassion for those who sincerely lament their doubt, who regard it as the ultimate misfortune, and who, sparing no effort to escape from it, make their search their principal and most serious business. But as for those who spend their lives without a thought for this final end of life . . . I view them very differently. This negligence in a matter where they themselves, their eternity, their all are at stake, fills me more with irritation than pity. It astounds and appalls me; it seems quite monstrous to me. I do not say this prompted by the pious zeal of spiritual devotion. I mean on the contrary that we ought to have this feeling from principles of human interest and self-esteem. . . . How can such an argument as this occur to a reasonable man?: "I do not know who put me into the world. . . . All I know is that I must soon die, but what I know least about is this very death which I cannot evade. Just as I do not know whence I come, so I do not know whither I am going. . . . And my conclusion from all this is that I must pass my days without a thought of seeking what is to happen to me . . . and allow myself to be carried off limply to my death, uncertain of my future state for all eternity." Who would wish to have as his friend a man who argued like that? Who would choose him from among others as a confidant in his affairs? Who would resort to him in adversity? To what use in life could he possibly be turned? It is truly glorious for religion to have such unreasonable men as enemies. . . . With everything else they are quite different: they fear the most trifling things, foresee and feel them; and the same man who spends so many days and nights in fury and despair about losing some office or at some imaginary affront to his honour is the very one who knows that he is going to lose everything through death but feels neither anxiety nor emotion. It is a monstrous thing to see one and the same heart at once so sensitive to minor things and so strangely insensitive to the greatest. It is an incomprehensible spell, a supernatural torpor.

The Alternative: Passionate Truth-Seeking

To render [diverting] passions harmless let us behave as though we had only a week to live. . . .

There are only three sorts of people: those who have found God and serve him; those who are busy seeking him and have not found him; those who live without either seeking or finding him. The first are reasonable and happy, the last are foolish and unhappy, those in the middle are unhappy and reasonable. . . .

Nature has nothing to offer me that does not give rise to doubt and anxiety. If I saw no sign there of a Divinity I should decide on a negative solution; if I saw signs of a Creator everywhere I should peacefully settle down in the faith. But seeing too much to deny and not enough to affirm, I am in a pitiful state. . . . My whole heart strains to know what the true good is in order to pursue it: no price would be too high to pay for eternity. . . .

Truth is so obscured nowadays and lies [are] so well established that unless we love the truth we shall never recognize it.

Three Places to Search; Three Metaphysical Levels

The infinite distance between body and mind symbolizes the infinitely more infinite distance between mind and charity. . . . They are three different orders differing in kind. . . . All bodies, the firmament, the stars, the earth, and its kingdoms are not worth the least of minds, for it knows them all and itself too, while bodies know nothing. All bodies together and all minds together and all their products are not worth the last impulse of charity. This is of an infinitely superior order. Out of all bodies together we could not succeed in creating one little thought. It is impossible, and of a different order. Out of all bodies and minds we could not extract one impulse of true charity. It is impossible, and of a different, supernatural, order. . . .

Philosophers: they surprise the ordinary run of men. Christians: they surprise the philosophers.

The Heart as an Epistemological Subject

We know the truth not only through our reason but also through our heart. It is through the latter that we know first principles. . . .

It is the heart which perceives God and not the reason. That is what faith is: God perceived by the heart, not by the reason. . . .

The heart has its reasons, of which reason knows nothing. We know this in countless ways. I say that it is natural for the heart to love the universal being or itself, according to its allegiance, and it hardens itself against either as it chooses. You have rejected one and kept the other. Is it reason that makes you love yourself?

The Relation between Faith and Reason

Two excesses: to exclude reason, to admit nothing but reason. . . .

One must know when it is right to [skeptically] doubt, to [rationally] affirm, to [faithfully] submit. Anyone who does otherwise does not understand the force of reason. Some men run counter to these three principles, either affirming that everything can be proved, because they know nothing about proof, or doubting everything, because they do not know when to submit, or always submitting, because they do not know when judgment is called for. . . .

Reason would never submit unless it judged that there are occasions when it ought to submit. It is right, then, that reason should submit when it judges that it ought to submit. . . .

Reason's last step is the recognition that there are an infinite number of things which are beyond it. It is merely feeble if it does not go as far as to realize that.

Why God Hides

God wishes to move the will rather than the mind. Perfect clarity would help the mind and harm the will. Humble their pride. . . .

There is enough light for those who desire only to see, and enough darkness for those of a contrary disposition. . . .

If there were no obscurity man would not feel his corruption; if there were no light man could not hope for a cure. Thus it is not only right but useful for us that God should be partly concealed and partly revealed, since it is equally dangerous for man to know God without knowing his own wretchedness as to know his wretchedness without knowing God. . . .

Knowing God without knowing our own wretchedness makes for pride. Knowing our own wretchedness without knowing God makes for despair. Knowing Jesus Christ strikes the balance because he shows us both God and our own wretchedness. . . .

If he had wished to overcome the obstinacy of the most hardened, he could have done so by revealing himself to them so plainly that they could not doubt . . . as he will appear on the last day. . . . This is not the way he wished to appear when he came in mildness. . . . The way of God, which disposes all things with gentleness, is to instill religion into our minds with reasoned arguments and into our hearts with grace; but attempting to instill it into hearts and minds with force and threats is to instill not religion but terror.

The Wager

Either God is or he is not. But to which view shall we be inclined? Reason cannot decide this question. Infinite chaos separates us. At the far end of this infinite distance a coin is being spun which will come down heads or tails. How will you wager? Reason cannot make you choose either, reason cannot prove either wrong.

Do not then condemn as wrong those who have made a choice, for you know nothing about it. "No, but I will condemn them not for having made this particular choice, but any choice; for although the one who calls heads and the other one are equally at fault, the fact is that they are both at fault. The right thing is not to wager at all."

Yes, but you must wager. There is no choice, you are already embarked.

Which will you choose then? Let us see. Since a choice must be made, let us see which offers you the most interest.

You have two things to lose: the true and the good; and two things to stake: your reason and your will, your knowledge and your happiness; and your nature has two things to avoid: error and wretchedness.

Since you must necessarily choose, your reason is no more affronted by choosing one rather than the other. That is one point cleared up.

> But your happiness? Let us weigh up the gain and the loss involved in calling heads that God exists. Let us assess the two cases: if you win you win everything, if you lose, you lose nothing.
>
> Do not hesitate then: wager that he does exist. . . .
>
> Thus our argument carries infinite weight, when the stakes are finite in a game where there are even chances of winning and losing and an infinite prize to be won. . . .
>
> What harm will come to you from choosing this course? You will be faithful, honest, humble, grateful, full of good works, a sincere, true friend. It is true you will not enjoy noxious pleasures, glory and good living, but will you not have others? . . .
>
> I tell you that you will gain even in this life, and that at every step you take along this road you will see that your gain is so certain and your risk so negligible that in the end you will realize that you have wagered on something certain and infinite for which you have paid nothing.

For a practical, commonsensical modern defense of Pascal's wager, see William James on "The Will to Believe" in vol. 4, chap. 79.

For a contemporary attempt to (1) organize the *Pensées* into a logical and practical order, and to (2) unpack their existential, personal "bite," see my *Christianity for Modern Pagans: Pascal's "Pensées" Edited, Outlined & Explained.*

57

BARUCH SPINOZA

AD 1632–1677

Spinoza's family were Jews from Portugal who during the previous century had become prosperous businessmen in Amsterdam, a refuge of tolerance in an age of religious persecution. "Benedictus" was his Christian name, though he was not a Christian; "Baruch" was his Jewish name, though he was solemnly excommunicated from the Jewish community for his heretical views.* He was not an

* His heresies included the notion that God had a material body (the universe), and that angels, immortality, and free will were illusions. This was the solemn ritual of excommunication, as described by Willis: "During the reading of the curse, the wailing and protracted note of a great horn was heard to fall in from time to time; the lights, seen brightly burning at the beginning of the ceremony, were extinguished one by one as it proceeded, till at the end the last went out—typical of the extinction of the spiritual life of the excommunicated man—and the congregation was left in total darkness." The formula of the excommunication, as translated by Van Vloten, read as follows: "With the judgment of the angels and the sentence of the saints, we anathematize, execrate, curse, and cast out Baruch de Espinoza, the whole of the sacred community assenting, in presence of the sacred books with the 613 precepts written therein, pronouncing against him the malediction wherewith Elisha cursed the children, and all the maledictions written in the Book of the Law. Let him be accursed by day and accursed by night; let him be accursed in his lying down and accursed in his rising up; accursed in going out and accursed in coming in. May the Lord never more pardon or acknowledge him; may the wrath and displeasure of the Lord burn henceforth against this man, load him with all the curses written in the Book of the Law, and blot out his name from under the sky. . . . Hereby then are all admonished that none hold converse with him by word of mouth, none hold communication with him by writing; that no one do him any service, no one abide under the same roof with him, no one approach within four cubits length [six feet] of him, and no one read any document dictated by him or written by his hand." Who cares passionately enough about *anything* to write such things anymore?

atheist; in fact, he was called "the God-intoxicated man." The most accurate label for his views is something like rationalistic pantheism.

He studied Talmud only until he was thirteen, and he found in traditional Jewish philosophers like Moses Maimonides, author of the medieval classic *Guide for the Perplexed*, only perplexity rather than guidance. He preferred the atomistic materialism of Democritus, Lucretius, and Epicurus, and above all the Stoics, to the philosophies of Plato and Aristotle. From the medieval Scholastics he took only their terminology and syllogistic method. Like Descartes, he tried to tighten and refine philosophy's method by modeling it after Euclid's geometry, since this alone gave him what he demanded: demonstrable certainty—a demand he shared with Descartes.

Like everyone in the seventeenth century, he was deeply influenced by Descartes, but disagreed with his matter-mind dualism. His master idea was that in the last analysis there was only one reality (that is monism) and this was God (that is pantheism). God and nature were one; the distinction between them came about only through mentally different points of view, when we distinguish "nature naturing" (*natura naturans*) and "nature natured" (*natura naturata*).

All who knew him testified that he was simple, modest, frugal, gentle, generous, and loyal. He made enough money to live on as a lens grinder. But his real world was the world of the mind. He so prized his freedom that he refused the prestigious chair of philosophy that the University of Heidelberg offered to him, even though he was promised complete freedom, because he feared that his views might "interfere with the established religion of the principality."

Religion, Faith, and Reason

This "God-intoxicated man" was the polar opposite of an atheist. Yet he was often called an atheist because he did not believe in the God of the Bible, the Creator. He was a pantheist. An atheist believes there is no Creator; a pantheist believes there is no creation. An atheist believes there is nothing above nature; a pantheist believes there is nothing below God. Spinoza's God was not the living, acting, personal God of Jewish, Christian, or Islamic religion. His God was simply "substance," or being itself. (See below, the section on his metaphysics.)

Yet at the same time he claimed to be also a good religious Jew, because he taught a kind of "two truth" theory similar to that of Averroes and Siger of Brabant (see vol. 2)—that faith, a religion of a personal God ("I AM"), divine revelation, miracles, divine law, free will, immortality, judgment, heaven, and hell were good myths for the masses, who could not rise to the philosophical abstractions that made them unnecessary for the enlightened philosopher.

Thus, Spinoza would agree with Pascal that there is a great gap between what Pascal called "the God of Abraham, Isaac, and Jacob" and "the God of the philosophers and scholars." But where Pascal chose the God of Abraham, known by the old faith, whose epistemic organ he located in the "heart" or intuitive mind ("The heart has its reasons, of which reason knows nothing"), Spinoza chose the God of the philosophers, known by the new Cartesian kind of mathematical reason.

His *Tractatus Theologico-Politicus* was the first influential modern source of "higher criticism" of the Bible, and of "demythologization," which classified everything in it that was supernatural or miraculous as myth, allegory, or metaphor.

This was done *not* on the basis of scientific or textual evidence, but on the basis of a prior philosophical conviction that the supernatural was unreal. In light of this philosophical premise, Spinoza had to radically reinterpret the textual data in the Bible if he wanted to claim that he accepted the religion of the Bible. Spinoza argued that his unorthodox views were in fact the views of the earliest Jews before the religion was perverted and changed into its present form: "I might even venture to say that my view is the same as that entertained by the Hebrews of old." This is also what Manicheans, Muslims, and Christian modernists said about the Christian Scriptures: that they are a later corruption of an originally Manichean, or Muslim, or modernist text (which is now, conveniently, totally lost and can only be "reconstructed"). See Augustine's critique of this in *Confessions*: "But they made no claim to produce any of the uncorrupted copies."

The fundamental problem with biblical Judaism for Spinoza was its metaphysical dualism of Creator versus creatures. This dualism stemmed from the distinctively Jewish notion of God *creating*, out of nothing, a world really distinct from himself by an act of omnipotent will. Ancient Hebrew even has a word for this unique concept that appears in no other ancient language: the word *bara'*. That verb always has God, not man, as its subject.

For Spinoza, God is not, as in the Bible, a person ("*I* AM"); this is only our projection. "I believe that a triangle, if it could speak, would in like manner say that God is eminently triangular. [Compare Xenophanes, vol. 1, chap. 14.] Neither intellect nor will pertains to the nature of God. . . . The mind of God is all the mentality that is scattered over space and time, the diffused consciousness that animates the world." (*Can* consciousness be "diffused" rather than centered in an "I"? Is this being misled by a material metaphor?)

Like later religious "modernists," Spinoza believed that all religions were one or could be made one, and that the polemics between Jews and Christians could be resolved by a compromise about Jesus: that he was not God but the best of men. Like the modernists, he opposed all dogmas and creeds and churches as divisive and hoped that their abolition would finally bring about universal human brotherhood.

Metaphysics

Spinoza's masterpiece is the *Ethics*, which begins with, and bases everything on, his metaphysics. The book could not be safely published in his lifetime because of its heretical theological views, but afterward it became cherished by Lessing, Herder, Schleiermacher, Novalis, Goethe, Wordsworth, Coleridge, Byron, Shelley, Fichte, Schelling, and Hegel. Yet it is one of the most difficult books ever written. Its style is that of Euclidean geometry, far more severely mathematical than Aquinas' *Summa*, which is loose by comparison. Every word counts, and it is long. Yet its summary is quite short and simple.

There are only three terms that cover everything that is:

A. substance,
B. attribute, and
C. mode.

Of these the first is by far the most important.

A1. "By 'substance' I mean that which is in itself and is conceived by itself; in other words, that the conception of which does not need the conception of another thing." In other words, *substance = the absolute*, both in being and in concept.

A2. This definition allows *only one substance*. Any second substance, in order to be second, would be relative to the first substance and thus would not be *substance* as Spinoza has defined it (i.e., absolute). Thus, he posits a monism or pantheism by definition.

A3. Substance must be *infinite* and not limited by or dependent on anything else in any way. This means it must have *an infinity of attributes*, since it is not qualitatively limited, and that it must be *eternal*, since it is not quantitatively limited by time.

A4. It is not immaterial, however. Both spirit and matter are real and are the only two of the infinite attributes of substance that we know. Thus it (God) and the material universe and the mind are one being, not three.

A5. It must also be the uncaused cause of everything, even itself. He calls it "causa sui" (cause of itself). This is a logical impossibility for an efficient cause. (How can something bring itself into existence? It would have to be metaphysically prior to itself.) But Spinoza means by "cause" not efficient or final cause but formal (and material) cause. It is the immanent form or formula for a thing's essence, as dogginess causes a dog to be a dog.

A6. Spinoza does not dismiss the plurality of beings in time and space as illusions, as some Hindu or Buddhist monists or pantheists do, but explains that they are (formally, not efficiently) generated by substance as conclusions are generated by axioms in geometry. This is not free creation but logical emanation or necessity, as in Plotinus. From it, Spinoza says, "infinite things in infinite ways, that is to say, all things, have necessarily flowed, or continually flow by the same necessity, in the same way as it follows from the nature of a triangle, from eternity and to eternity, that its three angles are equal to two right angles."

A7. Thus God and nature are identical. The only difference is how we look at it: from above (*natura naturans*, nature as active cause) or below (*natura naturata*, nature as receptive effect). God *is* nature and nature *is* God.

A8. Spinoza gives three arguments for the existence of this God. All are similar to Anselm's ontological argument. The first argument essentially repeats Anselm's. The second is that God's nonexistence could not be because this could not have a cause, and it could not have a cause because nothing could be great enough to cause God's nonexistence. The third is that if we admit that finite beings exist, we must admit that infinite Being exists, for the concept of finitude is meaningless without the concept of infinity. If only finite things exist, "it follows that things finite are greater than the absolutely infinite Being" (since that Being does not even have existence). And that is self-contradictory: that the finite is greater than the infinite.

In all these arguments Spinoza assumes that what is true of concepts is true of reality. This is one way of labeling the essential assumption of metaphysical rationalism: that reality is a (partial or imperfect) mirror of concepts rather than concepts being (partial or imperfect) mirrors of reality.

B1. "By 'attribute' I mean that which the intellect perceives of Substance, as constituting its essence." Attributes are answers to the question "What is it?" But all attributes are essential; nothing is accidental from God's point of view ("sub specie aeternitatis," from the viewpoint of eternity).

One is tempted to ask Spinoza how he as a mere creature has acquired God's point of view, but he would have a ready answer: nothing is a creature; everything is a "mode" of God (see point C).

B2. Infinite substance must have infinite attributes.

B3. The only two we know are thought and extension. Thus, Spinoza solves Descartes' mind-body problem at a cosmic level.

C. "By mode I understand the modifications of Substance or that which is another thing through which also it is conceived." This means all the concrete things that exist. To put the point in a crude and unfair but memorable image (from C.S. Lewis), God is like a pudding, its attribute is tapioca, and all things, including ourselves, are lumps of it.

To balance this probably unattractive exposition of Spinoza's monism, we should note its attractive and exhilarating aspect. But this comes out most clearly in our next section, Epistemology.

Epistemology: The "Coherence Theory of Truth"

1. Spinoza distinguishes four levels of human consciousness. They are (a) hearsay knowledge; (b) vague empirical experience; (c) clear, rational, deductive reasoning; and (d) the intellectual vision of eternal and necessary truth. These four steps are quite similar (though not identical) to the four steps of Plato's "divided line," and they lead us upward to perfect happiness through seeing things "sub specie aeternitatis," a kind of optimistic fatalism similar to that of Buddhism and Stoicism.
2. This is the heart of Spinoza's passion for philosophy: not just *explanation* and the search for rational certainty but ultimate meaning and *happiness*, a "beatific vision" to be attained not in heaven by divine grace but on earth through philosophical reasoning. Philosophy is for him what religion is for most people: the way to supreme happiness, the way of salvation (though not from sin but from ignorance, and not by divine grace, faith, or moral choice but by the intellectual understanding of the ultimate meaning of all things).

   Thus, philosophy is worth giving up the world for: "After experience had taught me that all things which frequently take place in ordinary life are vain and feeble . . . I determined at last to inquire whether there be anything which might be truly good, and able to communicate its goodness. . . . I determined, I say, to inquire whether I might discover and attain the power of enjoying throughout eternity continual supreme happiness" (*On the Improvement of the Understanding*).

   That is his great question. And here is his answer: "The greatest good is the union which the mind has with the whole of nature." For "nature" is just another word for "God," or the whole.
3. One's epistemology always matches one's metaphysics.* Thus Spinoza's monistic pantheism matches his "*coherence theory of truth*." Since reality is one, not two, therefore truth is the oneness, or coherence, of an idea within itself, or within a single system of ideas, rather than the correspondence between an idea and some other, second thing. Like the Hindu Upanishads, Spinoza believes that "the idea of oneness is the source of all truth; the idea of twoness is the source of all error."

   Most of his predecessors, including Descartes, had assumed the more commonsensical "*correspondence theory of truth*": that propositions are true when they correspond to objective reality. This theory fit Descartes' dualism

* Which comes first? Must we not first know *what is* to know what knowledge is? But must we not first know *how to know* before we can know being? This would later be called "the gnoseo-ontological circle."

between mind and matter, man and nature, subject and object, knower and known (though the correspondence theory is older and more widely held than the new Cartesian dualism).

But the occasionalists had shown that if Descartes' dualism were true, the world of matter could not act on minds to cause ideas that correspond to it.

Spinoza solved this problem by his monism: both the world with its things and our minds with their ideas are modes of the same single substance, God.

This monistic metaphysics requires a coherence theory of truth, which means that ideas are judged true not because they correspond to the material things and events that cause them (which for Spinoza is impossible) but because they cohere in a logical unity, or (to say the same thing more metaphysically) that they manifest the only true reality, God.

Thus, no idea is absolutely true except the idea of God. All other ideas are more or less true insofar as they manifest more or less of this unity. The bigger and more Godlike an idea is, the truer it is.

Thus, no idea is simply false.* (Spinoza, as a victim of intolerance, saw this idea as promoting tolerance for all ideas, since there is some truth in all of them.)

Spinoza's point is that there are levels of understanding anything. Another person, e.g., can be understood (a) as "just somebody"; or (b) as "Alice"; or (c) as "my sister whom I've lived with for twenty years, my closest friend"; or (d) as God understands Alice.

To understand any one thing or person completely, we would have to understand everything in the universe, because everything is related to everything in nature not externally and accidentally but intrinsically and essentially. Nature is not only one single system but one single thing, one substance, in which all apparently distinct things are really only modes of the same substance. Thus, to know any part of it rightly is to know the whole of it. It is like Tennyson's poem "Flower in the Crannied Wall":

Flower in the crannied wall,
I pluck you out of the crannies,
I hold you here, root and all, in my hand,
Little flower—but if I could understand
What you are, root and all, all in all,
I should know what God and man is.

---

* A Thomist critic would say that this theory makes sense regarding essences, but not regarding existence; i.e., it makes sense regarding concepts (the "first act of the mind" in Aristotelian logic) but not regarding judgments (the "second act of the mind"). Concepts (like "God," "one," or "evil") are never simply false, but more or less adequate, more or less clear. Falsity arises only when we make judgments (like "God is evil" or "God is not one").

Ethics

1. Spinoza begins his *Ethics* the same way Aristotle does, by defining "the good" as "the object of desire." The supreme good, or happiness, is simply the satisfaction of all desires. And this is the perfection, or actualization, or self-realization, of each person.
2. However, whereas for Aristotle (and for common sense) this realization or perfection must be attained by willing, choosing, and practicing the virtues, for Spinoza it is already there—everyone and everything is already perfect—so that the only actualization or self-realization that is necessary or even possible is mental, a realization of our already-existing eternal perfection through our divine identity.

   There are, in fact, *no real potentialities* at all for Spinoza. Everything is already actual; everything is eternal (not just everlasting but timeless, like a concept). This logically follows from monism, for since everything is, in the last analysis, one, therefore time, which *separates* things and persons and events, must be, in the last analysis, not real but only apparent.

   This is very similar to the *moksha* or *mukti* of Hinduism, expressed in the formula *tat tvam asi* ("thou art that"; your deepest identity, *Atman*, is identical to the divine identity, *Brahman*). It is not future but present and timeless. Buddhism makes a similar point: in the realization of *nirvana* or *satori* or *kensho*, it is not reality that changes but only your consciousness of it, from sleeping to waking ("enlightenment").
3. Since there is no time or potentiality, there is no free choice between potential futures. Free will is an illusion, even though common sense believes it is a necessary prerequisite for morality. (Kant expressed that common belief by saying that "*I ought* implies *I can*.")

   What we mistake for freedom, according to Spinoza, is only ignorance of the necessary causes that determine our choices and our future. Spinoza is a determinist. The mechanistic determinism that Descartes ascribed only to the material half of his cosmic dualism, Spinoza transforms into a *logical* determinism and sees in mind and spirit as well. There are no potentialities or possibilities; everything is either necessary or impossible. Neither man nor even God is free to choose among alternatives. The intellect is not like a navigator nor the will like a captain, so that the captain can obey or disobey the navigator's advice; in fact, "will and intellect are one and the same thing, for a volition is merely an idea which . . . has remained long enough in consciousness to pass over into action."

   Spinoza's argument for this surprising conclusion is that for anyone to say that God could have chosen differently and made things different (e.g., to have created or emanated a universe without any frogs in it) is to place a limit on God, who is unlimited. For this alleged possibility of a frogless universe would be either better than this one (in which case a perfect God would have necessarily chosen it) or worse (in which case it would have been impossible for Perfection to have chosen it). Leibniz argued that this must be "the best of all possible worlds." Spinoza agreed but thought there was only one possible world: this one.

Spinoza does speak of freedom, but this is only the freedom of self-determination, which is itself determined and necessary. It is merely the freedom from fear and ignorance, not from determinism, the freedom that comes from seeing that everything is necessary. This optimistic fatalism is similar to Stoicism's *amor fati* (love of fate), and teaches us "how we ought to behave with regard to things of fortune, or those which are not in our power. . . . It teaches us to bear each form of fortune because we know that all things follow from the eternal decree of God with the same necessity by which it follows from the essence of a triangle that its three angles are equal to two right angles."

To put this "existential bottom line" of Spinoza's into perspective, we might distinguish four possible philosophies of life:

- *Atheism*: There is no God and there are no real eternal necessities; therefore, we must live by our own wisdom, cleverness, and power, not his.
- *Paganism*: There are gods, who are unpredictable; therefore, we have much to hope for and much to fear.
- *Judeo-Christian theism*: There is a God of love and wisdom; therefore, we should live by our free choice of faith and trust in him and love for each other.
- *Pantheism*: There is nothing but God; therefore, all is necessary. We must learn to accept it.

4. *Immortality*, like freedom, is affirmed, but not in the commonsense version. There is no individual personal immortality, but only the immortality of the God who is all things, including ourselves. Individuals cannot hope to *become* immortal after death but only to become *aware* during their lifetime of the immortality they share with everything; they do this by realizing that they are only modes of the immortal God. Man is no more immortal than any other mode of God, but man alone can know this.

Medieval Christians prayed, "From a sudden and unprovided death, good Lord, deliver us." Socrates saw philosophy as "a rehearsal for death." Spinoza wrote, "The free man never thinks of death, but life."

Spinoza argues that personal life after death is impossible because it would require the survival of individual memory, but "the mind can neither imagine nor recollect anything save while it is in the body." So there is no Last Judgment, no hell, and equally no heaven. There are no eternal rewards or punishments, only the ones in this world. For just as there is no real difference between nature and God, there is no real difference between this life and a next life. He ends his *Ethics* by saying that "blessedness is not the reward of virtue, but virtue itself."

5. There is no absolute morality. There is neither a divine law nor a natural moral law but only eternal necessity everywhere. Petitionary prayer is an error. "By the help of God I mean the fixed and unchangeable order of nature."*

God is not a moralist. "Good" and "evil" are only human constructs, not an objective law or an obligation from a divine Other. "Whenever, then, anything in nature seems to us evil, it is because we have but a partial knowledge of things. . . . In fact, what our reason pronounces bad is not bad as regards the order and laws of universal nature. . . . As for the terms *good* and *bad*, they indicate nothing positive considered in themselves."

Can you imagine Spinoza preaching this to his descendants in Auschwitz?

---

* When Spinoza speaks of "nature," he seems to mystically exalt it into God, but when he speaks of "God," he seems to reduce God to the cosmic computer that is nature.

58

GOTTFRIED WILHELM LEIBNIZ

AD 1646–1716

The first of many great German philosophers, Leibniz was probably one of the four or five most sheerly intelligent men who ever lived. (Only Aristotle, Aquinas, Newton, and Einstein come to mind as rivals for that title.) He is often labelled the last universal genius in history, before the age of specialization. He was reading Scholastic philosophy at thirteen. As a teenager he assimilated the thought of Galileo, Boyle, Descartes, Pascal, and Spinoza (whom he met). He published a treatise at twenty that anticipated later crucial discoveries in logic and mathematics. He wrote tens of thousands of letters. He drafted schemes for the reunification of Protestant and Catholic Churches, as well as a pan-European alliance of states. He invented calculus three years before Newton did (which provoked charges of plagiarism from Newton's friends). He designed a new science of statistics and probability, invented symbolic logic, and conceived the idea of a universal computer language. Among many other things.

The rationalistic optimism typical of the Enlightenment could be summarized in the single word *calculemus* ("let us calculate"): if only we used reason (in the modern mathematical sense—the method of geometry, algebra, or logic), all darkness would be turned to light and mankind would be perfected.

Logic

Leibniz distinguishes two kinds of truths: the necessary and the contingent, or *truths of reason* and *truths of fact*. (These are essentially what Hume would later call "relations of ideas" and "matters of fact," and what Kant would later call "analytic" propositions, whose predicates are already contained within their subjects, and "synthetic" propositions, whose predicates add to their subject.) Necessary truths are known to be true by the law of noncontradiction alone (to deny them is to commit a self-contradiction), while contingent truths are not.

Thus, "All triangles are three-sided" and "Bachelors are unmarried" are truths of reason, but "The earth is round" and "Thousands of bachelors exist" are truths of fact.

This is put concretely in speaking of *possible worlds*. Some things are *impossible* in all worlds (universes), such as a four-sided triangle or a married bachelor. Some things are *necessary* in all worlds, such as triangles having three sides or bachelors being unmarried. And some things are *possible* in some worlds but not in others, such as a ten-foot-high man or an oval earth. Truths about such things are contingent. That a triangle is equilateral is possible, that a triangle is three-sided is necessary, and that a triangle is four-sided is impossible in all possible worlds. That a man is ten feet tall is possible in some worlds, that a man has reason is necessary in all possible worlds, and that a man has no body is impossible in all possible worlds.

Thus, whatever is actual is possible, but not everything possible is actual. Physics studies this actual world; metaphysics studies all possible worlds. A possible world is a world in which many contingent truths are "compossible" or possible together.

The law of noncontradiction is the test for truths of reason. *The Principle of Sufficient Reason* is the test for truths of fact. It states that for every contingent truth, there must be a reason or cause sufficient to rationally explain why this truth is true or why this effect exists.

"There are two basic principles of all reasonings, the principle of contradiction . . . and the principle that a reason must be given . . . or, in the common phrase, that nothing happens without a cause."

From the viewpoint of human reason there are many contingent truths and many possible worlds. Only empirical observation reveals that the earth is round or the sky is blue. However, according to Leibniz, from God's omniscient viewpoint all truths are necessary (i.e., all are "truths of reason" or "analytic propositions"). And therefore, since God sees things truly, each thing and each person already contains all of its or his or her attributes and actions, so that if we, like

God, understood the whole nature of each person or thing, we could deduce all attributes and acts that are truly predicable of them. For instance, if we knew the subject "Alexander," we could know the predicates "Macedonian king," "conqueror of the world," "successful with the phalanx," and "destined to despair and drink himself to death."

"I consider a true proposition as such that every predicate, necessary or contingent, past present or future, is contained in the concept of the subject."

This is a startling conclusion. Things are radically different than they seem. It seems to us as if our future is open and partly dependent on other beings as external causes. (E.g., Waldo is paralyzed only because a car crashed into him.) But Leibniz's logic deduces instead a kind of *deterministic fatalism*: each individual already has within his essence all his accidents, and every proposition that has that individual as its subject is really a necessary proposition, no matter what its predicate may be, even though we cannot know that necessity. So Waldo's paralysis comes not just from the car but from his essence.

Leibniz also deduces a *pluralism* in which each individual entity (which he calls a "monad") is "windowless," or closed to external dependency on other monads. We are all that we are not by external causes or relations but only by the internal necessity of our own nature.

This logic seems to contradict four commonsensical ideas: (1) free will, (2) the contingency of events, (3) the dependence of one thing on another, and (4) the externality of causal relationships. Leibniz's philosophy is thus a very useful challenge to your thinking if you want to maintain both logic and common sense (as, e.g., Aristotle does). After you finish reading this section on Leibniz, come back to this paragraph and evaluate these four non-commonsensical conclusions.

Metaphysics

If we had to summarize the metaphysics, or worldviews, of Descartes, Spinoza, and Leibniz in one word each, we could call them dualism, monism, and pluralism, respectively. Instead of reality being either mind or matter, as in Descartes, and instead of all things being modes of God or nature, as in Spinoza, reality is composed of many monads, or individual substances, for Leibniz.

1. All possible worlds must be composed of a plurality of entities, which are
   a. *individual* (i.e., divided from others but undivided in themselves);
   b. *windowless* (i.e., not related to or dependent on anything else, but self-contained and with no external relations, which seems to logically follow from the first); and
   c. *eternal*, since nothing else in the world could create or destroy them (this seems to logically follow from the second).

2. These monads are *not* the *material* atoms of Democritus or of the external world that was half of Descartes' dualism. Atoms are extended in space, but the essence of Leibniz's monads is not spatial extension or size but "force or activity" (or energy). This follows from (1b), for extension in space is an *external* relation.
3. All monads are spiritual, not material, since they are not extended. Thus (3) follows from (2). All things are made of mind, not matter.

   Leibniz argued, against Descartes, that if we accepted Descartes' dualism plus his principle of clarity and distinctness, then matter could not have any real connection to mind and could not act on mind to produce ideas; mind could not even know that matter exists.
4. The principle of "the identity of indiscernibles" states that if any two monads are identical in nature, they must be identical in number (that is, they must be one, not two). There can never be two totally identical twins, not even Tweedledum and Tweedledee in *Through the Looking-Glass* (whose author, by the way, was a professor of logic and mathematics at Oxford). Plurality is accounted for not by matter duplicating form (as in Aristotle) or by distinct acts of existence (as in Aquinas), but by form, nature, or essence. Everything has a different essence from every other thing.

   Contrast this with two previous philosophers, both more aligned with the commonsense opinion. Aristotle explained plurality by matter: two substances of the same nature can be like two copies of the same book, sharing the same form but different matter. Aquinas agreed and also used the real distinction between essence and existence to explain plurality, so that two things, with two different acts of existence, can have the same essence. Two animals can have the same form, or essence, or nature, or species, yet be two materially different bodies. Angels, having no material bodies, are different by form alone. What Aquinas says of angels, Leibniz says of all monads: that each is its own species; that there is only one member of each species; that Tweedledum is as different from Tweedledee as the species Dog is different from the species Cat.
5. Like Aquinas' angels, Leibniz's monads are arranged in a hierarchy. His "principle of continuity" states that there are no gaps or leaps between them; each differs from the next only minimally. In other words, they are like a series of positive integers. The "identity of indiscernibles" principle specifies that no place on the hierarchy or continuum can be filled by two monads; "the principle of continuity" specifies that every possible place is filled. So there can be one and only one example of each possible kind of entity. Everything is utterly unique. (Compare Duns Scotus' similar-but-not-identical principle of *haecceitas* or "thisness" in vol. 2, chap. 51.)

   Leibniz distinguished three kinds of monads: rational monads were human minds; sensory monads were animals; and "stunned" or "swooning" monads were unconscious, either inorganic or merely vegetative (think of surfer dudes). No monads are mere bodies. In fact, Leibniz calls them three kinds of "living souls"; everything is alive in some way.

6. Space is not an independently real material extension but a projection of monads, on the three levels of consciousness distinguished above. (Kant would say something similar about space: that it is not objectively, independently real but a form imposed by minds in the act of external sensation.)
7. Individual substances, whether planets, pansies, poodles, or people, are explained by a kind of metaphysical gravity called "virtual aggregation." Monads form aggregates or compound substances dominated by the superior monad. People are aggregates of all three levels of monads but dominated by the ruling monad of mind, reason, or spirit.
8. "Pre-established harmony" explains the *appearance* of interaction among monads, which Leibniz has denied can really exist. At the moment of creation, God pre-established a perfect synchronization of all monads, so that they are like billions of clocks all keeping the same time. None are externally related to any others; God is the only external agent. (This would be quite a shock to two lovers, and even more of a shock to two enemies who are killing each other.)

   Leibniz compared these harmonized monads to "several different bands of musicians and choirs, playing their parts separately, and so placed that they do not see or even hear one another. . . . [They] keep perfectly together, by each following their own notes, in such a way that he who hears them all finds in them a harmony. . . . Every substance expresses the whole sequence of the universe in accordance with its own viewpoint or relationship to the rest, so that all are in perfect correspondence with each other."*

Theology

Once this pre-established harmony is accepted, it proves the existence of a divine harmonizer and pre-establisher.

Another argument for God is similar to Augustine's: that eternal "truths of reason" require an eternal mind to know them.

Still another is a new version of Anselm's ontological argument: the "possible worlds version." It is similar to Duns Scotus' argument that if God is possible (which he is, since the concept of God contains no self-contradiction), he must actually exist because nothing could prevent this possibility from being actualized.

* Compare this with the Hindu image of the universe as a net of mirrored diamonds and contrast it with C.S. Lewis' image of the "great dance" at the end of *Perelandra*.

God is also proved by the Principle of Sufficient Reason, for nothing else explains why some possibilities become actualities and others do not, since monads cannot act on each other. (So it is really God, not Leibniz, who wrote the *Monadology*.)

This leaves us with a famous problem. If it is God who chooses, among possible worlds, which one to make actual, and if God is perfect, then this world must be "the best of all possible worlds." Leibniz is a Christian, not a Neoplatonist, so he believes God freely creates the world rather than necessarily emanates it; but God must have had a sufficient reason, and that reason must have been perfect. If another possible world were better than this one, he would have created it instead, for he always does what is best.

The obvious problem is that this is clearly *not* the best of all possible worlds.

1. There is no such thing as the best possible world for the same reason there is no such thing as the highest possible positive integer. One more good thing can always be added to a finite world, as one more number can always be added to any other number.
2. Voltaire, in *Candide*, satirized Leibniz's optimism in his fictional philosopher Dr. Pangloss, who explained the catastrophe of the 1755 Lisbon earthquake, which killed sixty thousand people, by noting that the undertakers were now fully employed.
3. If this is the best possible world, how awful all the others must be!
4. Schopenhauer the pessimist went so far as call this the *worst* of all possible worlds. (If point 3 makes Leibniz a pessimist, does that make Schopenhauer an optimist?)
5. The simplest refutation is the simple fact that evil exists. Even if, as Leibniz claims, physical evils are necessary in a finite world, moral evils are not, for they are blameworthy. (That is the point of the story of the fall in Genesis 3: it was a free choice. And that is the point of the Ten Commandments: we freely choose to disobey them.)

Leibniz answers these objections by arguing that evil is merely the absence of good, and that evils in the part are necessary for good in the whole: "If you look at a very beautiful picture, having covered up the whole of it except a very small part, what will it present to your sight . . . but a confused mass of colors, laid on without selection and without art? Yet if you remove the covering and look at the whole picture from the right point of view, you will find that what appeared to have been carelessly daubed on the canvas was really done by the painter with very great art." The twentieth-century American novelist Thornton Wilder, in *The Bridge of San Luis Rey*, uses the analogy of loose threads on the back side of a beautiful tapestry. They are all that we can see, while God sees the other side and therefore sees its perfection.

Using Leibniz's "modal logic," we can ask three questions about this vision: (1) Can this be proved (to be necessary)? (2) Can it be disproved (proved to be impossible)? (3) Can it be believed (to be possible)?

One can also ask: If God is maximally good, wise, and powerful, and therefore necessarily chooses the best of all possible worlds, is any other world, any world less good than this one, even possible? Apparently not. But wouldn't a world without dogs be less good than this one? And isn't that a possible world, since it contains no logical self-contradiction?

Freedom

Spinoza would say no to that question, for he would say that everything possible is actual and there are no unactualized possibilities at all. Thus, we have a fatalism and determinism. But Leibniz, too, seems to be a determinist because of his notions of "the best of all possible worlds" and the "pre-established harmony." Today most determinists are materialists ("determinism from below"); Leibniz, like Calvin, believes in a kind of predestination or "determinism from above." How can free will coexist with this divine determinism?

He claims that it can:

> Neither [God's] foreknowledge nor [his] predestination derogate from liberty. For God being moved by his supreme reason to choose, among many series of possible things or worlds, the one in which free creatures should make such or such resolutions (though not without his concourse), has thereby rendered every event certain and determined once and for all; but he has not derogated thereby from the liberty of those creatures; that simple decree or choice did not change, but only actualized, their free natures, which he saw in his Ideas. Neither does moral necessity derogate from liberty. For when a wise being, and especially God, who has supreme wisdom, chooses what is best, he is not on that account less free; on the contrary, not to be hindered from acting in the best manner . . . is the most perfect liberty. . . . The good inclines without necessitating.

But Leibniz's account of *human* freedom is that it is not, like God's freedom, the will's power to choose among genuine alternatives but the power of self-determination rather than determination by another; determinism from within rather than from without.* It is my own nature that determines all my actions.

* The traditional view is exactly the opposite: what Leibniz says about human freedom is true of God's freedom, and vice versa.

I am destined, but I am free from obstructions. What we commonsensically call freedom is only our ignorance of this determinism.

The problem with this answer is simply that that is not what most people mean by free will. Augustine distinguished two kinds of freedom, free will (*liberum arbitrium*), or free choice, and liberty (*libertas*), or self-realization. The first was a means to the second. Leibniz claims that we have the second but not the first.

Yet Leibniz is surely right in arguing that (1) God can infallibly foresee and predestine our free actions (see Boethius and Aquinas on this), and that (2) we are still free even when we do something that flows from our character and is predictable. A saint's generosity and hospitality is no less free for its being more predictable than that of a non-saint.

Leibniz is one of those philosophers who becomes richer and more complex with each rereading and rethinking. Even if you do not end up agreeing with him, you will end up with more mental muscle.

59

FRANCIS BACON

AD 1561–1626

Bacon was famous not only for his philosophy but also for:

1. His wide-ranging and very popular essays, which include many quotations that have become famous, e.g., "Some books are to be tasted, others to be swallowed, and some to be chewed and digested"; and "He that hath wife and children hath given hostages to Fortune; for they are impediments to great enterprises, either of virtue or mischief." He was never in love and wrote, "Great spirits keep out of this weak passion."
2. His political rise and fall: he became a lawyer and a Member of Parliament at twenty-three, Solicitor-General, Attorney-General, Lord Keeper of the Great Seal, Lord Chancellor, baron, and viscount, but was convicted of accepting bribes and dismissed in disgrace from all offices.
3. His idealization of science as the solution to all human ills, his contributions to the inductive logic that is central to the scientific method, and his insistence on and practice of the method of experiments. (He died of pneumonia that he caught while stuffing a chicken with snow to test the effectiveness of refrigeration.) In his utopian *New Atlantis*, he called for international governmental organization of science and technology, the socialization of science for the collective conquest of nature and the enlargement of man's power.*

* Contrast C.S. Lewis' dystopian take on this ideal in the *Brave New World*–like novel *That Hideous Strength*. A good debate topic.

He was either an atheist who had to conceal his opinions in a time when they were socially dangerous, or a nominal believer who simply did not care much about God, the soul, or heaven. His interests and innovations are in science, not religion; this world, not the next; man, not God; power, not virtue; and matter, not spirit. All these changing interests characterized the Renaissance and early modern times in general, in a gradual way, but in Bacon they are unusually sudden, clear, and radical.

Bacon's New Means and New End

The two most radically new and influential points of his philosophy are closely connected as means and end, and both are summarized in books whose title begins with the word "new":

1. The new means is a new, inductive logic. (Induction reasons from many concrete particular examples to an abstract general principle and claims only probability; deduction reasons from principle to example and claims certainty.) Many of the rules and fallacies of induction were formulated by Bacon in *The New Organon*.

   The old *Organon* (instrument) was the title of the six books of Aristotle's deductive logic. Bacon pillories Aristotle as the source of most of the errors in science. Deductive logic, he says, with its definitions and syllogisms, is useless as a tool for new scientific discovery. He criticized deductive, rationalistic thinkers as spiders who spin webs from their own minds without contact with the real world. But he also criticized mindless, merely empirical data-gatherers as ants who do not know what to do with the data they gather.

   Bacon famously classified four typical kinds of fallacies:

   a. *Idols of the Tribe*: fallacies common to all men, inherent in human nature, such as sensory illusions, judging by feelings, and oversimplifying.
   b. *Idols of the Cave*: fallacies particular to one's unique personality.
   c. *Idols of the Market Place*: fallacies of language and communication, especially verbal ambiguities.
   d. *Idols of the Theater*: reifying words or ideologies; mistaking philosophical systems for realities.

   Like almost all English philosophers, Bacon not only emphasized induction in practice but was also an empiricist in principle. He formulated the empirical aspects of the scientific method more clearly than anyone had done before him, especially the role of observation and controlled experiment.

   A little later, Descartes formulated and used the mathematical and deductive aspects of the scientific method and tried to apply this to philosophy as well as science. Late medieval philosophers had worked out something very close to the modern scientific method in theory. But it was Bacon who more than any other individual is responsible for formulating this method, which is the single most important discovery in the history of science, since it is like a skeleton key that opens all the other doors.

The negative side of this emphasis is the tendency to exclude from philosophy as well as from science all that did not fit under this method, especially formal and final causes. While premoderns tended to do their science by methods appropriate to philosophy, moderns tended to do their philosophy by methods appropriate to science.

2. Bacon's new end, stated in many of his essays and exemplified in the utopian novel *New Atlantis*, is nothing less than a new *summum bonum*, a new answer to the most important of all questions, the question of mankind's purpose, goal, end, greatest good, or "meaning of life." Every thinker in the past (except the Sophists) had taught that this is some kind of conformity of the human soul to objective reality, however differently that reality was conceived, and that the means were inner, personal wisdom and virtue. For Bacon, the end is the conformity of objective reality (at least material reality) to the desires of the human soul, and the means is technology, or applied science. Machiavelli's end was power too, but only power over other men. Bacon's end is power over the universe, over nature. Nearly three centuries later, Nietzsche would explore this "will to power" as the essence of life.

For the ancients, knowledge of the truth was an end in itself. For Bacon it is only a means: "knowledge for power." Aristotle had ranked the sciences in a hierarchy, by the standard of the end for which truth is sought. The highest end was simply knowledge, the second was practice, and the third and lowest was power over material nature. Truth came first, then goodness, then utility. Bacon turns this hierarchy on its head and explicitly says that utility is a higher and more humanly appropriate end than truth for its own sake. In other words, technology is more important than philosophy, religion, or morality. "I asked myself what could most advantage mankind. . . . When I searched, I found no work so meritorious as the discovery and development of the arts and inventions." Knowledge is the means, power over nature the end.

This new answer to the most important of all questions most deeply defines the difference between modern Western civilization and all others in history. The old end was somehow to conform earth to heaven; the new end is to create heaven on earth, to abolish pain—"the relief of man's estate." That end requires technology, which requires science, which requires a better method, which requires inductive logic.

When this is combined with a focus on the body more than the soul, the result is that "physicians should be honored . . . as dispensers of the greatest earthly happiness that could well be conferred on mortals." Descartes also ranked medicine, not philosophy, theology, cosmology, ethics, or politics, as the single most important science.

Here is Bacon's defense against the charge that this new end of power is merely selfish:

> It would not be amiss to distinguish the three kinds, and as it were grades, of ambition in mankind. The first is of those who desire to extend their power in their native country; which kind is vulgar and degenerate. The second is of those who labor to extend the power of their country and its dominion among men; this certainly has more dignity, but not less covetousness. But if a man endeavor to establish and extend the power and dominion of the human race itself over nature, his ambition is without doubt both a more wholesome thing and a nobler.

Notice that what makes it "nobler" is not a different quality but a different quantity.

Man and Nature

With Bacon we see a new relationship between man and nature. Nature is no longer "Mother Nature" but a set of puzzles to solve or even an enemy to conquer. Bacon described the controlled experiment, science's most powerful tool, as a kind of torture: "We must put nature on the [torture] rack to compel her to bear witness" so that we can attain the hidden knowledge that gives us power over her. This is strikingly similar to Machiavelli's image of the relation between man and nature ("fortune") at the end of *The Prince*: "For Fortune is a woman and it is necessary to beat and coerce her."

When the Japanese mountain-climbing team climbed the world's second-highest mountain, K2, for the first time, they explained to the Americans why they stopped fifty feet short of the summit: it was out of respect for the mountain. The philosophy was in the verbs: while Westerners spoke of "conquering" it, they spoke of "befriending" it. They were not Baconians.

Ethics

Bacon's ethics, unsurprisingly, are Machiavellian. He writes, "We are beholden to Machiavelli, and writers of that kind, who openly and unmasked declare what men do in fact and not what they ought to do." He advised a judicious mixture of deceit and honesty, and practiced the same.

It is logically consistent with his new *summum bonum*. If technology rather than ethics is the highest end, then ethics can only be a means. And a means is relative to its end. The end does justify the means; that's what a "means" *means*.

But if this pragmatic dimension is subject to the ethical, then a good end does not justify an evil means. (Feeding the poor does not justify killing the rich.)

Bacon's psychology is implicitly materialist and an early version of behaviorism. He denied the idea of free will as well as the distinction between the will and the intellect that the idea of free will assumes. (Do you see why this is assumed?)

60

JOHN LOCKE

AD 1632–1704

Locke will formulate the basic principles of empiricism, which seem to him quite harmless and commonsensical.

Berkeley will criticize Locke for not embracing all the logical conclusions of his premises. At least one of these conclusions, for Berkeley, is very radical: that matter does not exist!

Hume will do to both Locke and Berkeley what Berkeley did to Locke: draw out the logical conclusion of both their premises. And that conclusion is skepticism.

Raised in a Puritan family, Locke learned the virtues of thrift, hard work, simplicity, and common sense. (To understand his personality, think of Dr. "Bones" McCoy in *Star Trek*.) Educated at Oxford, he was a tutor, a medical doctor, and a political diplomat and advisor to the Earl of Shaftesbury. He wrote on such diverse topics as politics (*Two Treatises of Government* and the famous *Letter Concerning Toleration*), theology (*The Reasonableness of Christianity*), and economics (*Some Considerations of the Consequences of the Lowering of Interest and the Raising the Value of Money*), as well as epistemology (*Essay Concerning Human Understanding*).

The common theme in all of Locke's writings is the simplification of human knowledge. For Locke, it is less complex and mysterious than we usually think it is. It is really bound to the inside of Plato's cave: "The simple ideas we receive from sensation and reflection are the boundaries of our thoughts, beyond which the mind . . . is not able to advance one jot; nor can it make any discoveries when it would pry into the nature and hidden causes of these ideas."

It was not logical consistency but instinctive common sense that prevented Locke from drawing the conclusion of skepticism from this premise of empiricism, as Hume did.

No Innate Ideas

Locke begins his *Essay Concerning Human Understanding* by refuting the rationalists' theory of "innate ideas," which he regards as the root error of rationalism and the source of "dogmatism." Later, Kant would try to find an alternative to both what he called "dogmatic" (rationalistic, Cartesian) and "skeptical" (empiricistic, Humean) epistemologies.

It is ironic for both Locke and Kant to accuse Descartes of "dogmatism," for Descartes insisted on beginning with universal methodic *doubt*. But what they had in mind as dogmatism was not Descartes' method but his claim that we have "clear and distinct ideas" that are not derived from sense experience but are "innate" in the mind.

Locke argues, against "innate ideas," that babies have none. However, the defenders of this theory did not claim that these ideas were *actually* and *consciously* present from birth, but only *potentially* and *unconsciously* present, so Locke refutes a "straw man." (Look it up!)

Locke also argues, from observation, that blind men have no ideas of colors, and that when any one of the five senses is destroyed, all the ideas that come through that sense cease.

Aristotle and Aquinas both make this point too, and both teach that all our ideas *begin* in sensation, but they do not say that they are *confined* to sensation because they have a theory of abstraction of universal forms from particular matter. Modern empiricists reject "abstract ideas" because they are nominalists, and thus they hold that there are no universal forms in reality to abstract.

Like Aristotle, Locke said that the mind at birth is a *tabula rasa*, a blank writing tablet, on which only the senses write information. Ralph Cudworth, one of the "Cambridge Platonists," argued, against Locke, that if the mind is merely a *tabula rasa* and "there is nothing in the intellect that was not first in the senses," atheism logically follows, since the idea of a God cannot be in the senses. Locke replied that the cosmological arguments for God do not depend on any "innate ideas."

The strongest argument for innate ideas is that everyone knows certain self-evident first principles such as the law of noncontradiction in logic and "do good, not evil" in ethics. No one is ignorant of them, no one denies them, and no one doubts them. Locke replied (1) that these are certain not because they are innate but because our minds do not permit us to think otherwise, (2) that universal consent is not the same as innateness, and (3) that such highly abstract ideas could not be present in the minds of children. (Hume's answer, later, would be that they are not "matters of fact" at all but empty tautologies, mere "relations of ideas.")

Ideas as Objects of Knowledge

The opening line of Book II of Locke's *Essay* defines an idea this way: "Idea is the object of thinking." In other words, we do not think things, we think ideas. Ideas are not *acts* of knowing or *means* of knowing but *objects* of knowing. What we know first of all are our own ideas.

Locke is not a skeptic (no certain knowledge) or a subjectivist (no knowledge of objective reality) or a solipsist (no knowledge of anything but yourself); but his premise seems to entail these conclusions, and it was only his common sense, not his logic, that prevented him from embracing these conclusions. For if all we know are our own ideas, it seems to follow that we do not know the real world outside of our own ideas. If we see only pictures of things, we do not see things, only pictures. How then can we possibly know which pictures correspond to real things and which do not? (Locke held a commonsensical "correspondence theory of truth": that an idea is true if it corresponds to a real thing or event.)

One may reasonably suspect that this problem—whether we can know that the world outside our own ideas really exists or not—has never been seriously questioned by any philosopher who is married, has children, and has had to deal with baby diaper poo. One may also wonder why that job description is true of only a small minority of great philosophers.

Locke avoided skepticism by affirming that "sensitive knowledge" bridges the gap between ideas and realities, and that although the objects of our knowledge are only our ideas, they include the idea that these ideas come into the mind from the outside world. But if this idea—that ideas come from the outside world—is only an idea, we cannot know whether *it* is objectively true either. Or, if Locke says that the entrance of an idea into the mind is *not* merely an idea, Locke is contradicting his first principle that the object of every act of knowing is an idea. To observe a man enter a hotel from the street, we must first see him in the street.

Locke was an empiricist but not a materialist. Like Descartes, he was a dualist: he held that both matter "out there" and mind "in here" are real, and that ideas come from two sources—external sensation and the mind's internal reflection on its own operations that were awakened by these sensations. He did not resolve the mind-body problem and explain how material things could cause mental effects any more than Descartes did.

The Subjectivity of Secondary Qualities

Locke distinguished two kinds of qualities in material things. "Primary qualities" are quantifiable, such as size, weight, motion, and shape. "Secondary qualities" are nonquantifiable: sensations of color, heat, hardness, odors, and sounds. (Later philosophers would call non-sensible qualities such as moral, religious, and aesthetic values "tertiary qualities.")

According to Locke, only primary qualities exist in the objective world; secondary qualities are subjective—they exist only in our minds. The hard, round, white, rolling snowball really is round and rolling but it is not really hard or white. Secondary qualities are the subjective *effects of* primary qualities; they are mental, not physical.

This is essentially Democritus' materialistic view of the world. Unlike Democritus and like Descartes, Locke added an inner, mental world; but objective reality is reduced to the quantitative and mathematical, and thus the physical. All qualities not detectable by the scientific method are deposited in the mind.

One of Locke's arguments for the subjectivity of secondary qualities such as heat was the "hands in water" experiment. Put your left hand in a bucket of hot water and your right hand in a bucket of cold water. Then remove both hands and plunge them into a third bucket of lukewarm water. Your left hand will tell you that the third bucket is cold, while your right hand will tell you it is hot. Since it cannot be both, and the hands are equal witnesses, it must be neither.

Berkeley would later argue that all the arguments for the subjectivity of secondary qualities apply equally to primary qualities. But rather than draw the commonsense conclusion that both were objective, he drew the conclusion that both were subjective.

The Critique of Substance

Locke does not draw as many radical or skeptical conclusions as Berkeley or Hume do from his premise of empiricism, but he does draw some. One is his critique of the idea of substance.

Inherited from Aristotle, the idea of "substance" is what is grammatically expressed as a noun. It means a being that possesses qualities, quantities, and other attributes; it is the "substratum" that supports them. For instance, a big, red, bouncing ball is a substance, but big, red, and bouncing are not.

Locke argues that we sense these attributes (or "accidents" as Aristotle calls them), but we do not sense the being that has them. If we know only what we sense, it follows that we do not know substance. Locke declares it a meaningless idea, a "something I know not what." He says of the qualities that we sense that "because we cannot conceive how they should subsist alone, nor one in another, we suppose them existing in and supported by some common subject, which support we denote by the name substance, though it be certain that we have no clear or distinct idea of that thing."

If this is true of bodies (material substances), it must be true of minds too (mental substances). But Locke's common sense would not let him deny the existence of selves, minds, egos, or souls. However, Hume would later draw that radical conclusion, thus ranging as far as possible from Descartes, who thought that the self was not only real but the most certain thing knowable ("I think, therefore I am").

Locke's Ethics

Locke abandons his empiricism in his ethics. First, like a rationalist, he says, "I am bold to think that morality is capable of demonstration, as well as mathematics; since the precise real essence of the things moral words stand for can be perfectly known." (But knowledge of real essences does not seem to fit an empiricist epistemology and its corresponding nominalist metaphysics.)

Although Locke was neither a materialist nor a hedonist, like them he identified the good (the most fundamental term in ethics) with pleasure: "Things are good or evil only in reference to pleasure or pain. That we call good which is apt to cause or increase pleasure, or diminish pain in us." That is consistent with Locke's empiricism but not, it seems, with the rest of Locke's ethics.

Locke distinguishes three kinds of laws: *the law of (social) opinion*, *civil law*, and *divine law*. The law of opinion is a community's judgments about moral good and evil. This changes somewhat, though not completely, from one culture, time, and place to another. Civil law tends to follow the law of opinion, although not totally. Only divine law is unchanging and universal, and "this is the only touchstone of moral rectitude." Locke says we can all know this divine law by the (innate!) light of natural reason: "That God has given a rule whereby men should govern themselves, I think there is nobody so brutish as to deny." (Locke did not live in the twenty-first century!)

Unlike Aristotle, Augustine, and Aquinas, Locke does not speak of a natural moral law in his ethics (it is identified with divine law); but he does speak of it in his politics, as part of the "state of nature."

Locke's Political Philosophy

Locke both agrees and disagrees with Hobbes. He agrees that man is not by nature a political animal, as Aristotle claimed, and says that the state (civil society) is created by the artifice of the "social contract." So there is a distinction between "the state of nature" and "the state of civil society."

Even if there were no historical "state of nature" before civil society, the fact that we choose to live in our civil society rather than leave it constitutes tacit consent to the "social contract."

But Locke disagrees with Hobbes about this "state of nature." It is not egotistic and amoral, a state of war of each against each that is "solitary, poor, nasty, brutish, and short," as Hobbes said. Instead, Locke inherits the tradition of natural law from Richard Hooker (1553–1600), and says that morality is natural to man, and naturally known (by "natural reason"). "Reason, which is that law, teaches all mankind who will but consult it, that, being all equal and independent, no one ought to harm another in his life, health, liberty, or possessions."

Locke also includes in the natural law the notion that each person has intrinsic value because he has been created by God in his image. Thus, natural rights are not given by man, or the state, but by God; therefore they are inalienable, and each right brings a corresponding duty to respect it.

Kant, later, will teach a similarly high, idealistic, and personalistic ethics, but without a metaphysics of God and natural law and without an epistemological realism (that we can know objective reality as it really is) as its basis. Kant said that he demoted theoretical reason to make room for practical (moral) reason.*

Locke says that the state is invented not to give man rights but to enforce them and to adjudicate disputes about them. Disputes arise because the three kinds of laws do not always coincide, and the reason for this is that people tend to foolishly choose immediate and lesser goods (pleasures) over the greater, long-range, and lasting goods.

The distinctive Lockean emphasis in political philosophy is the concept of the right of *property*. Locke has a broad definition of property: it includes people's "lives, liberty, and estates, which I will call by the name property," since these are all proper to every man by nature. Locke believes that this is self-evident by the light of natural reason (even though this sounds suspiciously close to "innate ideas").

Since rights are natural and inalienable, the state must rest on the free consent of the governed. "Men being . . . by nature free, equal, and independent, no one can be put out of this estate and subjected to the political power of another without his consent." Many of the fundamental ideas of the American Constitution and Declaration of Independence are obviously influenced by Locke.

---

* A suggestion: since philosophers are usually less skeptical about their ethics than about their epistemology, perhaps they should deduce their epistemology from their ethics instead of vice versa.

61

GEORGE BERKELEY

AD 1685–1753

Like most great philosophers, Berkeley was a child prodigy. All his great philosophical works were written while he was in his twenties. Born in Ireland, he was educated at Trinity College, Dublin. He was an Anglican priest, and in 1734 he became the bishop of Cloyne, Ireland. He is buried in Oxford.

He was a typical Enlightenment figure, fascinated with the new science and eager to experiment. He watched an eruption of Mount Vesuvius dangerously close-up; had himself hanged (by a friend) and revived at the last minute to see what a near-death experience felt like (he felt nothing); crawled through Italian caves to find new species of tarantulas; and wrote extensively on the medical benefits of tar-water, supposedly proven by scientific experiments.

He proposed numerous thought experiments that have fascinated later analytic philosophers, especially that of thinking without language. He wrote, "I shall . . . endeavor, as far as I am able, to take off the mask of words, and obtain a naked view of my own particular ideas." In the twentieth century Wittgenstein would propose something similar but less radical: a therapeutic purging of the supposed philosophical deceptions inherent in language. Berkeley tried to purge language itself from human thought, in an attempt to return to the immediate experience of the world that preverbal infants have, but with an adult intelligence. (Sounds like Zen Buddhism!)

He traveled to America and lived in Newport, Rhode Island, for three years, planning to found a college in Bermuda whose purpose would be "the reformation of manners among the English in our western plantations and the propagation of the Gospel among the American savages." It failed to raise enough funds. Later, a California city and university, which are near better beaches for surfing than those in Bermuda, were named after him. But *that* name is pronounced "Berk-lee"; the philosopher's is "Bark-lee." Remember that when you read the poem four pages ahead.

Berkeley's Big Idea

Berkeley is famous for a single idea. The idea is a startling one: that *esse est percipi*, "to be is to be perceived."

To understand this, we must first remember that for Berkeley, as an empiricist, mental conception was not distinct in kind, only in degree, from sensory perception. Thus "to perceive" meant for him simply "to be aware of."

If "to be is to be perceived," then *nothing exists that is not perceived.*

This is startling because nearly everyone in the world believes the opposite: that the world of material substances exists even when no one perceives it. When a tree falls in the forest and no one hears it, is there noise? Some say yes and some say no depending on what they mean by "noise": is "noise" the subjective experience of hearing or the sound waves that are the objective physical causes of it? But almost no one says the tree doesn't even exist if no one perceives it. Berkeley does. Berkeley denied the existence of matter, in the usual sense of the word.

When Boswell told Samuel Johnson about Berkeley's philosophy, Johnson replied by kicking a stone and saying, "I refute him thus."

However, all he accomplished was a wounded toe, not a wounded philosophy. For Berkeley maintained that *esse est percipi* did not contradict common sense at all, as it seemed to, since it did *not* entail the consequence that trees, horses, books, or chairs pop into and out of existence as we turn our eyes to or away from them. For if we believe his philosophy, he wrote, "we are not deprived of any one thing in nature. Whatever we see, feel, hear, or any wise conceive or understand, remains as secure as ever, and is as real as ever. There is a *rerum natura* [natural reality], and the distinction between realities and chimeras retains its full force. . . . I do not argue against the existence of any one thing that we can apprehend, either by sense or reflection. . . . The only thing whose existence we deny is that which philosophers call matter, or corporeal substance."

Relation to Locke

Berkeley maintained that his conclusions, so apparently contradictory to common sense, followed logically from the principles of his empiricist predecessor Locke, who, ironically, was widely regarded as the most commonsensical of philosophers.

For Locke began his *Essay Concerning Human Understanding* by defining an "idea" as "the object of perception." Ideas are what we are immediately aware of, whether these ideas are sensory, like "red," or non-sensory, like "two."

(Contrast Aquinas [*ST* 1.85.2; also vol. 2, chap. 50, "Epistemology," no. 10], who says that ideas and perceptions are not the *objects* [*quod*] of awareness but the *means* [*quo*] of awareness; that we know real material things, not just our ideas of them.)

If all that we know are our own ideas, as Locke says, and if both our minds and our ideas are mental rather than physical, then we do not and cannot know anything nonmental. Therefore, we have no reason to claim that matter independent of mind exists at all.

Arguments

Berkeley has many ingenious arguments for this startling conclusion, especially in his most popular work, *Three Dialogues between Hylas* ("matter-guy") *and Philonous* ("mind-lover"):

1. The idea of matter is *meaningless*. For matter, in the popular sense of the word, is a radically different kind of reality than mind, spirit, or thought. Descartes had defined both matter and mind as "clear and distinct ideas." But if the objects of all knowledge are ideas, which are mental, it is literally meaningless to assert that there is in knowledge also something that is not ideas and has nothing in common with ideas.

   People say that our sensory images and ideas are "copies" of material things, or that they "correspond to" material things—and Locke follows this popular usage—but how could a mental experience like a color or a sound be an image of, or correspond to, or have anything in common with, something that is not a mental experience at all? A color can only be "like" another color, an idea "like" another idea, especially if Descartes is right in totally separating these two "clear and distinct ideas" of matter and mind.
2. As an empiricist, Berkeley begins with the premise that all knowledge is in empirical experience (inner or outer). Thus, it is *self-contradictory* to assert the popular belief in the existence of something (matter) that is by definition *not* in experience (sensation) but outside it (since experience is mental and matter is not).

   But can't we imagine things existing without anyone seeing them? No, says Berkeley, for you are mentally seeing them! Remember, as an empiricist, Berkeley cannot maintain that there is also another level of awareness—namely, intellectual conception—that is independent of experience (i.e., independent of both sensory perception and imagination). So he cannot say that we know what we do not *perceive* or imagine.

> But, say you, surely there is nothing easier than to imagine trees, for instance, in a park or books existing in a closet, and nobody by to perceive them. I answer: You may do so, there is no difficulty in it; but what is all this, I beseech you, more than framing in your mind certain ideas [remember Locke's first premise, that all we know directly are ideas] which you call "books" and "trees," and at the same time omitting to frame the idea of anyone that may perceive them? But do not you yourself perceive or think of them all the while? . . . To make out this [i.e., to defend the common idea of matter existing outside thought], it is necessary that you conceive them existing unconceived. . . . The mind, taking no notice of itself, is deluded to think it can conceive bodies existing unthought-of.

In other words, is it not a logical contradiction to *think* that anything exists when *no one thinks of it*?

(Can you find the grammatical ambiguity in that last sentence? Which verb does the adverbial phrase beginning with "when" modify? Does the logical distinction between the first two acts of the mind, conceiving and judging, clarify this?)

3. It is *inconsistent with Locke's proof of the subjectivity of secondary qualities*, which Berkeley considered conclusive proofs. Berkeley argued, against Locke's assertion that primary (quantifiable) qualities are objective while secondary (nonquantifiable) qualities are subjective, that the very same arguments that proved the subjectivity of secondary qualities also proved the subjectivity of primary qualities. (See Locke's "hands in water" experiment, chap. 60, "The Subjectivity of Secondary Qualities.") The two kinds of qualities cannot be separated. E.g., we cannot perceive, or even imagine, a colored surface without any size or shape, or a real thing with size and shape but no color. We can only conceive such abstract geometrical lines and figures, but these are not real; Berkeley's empiricism and nominalism rejects all universal "abstract ideas."

   Locke had tried to preserve the objective reality of only those aspects of the material world that the new quantitative physical science recognized (i.e., "primary qualities" like shape and size), while relegating all other, nonquantifiable qualities like color, taste, and sound to subjective, mental status. He maintained that our subjective perceptions of secondary qualities like color were caused by objectively real particles of matter that really possessed only primary qualities like shape and size. This was a convenient "two worlds" theory for previous philosophers like Descartes and Locke, who wanted to affirm that Newtonian science was objective, that physics could not be reduced to psychology. Berkeley uncomfortably demolished this comfortable dualism.

4. We cannot separate *any* of the ingredients in an experience from each other. E.g., when we put our hand into a fire, we feel heat and pain all at the same time. There is no reason to call the heat objective and the pain subjective, as we usually do. Since pain is obviously subjective—no one thinks pain is "out there"—therefore heat is too. Both must exist only in the mind.

Nominalism

Locke had denied that there are any universal *realities* but had admitted the meaningfulness and usefulness of universal *ideas* (i.e., abstract, general ideas like "human nature" or "triangularity" or "justice"). Berkeley, as a more consistent nominalist, goes further and denies all "abstract ideas," including matter, substance, number, geometrical figure, time, and qualities. He says these are all fictions, and our mental life is lived largely among these verbal fictions. "'Tis not to be imagined what a marvelous emptiness and scarcity of ideas that man shall discover who will lay aside all words in his meditations." For most words, except for proper nouns, are universal rather than singular.

Hume, who came immediately after Berkeley, would praise Berkeley for his consistent nominalism. He spoke of him as "a great philosopher [who] . . . asserted that all general ideas are nothing but particular ones. . . . I look upon this to be one of the greatest and most valuable discoveries that has been made." Hume would draw an even more radical conclusion from Berkeley's nominalism in rejecting two more "abstract ideas" (viz., *causality*, the fundamental principle of all scientific and commonsensical explanations, and *the self*, mind, soul, or spiritual substance). The same argument that Berkeley used to reject Locke's notion of *material* substance (viz., the argument that by empiricist standards "material substance" or substratum is unperceivable, and therefore inconceivable), Hume used to reject *spiritual* substance, self, soul, or mind. So we can sum up Berkeley and Hume by "No matter; never mind."

Locke had already reduced the idea of substance to a "something we know not what," since all "whats" are *qualities*; but he did not reduce it to nothing whatever, since he thought, commonsensically, that there had to be *something* that held together the qualities. Berkeley disagreed. He drew the logical conclusion from Locke's definition of substance that an "I know not what" is indistinguishable from nothing at all.

You can see that the operative bottom-line difference between Locke and Berkeley is that Berkeley preferred logical consistency to common sense. (Can these two contradict each other? If so, which do you choose? Why? See Thomas Reid [chap. 63] on this issue.)

All of these mainline modern philosophers, from Descartes through Hume, are using Ockham's Razor, the principle of simplicity: that we should always prefer the simplest, sparest explanation, in philosophy just as in science. And therefore their worldviews keep shrinking from one philosopher to the next. Finally, with Hume, we will reach a point of nearly nothing, a nearly universal skepticism.

God

Berkeley thought his philosophy to be the definitive refutation of atheism. For if we accept his principles, God is absolutely necessary to maintain nature in existence when no human mind perceives it. "When I deny sensible things an existence outside of the mind, I do not mean my mind in particular, but all minds. Now it is plain that they have an existence exterior to my mind, since I find them by experience to be independent of it. [Is that possible, on his principles?] There is therefore some other mind wherein they exist, during the intervals between the times of my perceiving them."

In other words,

Bishop Berkeley
whispered darkly:
"If God don't see ya,
you don't be ya."

Or, more elegantly, in the words of Ronald Knox,

There was a young man who said, "God
Must think it exceedingly odd
If He finds that this tree
Continues to be
When there's no one about in the Quad."

Reply:

Dear Sir: Your astonishment's odd:
I am always about in the Quad.
And that's why the tree
Will continue to be,
Since observed by
Yours faithfully,
God.

And since human minds are temporal and intermittent, and often diverted from perceiving, God's mind must be eternal, omnipresent, and omniscient, knowing all things and thus keeping them in existence.

Thus, the only two things that exist are God and our minds. Everything else—the whole universe—is a kind of indirect mental telepathy between our minds and the divine mind.

Problems

Two theological problems seem to arise here. First, Berkeley seems closer to some form of Hinduism or Buddhism than to Christianity, central to which are the doctrines of creation and Incarnation, which make Christianity the most materialistic religion in the world. Second, why would not Ockham's Razor dictate pantheism as the simplest of all hypotheses? How can Berkeley prove the existence of other human minds? This is a surprisingly tricky problem for one who demands logical proofs for everything and refuses to accept the authority of common sense.

A logical problem also arises. If "to be is to be perceived," then the perceiver must also exist (since a nonexistent perceiver cannot perceive), and since *all* "to be" is "to be perceived," then *that* "to be" must also be perceived by another perceiver, et cetera et cetera ad infinitum, necessitating an actually infinite number of perceivers at once, at every time. This is as impossible as the infinite regress of efficient causes in Aquinas' cosmological arguments. If, on the other hand, the perceiver (or subject) exists but cannot be perceived (as an object of perception), then *esse est percipi* is not universally true.

62

DAVID HUME

AD 1711–1776

If you want to understand most contemporary philosophers who write in English today, you must know Hume. For most of these philosophers identify themselves as "analytic philosophers," and Hume is the single most important source of this philosophical school or method.

He is also the most formidable, challenging, and difficult-to-refute skeptic in the history of human thought. His logic is powerful. Once you grant his apparently commonsensical and attractive premises, it is difficult or impossible to avoid his radical and non-commonsensical skeptical conclusions.

Life

Hume's life, like that of most philosophers, was not spectacular. Born in Edinburgh as David Home (it was pronounced "Hume," so he changed the spelling), he entered the University of Edinburgh at eleven, leaving at fifteen without a degree. His father had died when he was an infant, and he was raised by his strict Presbyterian mother. This included three-hour church services and long daily family prayers. He lost his childhood faith in religion very early. His family pressured him to study the lucrative profession of law, but when he discovered philosophy, he says (in his autobiography) that "there opened up to me a new Scene of Thought. . . . The Law, which was the Business I designed to follow, appeared nauseous to me, and I could think of no other way of pushing my Fortune in the World but that of a Scholar and Philosopher."*

His earliest and most important philosophical influence was Francis Hutcheson, a Scottish ethicist at the University of Glasgow who taught that morality is based on neither reason nor faith, neither natural nor divine law, but feeling and sentiment. Hume conceived the project of extending this "subjectivist" principle to all our mental activity, not just morality. This would undermine nearly all previous philosophy. He was eighteen at the time!

For six months Hume worked feverishly on his new "science of thought." The result was a nervous breakdown that remained so severe that for nine months he could not follow a train of thought. He tried working for a businessman but found it "unsuitable." At twenty-three he settled in France, at La Flèche, home to the prestigious Jesuit university where Descartes had studied. He lived in a tiny apartment on a country estate where he could use the college library, and he completed his *Treatise of Human Nature* in 1737, at age twenty-six. He returned to London and found a publisher, but only by (in his own word) "castrating" his book of its most offensive attacks on religion. He was bitterly disappointed when it found few readers and no favorable reviewers. He wrote that his book "fell deadborn from the press."

His next disappointment was being turned down for a professorship at both Edinburgh and Glasgow because of his skepticism and apparent atheism. He became a private tutor to various wealthy persons. His first pupil was literally insane. When he returned to Paris (the Mecca for atheists), he was suddenly famous and successful and fulfilled what he called his "ruling passion—the love of literary fame." He was known as "le bon David." He abandoned philosophy (once skepticism is established, what else can one say?) and wrote a long history of Great Britain, which brought him fame and fortune there. He retired on a large pension and had a fine house built in Edinburgh, on St. David's Street. Some claim the street was named for him; some not.

He was a gentle man, personally beloved by all who met him (except the volatile and paranoid Rousseau—see chap. 71, "His Life"). He did not *look* like a philosopher. Lord Charlemont described him this way: "His face was broad and fat, his mouth wide, and without any other expression than that of imbecility. His eyes vacant and spiritless and the corpulence of his whole person was far better fitted to communicate the idea of a turtle-eating alderman than of a refined philosopher.† His speech in English was rendered ridiculous by the broadest Scotch

* I have taken the liberty to modernize Hume's florid punctuation in quoting him but have not altered any of his words or capitalizations.

† When you compare Scottish and French cooking, you know why he put on a lot of weight in France.

accent, and his French was, if possible, still more laughable, so that wisdom never before disguised herself in so uncouth a garb."

Hume and Benjamin Franklin would party together in Paris with "bluestocking ladies" on their laps. But Hume was as un-clever with the ladies as Rousseau was clever. Once at a party game he was put between two beautiful women and told to play the part of a sultan trying to win the love of his slaves. He could do nothing but slap his knees and belly and say, over and over, "Well, young ladies, well, there you are, then. Well, there you are." After fifteen minutes the ladies left.

Like Kant, he never married, though he did fall in love once, when he was fifty-two, with a married but separated woman, Madame de Boufflers. She fell out of love with him and in love with a prince whose mistress she had been, but he remained loyal and friendly to her until his death. Five days before he died, he wrote her a letter of condolence for the death of her husband.

He died peacefully, of cancer, in his home. Boswell, Samuel Johnson's biographer, visited him shortly before he died, because he could not believe an intelligent man could die peacefully and without either faith or fear, with no hope of life after death. But Hume maintained his skepticism to the end, moved only by logical consistency. He called life after death "a most unreasonable fancy." When asked whether he did not at least hope there was a heaven, he answered, "Not at all; it is a most gloomy thought."

Hume's Historical Situation

Hume lived at the height of the Enlightenment. Philosophically speaking, the year 1637 is probably the best candidate for the year of its beginning—the publication of Descartes' *Discourse on Method*. In one sense the "Enlightenment" has not yet ended, for most intellectuals in the Western world still put their faith in science and not in the "pre-scientific" philosophy of the Catholic Middle Ages. But in another sense the "Enlightenment" is over, for the faith that reason, especially scientific reason, is self-evident, self-validating, and able to solve all theoretical and practical problems—this faith was given its philosophical death blow by Hume, reason's greatest critic. So perhaps the year of his death, 1776, is the best candidate for the end of the "Enlightenment." Or perhaps it is 1831, the death of Hegel, the last great rationalist system-builder.

The two centuries between 1637 and 1831 saw a jungle growth of philosophy, of science, and of optimism about reason. Newton had apparently unlocked nature's last secrets. Alexander Pope was *not* being satirical or ironic when he wrote:

> Nature and nature's laws lay hid in night;
> God said: Let Newton be! and all was light.

Locke had already argued, as early as 1664, that the laws of nature must govern human reason and human life as well as the rest of the universe (Hume agreed), and he had attempted to map these laws in epistemology (as did Hume). The result was a rational, scientific empiricism whose premises Hume inherited and took to their more radical but logical conclusions.

Locke also applied this philosophy of natural reason to ethics, and the result was a philosophy of universal rights. He wrote, "Reason . . . teaches all mankind who will but consult it, that, being all equal and independent, no one ought to harm another in his life, health, liberty, or possessions." This was the rational "Enlightenment" ethic that justified England's "Glorious Revolution," or "Bloodless Revolution," of 1688 that replaced absolute monarchy with representative democracy. It also would inspire, in significantly different ways, both the American (1776) and French (1789) Revolutions.

Hume, beginning with Locke's epistemological premises, would radically undermine Locke's claims for the power of reason both in epistemology and in ethics. He would cut the epistemological legs out from under the "Enlightenment."

In philosophy, both rationalists and empiricists claimed Newton as their model. But they were philosophical opposites. Rationalists (Descartes, Spinoza, and Leibniz) produced quasi-mathematical systems of cosmology and metaphysics, while empiricists (Bacon, Hobbes, Locke, Berkeley, and Hume) were skeptical of metaphysics and largely confined themselves to epistemology.

The empiricists focused especially on two questions that would begin the move toward skepticism that culminated in Hume. The first question was directed to all claims to rational knowledge; it was simply *How do we know that?* The second question was *What are the limits of human knowledge?*

Hume's Bottom Line: Limiting Human Knowledge

Here, in two paragraphs, is the upshot or bottom line of all of Hume's philosophy. It is exactly the opposite of that of Plato's cave or of Hamlet's "There are more things in heaven and earth, Horatio, than are dreamt of in your philosophy." For Hume there are far fewer.

> Nothing, at first view, may seem more unbounded than the thought of man, which . . . is not even restrained within the limits of nature and reality. To form monsters, and join incongruous shapes and appearances, costs the imagination no more trouble than to conceive the most natural and familiar objects. And while the body is confined to one planet, along which it creeps with pain and difficulty, the thought can in an instant transport us into the most distant regions of the universe, or even beyond

> the universe. . . . Nor is any thing beyond the power of thought except what implies an absolute contradiction.
>
> But though our thought seems to possess this unbounded liberty, we shall find, upon a nearer examination, that it is really confined within very narrow limits, and that all this creative power of the mind amounts to no more than the faculty of compounding, transposing, augmenting, or diminishing the materials afforded us by the senses and experience. When we think of a golden mountain, we only join two consistent ideas, *gold* and *mountain*, with which we were formerly acquainted. . . . In short, all the materials of thinking are derived either from our outward or inward sentiment: the mixture and composition of these belongs alone to the mind and will. Or, to express myself in philosophical language, all our ideas or more feeble perceptions are copies of our impressions or more lively ones.

For Hume it is not the cave that is the illusion; it is the world outside the cave. Hume set out to destroy Plato's philosophy of two worlds (matter and Forms), two parts of human nature (body and soul), two powers of knowledge (sensation and reason), and two degrees of certainty (opinion and knowledge). The second level, in each case, does not exist for Hume. Plato's "divided line" leads not to wisdom but to nothing.

This is closely connected, in Hume's mind, with the "Enlightenment" project of refuting "superstition" (supernatural religion, most especially Catholicism, which Hume, like Hobbes [see chap. 70, "Hobbes' 'Political Correctness'" and "Hobbes on Religion and Politics"], always regarded as his primary enemy) by undermining its epistemological assumptions. Hume even uses the military language of spiritual "war" and "enemies" in referring to this philosophical project. He says that philosophies that go beyond strict empiricism and make metaphysical claims

> are not properly a science, but arise either from the fruitless efforts of human vanity, which would penetrate into subjects utterly inaccessible to the understanding, or from the craft of popular superstitions. . . . And many, through cowardice and folly, open the gates to the enemies and willingly receive them with reverence and submission, as their legal sovereign. But is this a sufficient reason why philosophers should . . . leave superstition still in possession of her retreat? Is it not possible to draw an opposite conclusion, and perceive the necessity of carrying the war into the most secret recesses of the enemy?

Like Hobbes, Hume sees his philosophy in terms of spiritual *warfare*.

Hume's Three Basic Premises

Though Hume is an empiricist, not a rationalist like Descartes, his philosophy is a deductive system in that everything follows from his three basic premises, just as in Descartes everything follows from "Cogito ergo sum." Here are the premises:

1. Like Locke, Hume assumes that the first and immediate objects of all thinking are not real things but ideas, or perceptions. (What Locke calls "ideas," Hume calls "perceptions" or "perceptions of the mind.") Hume does not specify this assumption in the *Enquiry Concerning Human Understanding*, from which we are quoting here, but simply assumes it. But in the *Treatise of Human Nature* he says that "properly speaking, 'tis not our body we perceive when we regard our limbs and members, but certain impressions, which enter by the senses." This is his most fundamental questionable assumption that entails his radically skeptical conclusion: that we do not know anything outside our own impressions and ideas.*
2. Hume then divides "perceptions" into "impressions" and "ideas": "We may divide all the perceptions of the mind into two classes or species, which are distinguished by their different degrees of force and vivacity.† The less forcible and lively are commonly denominated Thoughts or Ideas. The other species want a name in our language. . . . Let us, therefore . . . call them Impressions. . . . By the term *impression* I mean all our more lively perceptions, when we hear, or see, or feel, or love, or hate, or desire, or will."
3. Hume's next move—the most crucial one—is to make ideas totally dependent on impressions, in fact mere images or feeble copies of impressions: "All our ideas or more feeble perceptions are copies of our impressions or more lively ones."

   This is his radical empiricism.

   Since all ideas are copies or images of impressions, Hume's strategy in critiquing all ideas is to demand: "Show me the impression it was copied from." If none can be found, the idea is dismissed as meaningless: "When we entertain, therefore, any suspicion that a philosophical term is employed without any meaning or idea (as is but too frequent), we need but enquire,

---

* For a critique of this assumption and an alternative to it, see the beginning of the Locke chapter. Hume's assumption here logically seems to lead to *solipsism* (the belief that we can know nothing but ourselves). Solipsism may be believable but it is certainly not livable by any Humean being. In fact, Dostoevsky and C.S. Lewis identify it as the psychology of hell!—see Fr. Zosima's reflections on hell halfway through Dostoevsky's *The Brothers Karamazov* and chapter 8 of Lewis' *The Problem of Pain*.

† Hume means by "species" merely "conventional classes," not "natural kinds." Natural kinds are distinguished not by mere differences of degree (like "smart men" vs. "stupid men" or "bright colors" vs. "dull colors") but only by differences in kind, in essential nature (like "men [rational animals]" vs. "brutes [irrational animals]" or "colors" vs. "shapes").

from what impression is that supposed idea derived? And if it be impossible to assign any, this will serve to confirm our suspicion. By bringing ideas into so clear a light, we may reasonably hope to remove all dispute which may arise concerning their nature and reality."

This goal was Descartes' dream too, and the dream of the "Enlightenment": to eventually end all disputes or differences of opinion in philosophy, as was being done in science. (Is this possible? If so, why has it never been done? If not, why not?)

As we shall see shortly, this Humean principle that all meaningful ideas are copies of sense impressions logically eliminates all ideas that are *not* copied from impressions, including God, the soul, the self, immortality, substance, moral good and evil, and causality. All these ideas are not merely false but meaningless! Metaphysics, science (which depends on the principle of causality), ethics, and religion are all, in the last analysis, reduced to subjective feeling. They are not rational.

Hume will show that these very radical conclusions follow from the principle that all ideas are copies of impressions. Hume's logic is tight. If his premises are true, his radical conclusions are also true. If his conclusions are not true, his premises are not true either. So his argument may be regarded as either (a) a demonstration of skepticism, as was his intention, if one thinks his premises more obviously right than his conclusions obviously wrong, or (b) as a *reductio ad absurdum* (reduction to absurdity) of his premises, if one thinks his conclusions more obviously wrong than his premises obviously right. One cannot, however, comfortably accept his premises without his conclusions, as many of his predecessors did.

Here is how Hume proves his crucial empiricist premise that all ideas are copies of impressions:

> To prove this, the two following arguments will, I hope, be sufficient. First, when we analyze our thoughts or ideas, however compounded or sublime, we always find that they resolve themselves into such simple ideas as were copied from a precedent feeling or sentiment. Even those ideas which, at first view, seem the most wide of this origin are found, upon a nearer scrutiny, to be derived from it. The idea of God, as meaning an infinitely intelligent, wise, and good Being, arises from reflecting on the operations of our own mind, and augmenting, without limit, those qualities of goodness and wisdom. We may prosecute this inquiry to what length we please; where we shall always find that every idea which we examine is copied from a similar impression. Those who would assert that this position is not universally true nor without exception, have only one, and that an easy method of refuting it: by producing that

idea which, in their opinion, is not derived from this source. It will then be incumbent on us, if we would maintain our doctrine, to produce the impression or lively perception which corresponds to it.

Second, if it happen, from a defect of the organ, that a man is not susceptible of any species of sensation, we always find that he is as little susceptible of the correspondent ideas. A blind man can form no notion of colours; a deaf man of sounds. Restore either of them that sense in which he is deficient; by opening this new inlet for his sensations, you also open an inlet for the ideas; and he finds no difficulty in conceiving these objects.*

The Inner Gravity of Ideas: Association

Here is where Hume attempts to be the Newton of the mind. Newton formulated the fundamental principle binding all physical things together in his law of universal gravitation, and Hume formulates what he claims to be the three principles of mental gravitation that bind together all mental things, all ideas.

> Though it be too obvious to escape observation that different ideas are connected together, I do not find that any philosopher has attempted to enumerate or class all the principles of association; a subject, however, that seems worthy of curiosity. To me, there appear to be only three principles of connexion among ideas, namely *Resemblance*, *Contiguity* in time or place, and *Cause or Effect*.
>
> That these principles serve to connect ideas will not, I believe, be much doubted. A picture naturally leads our thoughts to the original (Resemblance). The mention of one apartment in a building naturally introduces an inquiry or discourse concerning the others (Contiguity). And if we think of a wound, we can scarcely forbear reflecting on the pain which follows it (Cause and Effect).

This last one is by far the most important and is the foundation of all scientific reasoning as well as common sense. Hume's attack on the very notion of causality (below, "Hume's Critique of Causality") is an attack on the belief that either science or common sense can give us knowledge (as distinct from opinion) about the real world.

Hume's three laws of association of ideas seem at first to be simply an uncontroversial observation of mental data, but there is a hidden questionable

* This is not an original argument: it was used by Aristotle and Aquinas, who were *neither* empiricists *nor* rationalists, to refute Plato's rationalistic notion of innate ideas.

assumption here: that these mental data, or ideas, are like atomistic particles rather than continuous waves; that they do not come already "associated" but require mental activity on our part to associate them.

Hume explains complex ideas by our power to join simple ideas together. Thus, we can imagine things we have never seen, like a golden mountain or a talking horse, only because we *have* seen mountains, gold, horses, and talking. We can imagine a missing shade of blue, which we have never seen before, halfway between medium blue and light blue, simply by extrapolation or projection, as on a graph. (This is also Hume's explanation of the origin of our idea of God: our projection, toward infinity, on a curve, like a hyperbola, made up of a finite number of points of experienced finite perfections. See quote above in "Hume's Three Basic Premises," no. 3.)

Hume's New Logic: Relations of Ideas vs. Matters of Fact

When Hume spoke of "the association of ideas," he meant by "ideas" not *propositions* but terms, or concepts. When he speaks now of "relations of ideas" versus "matters of fact," he speaks of two kinds of *propositions*, which *relate* subject terms and predicate terms together. The following distinction between these two classes of propositions is absolutely crucial, not only for Hume but also for subsequent analytic philosophers:

> All the objects of human reason or enquiry may naturally be divided into two kinds, to wit, *Relations of Ideas* and *Matters of Fact*. Of the first kind are the sciences of Geometry, Algebra, and Arithmetic, and in short, every affirmation which is either intuitively or demonstratively certain. *That the square of the hypotenuse is equal to the square of the two sides*, is a proposition which expresses a relation between these figures. *That three times five is equal to the half of thirty*, expresses a relation between these numbers. Propositions of this kind are discoverable by the mere operation of thought, without dependence on what is anywhere existent in the universe. . . .
>
> Matters of fact, which are the second objects of human reason, are not ascertained in the same manner; nor is our evidence of their truth, however great, of a like nature with the foregoing. The contrary of every matter of fact is still possible, because it can never imply a contradiction, and is conceived by the mind with the same facility and distinctness as if ever so conformable to reality. *That the sun will not rise tomorrow* is no less intelligible a proposition, and implies no more contradiction, *than that it will rise*. We should in vain, therefore, attempt to demonstrate its falsehood. Were it demonstrably false, it would imply a contradiction, and could never be distinctly conceived by the mind.

What Hume means by "matters of fact" here is not simply anything that is true, but propositions that can be verified by sense observation. Thus, as we shall see below, the existence or nonexistence of God, the self, the soul, moral laws, immortality, universals, substances, and causality are *not* "matters of fact" for Hume. They are neither true nor false; they are simply not *knowledge*. At most they are subjective psychological habits or feelings.

It's not merely that Hume is agnostic about these things, that he thinks they can't be *proved*. How many craters ten miles or more in diameter there were on the moon ten million years ago can't be proved or known, but it is an objective fact. The above items are not matters of objective fact at all for Hume. For him it is a *linguistic confusion* to wonder whether there is a God and whether we can prove or disprove his existence, or whether Plato is right or wrong when he argues in the *Republic* that "justice is more profitable [to the soul] than injustice." It is impossible in principle to do this, by Hume's new, narrower logic. It eliminates as meaningless just about everything interesting that all previous philosophers had ever said.

The historical import of this abstract logic is intense and immense. It demolishes all claims for meaningful knowledge of objective reality, not just in religion and metaphysical philosophy but also in common sense and even in science. Modern science had apparently shown the power of human reason to penetrate into nature and find certain universal principles, such as Newton's laws of motion. But Hume is pulling reason and nature apart. He is confining reason to the kind of thing a computer can do (determining whether two ideas are logically consistent or inconsistent with each other—which is all that he means by "relations of ideas"), and he is confining our knowledge of nature to the kind of thing an animal can do (sense observation of "matters of fact" that are contingent and can be determined as true or false not by logical analysis but only by sense experience). We are only apes with computers.

Because of the radical influence of this idea, and because of the catastrophic difference it makes, we must go into it in more detail, even though this detail is very abstract and technical. For Hume's confinement of all human knowledge to "relations of ideas" and "matters of [empirical] fact" is the single most enduring and influential idea in all of Hume. It is the basis for modern "analytic philosophy" and its new logic ("symbolic logic" or "mathematical logic" or "propositional logic"), which replaces the old Aristotelian logic that (a) began with terms rather than propositions and with the "first act of the mind," *understanding* the meaning of a term, which is something no computer can do; (b) classified predicates as five different relations to their subjects, as genus, species, difference, property, or accident; and (c) implicitly assumed a realism rather than a nominalism of universals.

Hume divides all propositions into only two classes:

1. "Relations of ideas" are what Kant later called "analytic propositions." They are true by definition, by the law of noncontradiction alone; it is contradictory to deny them. "Red things are red," "Red things are things," "Red unicorns are red," and "Red unicorns are unicorns" are all "relations of ideas." Their predicates are necessary and essential to their subjects.
2. "Matters of fact" are what Kant called "synthetic propositions." They are known to be true only by sense observation. Their predicates are not necessary or essential to their subjects, but accidental. "Tomatoes are red," "Unicorns do not exist," and "Tomatoes are healthy" are all "matters of fact."

Aristotle would say that there is also a third kind of proposition. The predicate of the first kind of proposition is always the *genus*, *species*, or *specific difference* of the subject; and the predicate of the second kind of proposition is always an accident of the subject; but there is a third possibility—a predicate may also be a *property*, or "proper accident" of its subject (e.g., "All men are mortal" or "Justice is always profitable to the soul"). These propositions are known to be true not merely by the law of noncontradiction, like Hume's "relations of ideas," nor merely by sense observation, like Hume's "matters of fact," but by intellectual understanding, or wisdom: if you truly understand human nature, you know that mortality is always a property of it, and if you truly understand virtue and its relation to the soul, you know that the virtue of justice always profits the soul.

This assumes that there *are* such universal essences or forms or natures as human nature, body, soul, and justice. But that is metaphysical realism rather than nominalism. Nearly all modern philosophers (except the rationalists) are nominalists. That is why they prefer modern symbolic logic to Aristotelian logic. Logic is *not* philosophically neutral.

Hume's Critique of Causality

Immediately after announcing the division between "relations of ideas" and "matters of fact," Hume proceeds to his most radical skeptical application of this principle, viz., his famous critique of causality. It is important to see the logical connection between these two points, the premise (the last section) and the conclusion (this section). It is *because* "the contrary of every matter of fact is still possible, because it can never imply a contradiction" that Hume next says, "It may, therefore, be a subject worthy of curiosity to enquire what is the nature of that evidence which assures us of any real existence and matter of fact, beyond the present testimony of our senses or the records of our memory."

His answer is that

> all reasonings concerning matter of fact seem to be founded on the relation of *Cause and Effect*. By means of that relation alone we can go beyond the evidence of our memory and senses. If you were to ask a man why he believes any matter of fact which is absent—for instance, that his friend is in the country, or in France—he would give you a reason; and this reason would be some other fact, as a letter received from him, or the knowledge of his former resolutions and promises. A man, finding a watch or any other machine in a desert island, would conclude that there had once been men in that island. All our reasonings concerning fact are of the same nature.
>
> And it is constantly supposed that there is a connection between the present fact and that which is inferred from it. Were there nothing to bind them together, the inference would be entirely precarious. The hearing of an articulate voice and rational discourse in the dark assures us of the presence of some person. Why? Because these are the effects of the human.
>
> If we would satisfy ourselves, therefore, concerning the nature of that evidence which assures us of matters of fact, we must enquire how we arrive at the knowledge of cause and effect. . . .
>
> I shall venture to affirm, as a general proposition, which admits of no exception, that the knowledge of this relation is not, in any instance, attained by reasonings *a priori*, but arises entirely from experience, when we find that any particular objects are constantly conjoined with each other. Let an object be presented to a man of ever so strong natural reason and abilities; if that object be entirely new to him, he will not be able, by the most accurate examination of its sensible qualities, to discover any of its causes or effects. Adam, though his rational faculties be supposed, at the very first, entirely perfect, could not have inferred, from the fluidity and transparency of water, that it would suffocate him, or from the light and warmth of fire, that it would consume him. No object ever discovers, by the qualities which appear to the senses, either the causes which produced it or the effects which will arise from it; nor can our reason, unassisted by experience, ever draw any inference concerning real existence and matter of fact. . . .
>
> We fancy that were we brought on a sudden into this world, we could at first have inferred that one billiard-ball would communicate motion to another upon impulse. . . . Such is the influence of custom. . . . But . . . the mind can never possibly find the effect in the supposed cause by the most accurate scrutiny and examination. For the effect is totally different from the cause [Is this true? Look at examples], and consequently can never be discovered in it. Motion in the second

> billiard-ball is a quite distinct event from motion in the first, nor is there any thing in the one to suggest the smallest hint of the other. . . . Every effect is a distinct event from its cause. It could not, therefore, be discovered in the cause.

Also, Hume points out, causality itself, the causal *connection*, is not something we can ever sense. What color or shape is it?

> We are never able, in a single instance, to discover any power or necessary connexion, any quality which binds the effect to the cause and renders the one an infallible consequence of the other. We only find that the one does actually in fact follow the other. . . . All events seem entirely loose and separate. One event follows another, but we never can observe any tie between them. They seem conjoined, but never connected. And as we can have no idea of anything which never appeared to our outward sense or inward sentiment [Hume's empiricist premise], the necessary conclusion seems to be that we have no idea of connexion or power at all, and that these words are absolutely without any meaning.

Hume's argument so far amounts to this:

1. All matters of fact are contingent; that is, their opposite is logically possible, and not self-contradictory.
2. It is our reason and only our reason that tells us which "relations of ideas" are and which ones are not contradictory, but it is our senses and only our senses that tell us "matters of fact."
3. Therefore, all our knowledge of matters of fact come not from our reason but from sense experience.
4. But we *believe* we have knowledge of matters of fact that lie beyond our present, immediate sense experience.
5. Is this belief true? If this is true, it can only be by reasoning from what we sense to what we do not sense by the principle of cause and effect. That is, we think we can deduce the unseen causes and effects of what we see.
6. But we cannot do this deduction, because of point 3 above. We cannot know what we have not experienced, viz., unseen past causes or future effects.
7. Another reason is that we cannot sense causality itself.
8. Therefore, our belief that we have such knowledge is only subjective, not objective; it is due to custom and habit, not reason. It is just a feeling in us. We expect the sun to come up tomorrow only because we have seen it happen so many times in the past. All we can know is our own mental habits, not the real causes of sunrise *or of any other event in the universe*!

If you disagree with this radical, skeptical conclusion, Hume argues, you must answer the following question:

> These two propositions are far from being the same, [1] *I have found that such an object has always been attended with such an effect*, and [2] *I foresee that other objects, which are in appearance similar, will be attended with similar effects*. I shall allow, if you please, that the one proposition may justly be inferred from the other; I know in fact that it always is inferred. But if you insist that the inference is made by a chain of reasoning, I desire you to produce the reasoning. The connexion between these propositions is not intuitive. There is required a medium, which may enable the mind to draw such an inference, if indeed it be drawn by reasoning and argument. What that medium is, I must confess, passes my comprehension; and it is incumbent on those to produce it who assert that it really exists and is the origin of all our conclusions concerning matter of fact.

The usual answer to Hume's question here is called "the principle of the Uniformity of Nature": that the future will resemble the past, that the laws of nature will continue to operate.* But Hume asks *how we can know that principle*. On the basis of his epistemology, we can't; for it is not a "relation of ideas," since its denial is not self-contradictory; nor is it a "matter of fact," since we cannot sense, in the present, the future unchangingness of these laws of nature.

> We have said that all arguments concerning existence are founded on the relation of cause and effect; that our knowledge of that relation is derived entirely from experience; and that all our experimental conclusions proceed upon the supposition that the future will be conformable to the past. To endeavor, therefore, the proof of this last supposition by . . . arguments regarding existence, must be evidently going in a circle, and taking that for granted which is the very point in question. . . . For all inferences from experience [pre]suppose, as their foundation, that the future will resemble the past, and that similar powers will be conjoined with similar sensible qualities.

Hume is here casting doubt on the rationality of belief in science as much as belief in religion. Unseen physical and natural causes and effects are just as much forever beyond the grasp of our reason as spiritual or supernatural ones. Newton's principles are just as doubtable as Aquinas'.

---

* Is there another answer? Is there one in the Aristotelian "Four Epistemologies" diagram in the introduction?

This was the most total and the most consistent skepticism the world of thought had ever seen. It had to be answered. The immediate answer would come from Kant. But the answer would be, in a different way, even more skeptical than the question.

Essentially, it would be this: the subjectivity that Hume took to be the problem, Kant would take to be the answer. Hume reduced causality from a known objective fact to a subjective mental habit, and from this premise he derived the conclusion of skepticism, because he assumed a second premise, a premise that every philosopher before Kant had assumed and that Kant would deny: that the proper work of human reason is to know objective reality, or "things-in-themselves," as Kant would call them.

Kant (1) generalized Hume's reduction of causality to subjectivity to the reduction of *all* human knowledge to subjectivity, but he (2) denied that this entailed the conclusion of skepticism, for he said that this is all that human reason could ever do, that this was its proper work: to create, not to discover, the forms and structures and order of the world. (We haven't studied Kant yet, so if you don't understand this yet, don't worry. Perhaps you should worry if you *do*.)

Hume's Solution: Causality is Only Custom

Hume's empiricism limits our knowledge to our experience. We know only what we experience. But we do not experience causality itself, because causality is not an empirical thing or event but the relationship between the two events that we call the "cause" and the "effect." A relationship between two empirical things is not itself empirical. Hume calls this supposed nonempirical relationship a "necessary connection" and a "secret [invisible] power" that emanates from the cause so as to produce the effect, as one billiard ball communicates motion to a second, or as a mother gives birth to a baby. We think the movement of the second billiard ball is really dependent on that of the first, and the baby on the mother; but we do not see "dependence," only balls, babies, and mothers. We do not see the causal relationship.

But we do think in terms of causality. Why? What is the origin of this thinking? Not either reason or experience but a feeling, an instinct, a habit, a "custom."

> He immediately infers the existence of one object from the appearance of the other. Yet he has not, by all his experience, acquired any idea of knowledge of the secret power [causality] by which the one object produces the other, nor is it by any process of reasoning that he is engaged to draw this inference. But still he finds himself determined to draw it . . . though . . . his understanding has no part in the operation. . . . [Therefore] there is some other principle which determines him to form such a conclusion.

> This principle is Custom or Habit. For wherever the repetition of any particular act or operation produces [really "*causes*"?] a propensity to renew the same act . . . we always say that this propensity is the effect [a real "*effect*"?] of Custom. . . . All inferences from experience, therefore, are effects of custom, not of reasoning.

Causality is reduced to a purely subjective habit of thought. All science is thus reduced to psychology.

Kant would pick up on this answer and modify it in just one important way: for him, this habit or custom, though just as subjective as it is for Hume, is universal and necessary and therefore rational. Causality, for Kant, will become a "category" of rational thought, but he will agree with Hume that it is not a known aspect of objective reality. In fact, Kant will cut us off even more from any knowledge of objective reality than Hume did. For he will maintain that even immediate sense experience is only a mental projection of our subjective (but universal and necessary) categories such as space and time and causality out onto a reality ("things-in-themselves") that we can never know as it is in itself, like the constant projection of a movie onto a screen from the projecting machine that is our own minds.

Hume's Critique of Substance and Self

From Hume's simple, apparently innocent premise of empiricism, he deduces the radical consequence that no substance, including the self, can be known:

1. If we do not know what we do not sense (Hume's empiricist premise),
2. and if we sense only qualities but not any underlying substance holding these qualities together,
3. then we do not know any substance.
4. But we think of ourselves not just as bundles of qualities but as a single being or entity (what Aristotle meant by a "substance" that *has* those many qualities), as "I"—either
   a. single material substances, if we are materialists like Hobbes, or
   b. single spiritual substances, if we are spiritualists like Plato, or
   c. two separate substances, if we are dualists like Descartes, or
   d. a single substance composed of matter (body) and form (soul), if we accept Aristotle and Aquinas' anthropology of hylomorphism or (to use current terms) psychosomatic unity.
5. All four of these concepts of ourselves are wrong, according to Hume. We know no self, since we know no substance. As far as we know, there is no self. We do not exist. Only our thoughts and perceptions and experiences exist.

There's nobody there to know them. There's nobody home. Descartes argued, "I think, therefore I am"; Hume replies, "I think that I am not." There is no Humean being.

Hume's strict empiricist premise necessitates this conclusion. We know only what we sense, and we do not sense the self, the senser, only the sensed objects. Meaningful ideas must be copies of impressions; therefore, there is no meaningful idea of the self, for

> from what impression could this idea be derived? The question is impossible to answer. . . . It must be some one impression that gives rise to every real idea. But self or person is not any one impression, but that to which our several impressions and ideas are supposed to have a reference. If any impression gives rise to the idea of the self, that impression must continue invariably the same through the whole course of our lives, since self is supposed to exist after that manner. But there is no impression constant and invariable. . . .
>
> All the nice and subtle questions concerning personal identity can never possibly be decided, and are to be regarded rather as grammatical than as philosophical difficulties.

This is Hobbes' linguistic ploy (see chap. 70, "Hobbes vs. Descartes: the 'Meaningless Language' Argument"): dissolving rather than solving metaphysical questions by declaring them linguistically meaningless—a technique of many early (and some late) analytic philosophers. The self for Hume is not so much *false* or *nonexistent* as *meaningless*, since it is not an idea copied from any impression.

At this point, if not before, most readers will turn to common sense, as Reid did (see next chapter) and argue that if Hume has not made a mistake in his reasoning, then far from proving his radically skeptical and anti-commonsensical conclusion from his empiricist premise, as he thinks he has done, he has refuted his premise. For if any premise leads to such absurd conclusions, it must be false. Contrary to his own intentions, Hume has not established but *refuted* his own empiricism. His whole philosophy is an elaborate *reductio ad absurdum*. For if there *is* no Hume, then with "hume" are we arguing when we argue with Hume?

Hume's answer is the same as Buddha's: there is no soul or self. Buddha calls this the *anatta* or "no-*Atman*" theory: I am only the coming-together of perceptions, like the knotting of strands (*skandhas*) of a rope. Its unity is only apparent, not real. "I may venture to affirm of the rest of mankind that they are nothing but a bundle or collection of different perceptions, which succeed each other with an inconceivable rapidity, and are in a perpetual flux and movement. . . . The mind is a kind of theatre, where several perceptions successively make their appearance." A modern movie theater is an even better image than Hume's stage theater. The movie seems real, but it is only a rapid succession of images, twenty-four frames per second, too fast for us to see the gaps between them, but none of them is substantial. Nothing holds successive perceptions together, not even memory, for there is no subject or agent to do the remembering. Life is a movie without a projector.*

Empiricists have always had a problem accounting for *other minds* (selves, I's, subjects, souls, persons, or egos). But Hume has no such problem: they are in the same position as his own mind. They do not exist.

It sounds like a very bad knock-knock joke:

"Knock, knock."
"Who's there?"
"Nobody."
"Nobody who?"
"Nobody you."

Hume has (2) an *a posteriori* and experiential argument for the "no-substance" theory of the self, as well as (1) the above *a priori* deductive argument from the premise of empiricism and its denial of any kind of substance. He argues that he can never catch "himself" as an observed object, no matter how hard he tries: "For my part, when I enter most intimately into what I call *myself*, I always stumble upon some particular perception or other, of heat or cold, light or shade, love or hatred, pain or pleasure. I can never catch *myself* at any time without a perception, and never can observe anything but the perception."

But Hume's inability to innerly "see" himself as an object is exactly what we should expect if the commonsensical belief in a substantial self or subject were true. The subject is not an object, any more than the projecting machine in the movie theater is one of the images projected on the screen. The seer is more than the seen.†

This insubstantiality of the self also entails the conclusion that there can be no life after death:

> And were all my perceptions removed by death, and could I neither think nor feel nor see nor love nor hate after the dissolution of my body, I should be entirely annihilated. . . . If anyone, upon serious and unprejudiced

---

* For a powerful concrete case for the need for a substantial self, read Robert Bolt's play about Thomas More, *A Man for All Seasons*, especially his comments, in his preface, on the dissolution of the substantial self in modern life. And see the Academy Award–winning movie based on this play.

† One may ask, How then do we know this non-object? One possible answer is what Marcel calls "recollection" (see vol. 4, chap. 77).

> reflection, thinks he has a different notion of *himself*, I must confess I can reason no longer with him. All I can allow him is that . . . we are essentially different in this particular. He may, perhaps, perceive something simple and continued, which he calls *himself*, though I am certain there is no such principle in me.

Like Hobbes, Hume's "comeback" against traditional metaphysical beliefs is not a logical refutation but a linguistic one: he finds your terms meaningless. This is a powerful and intimidating debating technique because it cannot be answered. Hume is demanding that you meet him on his own empiricist terms, not any others; nor is he prepared to debate those terms. He demands that you show him what he, from the beginning, insists that his mind simply cannot take in or understand. His criterion for meaning is too narrow, but he will not expand it. He is in Plato's cave, and he will not come out. And the cave is too small to contain the world outside it.* Like a child, he can simply say, "I just don't understand you"—and seem not childish but sophisticated! Is this "serious and unprejudiced reflection"?

Hume's Critique of Free Will

Free will was a problematic concept for Hume's contemporaries because it seemed to find no place in Newton's deterministic clockwork universe. If every event had determining causes, human choices must also have determining causes—in which case, it seemed, they were not free.

Hume argues that free will does not contradict deterministic causality. In fact, "according to any reasonable sense which can be put on these terms . . . the whole controversy [between free will, or liberty, and necessity, or causal determinism] has hitherto turned merely upon words." Again he turns to the linguistic ploy: the problem is linguistically dissolved rather than logically solved.

His two linguistic ploys are

1. to deny the usual notion of physical determinism as real necessary causal connection (see his critique of causality above) and to redefine natural causality as merely observed repetition rather than real causal connection; and
2. to deny the usual notion of human free will as the spirit or soul actively initiating an action on its own, from within, rather than just passively transmitting a chain of determining causes from without, from biological heredity or physical environment. Hume redefines human freedom as

---

* See C.S. Lewis' satire on this in *The Silver Chair*. Hume is like the Witch of the Underland, and Reid (next chapter) will be like Puddleglum.

> simply unimpeded movement, the physical ability to do what you desire to do. This makes it the same *kind* of thing as happens in animals, or even in minerals. Hume sees no difference between inorganic physical causality (e.g., clouds causing rain) and human causality (e.g., a man causing a murder), for "in neither case, material or intelligent, is there any *constraint* observed." If the man is chained, he cannot cause the murder, and if the rain is impeded by a tent roof, it cannot wet the ground beneath it.

He then argues that there is no contradiction between human free will and Newtonian deterministic physics, because on the human side free will does not mean something uncaused, and on the side of nature causality does not mean necessity but simply regularity. Thus, Newtonian determinism and human free will are compatible. Contemporary philosophers call this view of free will "compatibilism." It presupposes that human free will is defined materialistically, merely as unimpeded power.

This is one of the reasons why Hume thinks that a Newtonian kind of science of human nature and human thought is just as possible as Newton's science of physics. Modern behaviorist psychologists often follow him here.*

Hume's Critique of God

Almost all of Hume's contemporaries, both friends and enemies, thought Hume was an atheist. This is why universities refused to employ him. Hume argued in print that his philosophy does not entail atheism, but this is pretty clearly a less-than-honest defensive ploy that Hume thought pragmatically necessary to avoid public trouble, for (1) Hume clearly says in his autobiography that he lost his religious faith before he began his writing career, and (2) the argument Hume uses in the *Enquiry* for the compatibility of his philosophy with Christianity is so weak that it may be deliberately intended to be ridiculous. He argues there that only a faith that *cannot* be defended by reason, in fact that contradicts reason (as he will say Christianity does when he claims to prove that miracles do not exist), i.e., only a faith that is shown by reason to be *false*, is the *true* faith (i.e., "our most holy religion"). He says this at the end of his refutation of miracles: "I am the better pleased with the method of reasoning here delivered, as I think it may serve to confound those dangerous friends or disguised enemies to the *Christian Religion*, who have undertaken to defend it by the principles of human reason. Our most holy religion is founded on *Faith*, not on reason; and it is a sure method of exposing it to put it to such a trial as it is by no means fitted to endure."

* For a critique of the applications of such a psychological science, see C.S. Lewis, *The Abolition of Man*, and Joseph Wood Krutch, *The Measure of Man*.

In his *Dialogues Concerning Natural Religion* he refutes all arguments for the existence of God, as we would expect him to do since he has already come to the conclusion that reason cannot prove anything at all about "matters of fact." He refutes first Descartes' arguments.

Descartes' main proof, in the *Meditations*, is essentially Anselm's ontological argument, which tries to prove the existence of God *a priori* by simply analyzing the *idea* or definition of God. Hume argues, commonsensically, that ideas prove only ideas; you need a fact to prove another fact. (That is essentially Aquinas' reason for rejecting Anselm's argument too.)

He also argues from his empiricist premise that ideas that cannot be traced back to impressions are meaningless—and this argument undercuts not just Anselm's or Descartes' but *all* arguments for God, since God is not an impression. "Our ideas reach no farther than our experience. We have no experience of divine attributes. I need not conclude my syllogism. You can draw the inference yourself." The only way to deny the conclusion is to deny one of the two premises.

Since the idea of God is not copied from any impression, it is neither true nor false but meaningless. This is even farther from theism than atheism is, just as "You are meaningless to me" is farther from "I believe in you" than "I don't believe in you" is.

Descartes tried to prove the existence of God as the only possible cause of our idea of him as an infinitely perfect being, since the imperfect cannot be the total or adequate cause of the perfect. Hume argues that we can explain our idea of God simply as a projection of our own finite perfections in the direction of infinity.

Hume answers all cosmological arguments for God, which argue from premises of observed facts about the cosmos to God as their only adequate cause, (1) by his critique of causality, and (2) by arguing that the universe, not God, could just as well be the first, uncaused cause, the eternal being.

The most popular argument for God in Hume's day was the argument from design. (Sometimes this is classified as one of the cosmological arguments, sometimes separately.) Science had discovered far more order or design in the universe than ever before, and design seems to imply an intelligent Designer. Paley famously argued that if we found a watch in the wilderness, we would infer, from its design, that it was made by an intelligent mind; but the universe has much more design and order in it than a watch; therefore, it is reasonable to believe that there is a great mind behind all this magnificent order in the universe.

Hume replies (1) that no argument from experience can ever establish a certainty; (2) that there is no proportion between an infinite cause and a finite effect; (3) that the argument depends on the analogy between human and divine designers, but we have no experience of the second half of that analogy; (4)

that it does not prove monotheism, for many human beings together design machines like watches; (5) that the world resembles a vegetable, which just grows by itself, more than a designed machine like a watch; (6) that apparent design could have arisen by a Humean anticipation of Darwinian "natural selection"; (7) that the universe could have emerged like a spider's web from a spider, not by intelligence but by instinct; (8) that the world is not like any one thing in it such as a watch, but is "entirely singular"; (9) that the concept of causality, whether mental or physical, cannot be applied beyond the realm of empirical appearances, to God and his relation to the universe that *contains* all appearances; (10) that the universe also contains much "undesign" (randomness); (11) that like many earlier and poorly working versions of the invention of the watch, "many worlds might have been botched and bungled, throughout an eternity, ere this system was struck out"; and (12) that the world contains also much bad design, i.e., what we call evil, both physical (pain) and moral (injustice). Twelve strikes should be more than enough to declare a batter out.*

Hume acknowledges that religious belief seems innate to mankind, but he explains its origin in the same way he explains the origin of the idea of causality: by subjective feelings, in this case the fear of death and the desire for immortality.

This seems to imply that Christianity is myth, not truth. Yet Hume also argues (probably for the sake of the censors) that his skepticism is a friend, not an enemy, of religion, and that "to be a philosophical skeptic is, in a man of letters, the first and most essential step towards being a sound, believing *Christian*, for a person seasoned with a just sense of the imperfections of natural reason will fly to revealed truth with the greatest avidity." (But why, one must ask, to Christianity rather than any other equally irrational belief, whether Zen Buddhism or the invisible flying spaghetti monster? Hume *can't* be serious here. Yet many "fideist" Christians have not only interpreted him seriously but agreed with him!)

Hume's Critique of Miracles

As we have seen, Hume claims that we cannot really know, by reason, any matter of fact. However, there seems to be one exception to this in Hume's mind: we can know that no miracle has ever happened as a matter of fact. Writing to a friend, Hume expressed great excitement and enthusiasm over the fact that he thought he had finally come up with an argument that refuted miracles. He saw this not as an impersonal scientific conclusion but as part of the spiritual war against superstition.

---

* If readers know Thomas Aquinas well, they may guess how he would defend his five cosmological arguments against these critiques.

1. He begins with an assumption that was later called "Clifford's Rule," after a twentieth-century Oxford logician: "A wise man . . . proportions his belief to the evidence." No evidence, no belief; weak evidence, weak belief; strong evidence, strong belief; certain evidence, certain belief.

   (Like Ockham's Razor, this is a good principle of scientific method, but when *other* people are involved, it is questionable because it does not allow us to take account of personal trust or loyalty. Should a judge treat his or her spouse at home the same way he or she treats an accused criminal in court?)
2. Next follows Hume's definition of a miracle: "A miracle is a violation of the laws of nature."

   (This, too, can be questioned, since it is only the *cause* of a miracle that is outside the natural order; once it happens, if it ever does happen, it becomes part of nature as a meteor from outer space becomes a rock on the earth's surface when it falls. Even a virgin birth follows the ordinary course of a nine-month pregnancy.)
3. The nub of Hume's argument comes next: that miracles, though not logically self-contradictory, are more improbable than anything else, for the following reason: "As a firm and unalterable experience has established these laws [of nature], the proof against a miracle, from the very nature of the fact, is as entire as any argument from experience can possibly be imagined."

   To speak of the testimony of experience as "unalterable" seems to beg the question: it seems to assume the conclusion he is trying to prove, viz., that no one has ever experienced a miracle (i.e., a violation of the laws of nature). Thus Hume says, "It is no miracle that a man, seemingly in good health, should die on a sudden: because such a kind of death, though more unusual than any other, has yet been frequently observed to happen." (Notice that Hume does not appeal to causality here, only to frequency of observation.) "But it is a miracle that a dead man should come to life, because that has never been observed." This *assumption*, that miraculous events like resurrections have never been observed, is precisely what believers deny and Hume must prove rather than assume.
4. His argument is linguistic rather than empirical when he goes on to say that "there must, therefore, be a uniform experience against every miraculous event, *otherwise the event would not merit that appellation*" (italics mine).

   "And as an uniform experience amounts to a *proof*, there is here a direct and full proof, from the nature of the fact, against the existence of any miracle."

   (It seems very strange that Hume here violates his own skeptical principles. He never calls any other historical or empirical claim for or against anything at all "a direct and full proof.")
5. Hume then adds his argument from probability, calculating that it is always more probable that those who claim to have witnessed miracles are either hallucinating or lying than that miracles actually happen, because we know

already that many people do hallucinate or lie but we do not know that miracles happen: "When anyone tells me that he saw a dead man restored to life, I immediately consider with myself whether it be more probable that this person should either deceive [lie] or be deceived [hallucinate], or that the fact which he relates should really have happened."

(*Why* is a miracle improbable? Because it is so unusual, so unique. But so is each individual human being who has ever lived. Yet they are real.)

6. He then gives reasons for doubting the veracity of all who claim to have seen miracles: "There is not to be found, in all history, any miracle attested by a sufficient number of men, of such unquestioned good sense, education, and learning, as to secure us against all delusion in themselves; of such undoubted integrity as to place them beyond all suspicion of any design to deceive others."

   (What about the thousands of saints, innocent children, and people of sound mind and morals who were bribed, pressured, threatened, persecuted, tortured, and martyred and yet maintained this claim?)

   "It forms a strong presumption against all supernatural and miraculous relations that they are observed chiefly to abound among ignorant and barbarous nations."

   (Why are they "ignorant and barbarous"? Why, because they believe in miracles! Again, arguing in a circle, or begging the question. Very surprising for such a logical thinker as Hume.)

   "Prodigies, omens, oracles . . . grow thinner every page in proportion as we advance nearer the enlightened ages."

   (Why are later ages more "enlightened"? Because they disbelieve in miracles. The circle again.)

   "Such prodigious events never happen in our days."

   (That is his conclusion; how can it be his premise? Circularity again.)

Hume lived in a society that was almost uniformly Christian, except among its intellectuals. He was quite familiar with Christianity and the crucial importance of the miracle of Christ's Resurrection for Christians. So in calling believers in miracles either deceived (fools) or deceivers (liars), he must here be thinking primarily of Christians, all of whom, from the Apostles to present-day believers, claim this miracle—Christ's Resurrection—as central and necessary to their religion (see 1 Cor. 15:12–19).

Hume's Critique of Morality

All societies, cultures, and religions in history have believed in some form of what is traditionally called the natural moral law, i.e., moral principles that are universal (for all human beings), absolute (inescapable obligations), and objective (not just subjective desires or feelings). There is only one exception: modern Western civilization. Denial of any natural moral law has increased each century, from the "Enlightenment" onward, and has spread from intellectuals and philosophers to the masses. Hume is one of the most influential philosophers in this development (i.e., in the rise of moral subjectivism and moral relativism), just as he is in the rise of modern "analytic" logic.

There is a close connection between these two developments. "The fact-value distinction" is a staple of modern analytic philosophers, and it stems from Hume's absolute distinction between "matters of fact" and "relations of ideas." Moral values fit into neither category; therefore, they are not rational.* They are mere feelings, emotions. That is Hume's bottom line in ethics.

This classification of moral values as feelings is based on the psychology, or anthropology, of human reason as weak and incapable of guiding the will, or the feelings ("passions"), or the actions:

"Nothing is more usual in philosophy, and even in common life, than to talk of the combat of passion and reason, to give the preference to reason, and to assert that men are only so far virtuous as they conform themselves to its dictates. . . .† In order to show the fallacy of all this philosophy, I shall endeavor to prove *first*, that reason alone can never be a motive to any action of the will; and *secondly*, that it can never oppose passion in the direction of the will."

Hume argues that mere knowledge of facts cannot motivate the will to act. E.g., even if I know that I must be morally good in order to be happy,‡ or, as Plato put it, that "justice is more profitable than injustice," this knowledge will not, as Plato thought, motivate me to be good or just unless I already seek happiness as my end; and this seeking is done not by the reason or *by the will*, but by feeling, emotion, or sentiment: "The ultimate ends [goods, values, purposes] of human actions can never, in any case, be accounted for by

---

* Before the eighteenth century, the word "values" was used to refer not to ethics but to economics. The word that was used in morality was "laws." But "laws" cannot be subjective to me; they impinge on my will, so that I must either obey or disobey them. But "values" is a more flexible term. Values can be either subjective or objective, either created or discovered, either freely chosen or bindingly "imposed."

† This is true. In fact, it is the very essence of classical morality, pagan as well as Christian. Hume will now undermine this essential foundation.

‡ Hume would not call this "knowledge" at all, but only "belief." Hume cannot say that anything moral is "knowledge" because moral qualities or values are not empirical. They are not "ideas" because they are not copied from any sensory "impressions." They are therefore cognitively meaningless. They are mere feelings, and therefore it is not logically possible to meaningfully argue about them. But this is what we always do: we argue about whether an act would be right or wrong, but we do not argue about whether a taste felt pleasant or unpleasant. So Hume is telling us that all the arguments about morality that have occupied nearly all philosophers and ordinary people throughout history are mistakes, linguistic errors, and cognitively meaningless.

reason,* but recommend themselves entirely to the sentiments and affections of mankind, without any dependence on the intellectual faculties."

Hume goes farther: "Reason is, and ought only to be, the slave of the passions, and can never pretend to any other office than to serve and obey them." (This is exactly what Hobbes said: see chap. 70, "Free Will," par. 3, and "Hobbes' Anthropology," no. 8.) Reason cannot make moral judgments at all! It can only calculate what things are likely to satisfy our desires, but it cannot judge any desires at all as right or wrong. In fact, Hume makes the astonishing claim that "'tis not contrary to reason to prefer the destruction of the whole world to the scratching of my finger." (See the previous footnote on the meaning of "reason" in Hume.)

Hume then proceeds to refute the traditional view that some human actions are in fact good or evil, right or wrong, by using his empiricist premise to reduce everything objectively real to merely sensory qualities:

> Take any action allowed to be vicious: Willful murder, for instance. Examine it in all lights, and see if you can find that matter of fact, or real existence, which you call *vice*. In whichever way you take it, you find only certain passions, motives, volitions, and thoughts. There is no other matter of fact in the case. The vice entirely escapes you, as long as you consider the object. You can never find it, till you turn your reflexion into your own breast, and find a sentiment of disapprobation, which arises in you, towards this action. Here is a matter of fact; but 'tis the object of feeling, not of reason. It lies in yourself, not in the object. So that when you pronounce any action or character to be vicious, you mean nothing but that from the constitution of your nature you have a feeling or sentiment of blame from the contemplation of it.

(But that is a very blatant confusion, and the confusion is in Hume, not in the rest of humanity, whom he is criticizing for linguistic confusion. For "blame" is not a feeling; it is a *judgment*. "That is a wicked act" does not *mean* "I feel in a blaming mood when I look at that." I may feel "non-blaming" and desire not to blame, yet I blame anyway. A good judge cannot go by his feelings! Nor can a defendant: "But judge, I don't *feel* guilty" is hardly an excuse for a crime.)

So for Hume, we do not feel good about justice or charity because they *are* good, or bad about injustice or cruelty because they *are* bad. They're not! They're value-free. Only because we feel good or bad when we contemplate them do we

* This conclusion follows from Hume's new, narrowed, "analytic" notion of "reason" as mere logical consistency ("relations of ideas," which are judged true or false by the law of noncontradiction alone), not wisdom or understanding. Contrast what nearly all pre-Humean philosophers meant by "reason."

(misleadingly) call *them* good or bad. The Nazis *felt* good about murdering the Jews, therefore they *called* it "good." The deed, in reality, was neither good nor evil. (A convenient philosophy for tyrants! In his philosophical musings, *Diuturna*, Mussolini explicitly identifies fascism with relativism.)

Hume then announces the absolute divide between is and ought, facts and values, truth and goodness that is, for him, fatal to traditional rational or philosophical ethics: "In every system of morality which I have hitherto met with, I have always remarked that . . . instead of the usual copulations of propositions, *is and is not*, I meet with . . . an *ought* or *ought not*. . . . What seems altogether inconceivable [is] how this new relation can be a deduction from others, which are entirely different from it."*

What moral principles can be used, then, if there really is no virtue or vice, no good or evil, no right or wrong? Hume reduces moral judgments to two: judgments about what is "agreeable or useful." Aristotle said, commonsensically, that "good" could mean three things: the virtuous, the pleasant, or the useful. Hume reduces these three to two. We can calculate what will give us pleasure and what will work. That is all. There is no more. We can't give ourselves or each other any reason to prefer saving a life to scratching our head. Moral judgments are just as irrational as judgments about the taste of foods. "I love violence" is related to "I love peace" as "I love spicy cheese" is related to "I love plain cheese."

This idea of Hume's gave Jeremy Bentham the basic premise for his new morality of utilitarianism (the reduction of the good to the useful). When he read Hume, Bentham wrote, "I felt as if scales had fallen from my eyes."

Hume thinks this does not lead to social destruction because he optimistically relies on the universality and strength of the feeling of sympathy, which works for community and communality in all of us. Hume did not live to see "the century of genocide."

What's Left?

Hume has set himself against universal common sense, against nearly all previous philosophy, and against all religion. He has undermined reason's power to know anything beyond sense impressions: metaphysics, religion, science, common sense, causality, substance, self, mind, soul, spirit, other minds, immortality, providence, freedom, God, miracles, and morality. He is the most complete skeptic in the history of philosophy.

His famous bottom line at the end of the *Enquiry* is:

---

* The answer to Hume's question is that moral reasoning does not deduce an "ought" from an "is" alone but from an "is" premise (e.g., "Murder is evil") plus an "ought" premise ("Evil ought not to be done"). This latter principle is traditionally held to be morally self-evident just as the law of noncontradiction is logically self-evident. Both were part of traditional "reason."

"When we run over libraries, persuaded of these principles, what havoc must we make? If we take into our hand any volume of school metaphysics, for instance, let us ask: *Does it contain any abstract reasoning concerning quantity or number? No. Does it contain any experimental reasoning concerning matter of fact and existence? No.* Commit it then to the flames. For it can contain nothing but sophistry and illusion."

By these very standards, the first book to go into the flames would be Hume's own work. For the statement that the only meaningful statements are one of these two—"relations of ideas" or "matters of [empirical] fact"—is itself neither one, and therefore, by its own standards, meaningless. "Commit it then to the flames. For it can contain nothing but sophistry and illusion." What is left? Only the flames.

Hume does not admit that this philosophy is self-contradictory and thus unthinkable. But he does admit that it is unlivable. He says that he is

> ready to reject all belief and reasoning, and look upon no opinion even as more probable or likely than another. Where am I, or what? From what causes do I derive my existence, and to what condition shall I return? Whose favor shall I court, and whose anger must I dread? What beings surround me? And on whom have I any influence, or who have any influence on me? I am confounded with all these questions, and begin to fancy myself in the most deplorable condition imaginable, environed with the deepest darkness and utterly deprived of the use of every member and faculty. [But to] whatever length anyone may push his speculative principles of skepticism, he must act . . . and live and converse like other men. . . . It is impossible for him to persevere in total skepticism or make it appear in his conduct.

His only solution to this radical disconnect is to abandon his philosophy in his life, to embrace a "double truth theory," in order to avoid depression and perhaps insanity:

> Most fortunately it happens that since reason is incapable of dispelling these clouds, nature herself suffices to that purpose, and cures me of this philosophical melancholy and delirium, either by relaxing the bent of mind, or by some avocation and lively impression of my senses, which obliterate all these chimeras. I dine, I play a game of backgammon, I converse and am merry with my friends; and when, after three or four hours' amusement, I would return to these speculations, they appear so cold and strained and ridiculous that I cannot find in my heart to enter into them any farther.

Four possible general answers to Hume:

1. One could throw old Aristotle into the conversation, as I have implicitly done, and I think he would quite hold his own with Hume, even on empiricist premises.
2. Reid (next chapter) will defend common sense against Hume, even on empiricist premises.
3. Pascal would say that Hume's heart is far wiser than his head; that "the heart has its reasons, of which reason knows nothing." That would be something like the answer of the later existentialists like Kierkegaard and Nietzsche.
4. But before they come on the scene, one more strictly rational attempt to answer Hume's great skeptical challenge appears, and his name is Immanuel Kant.

63

THOMAS REID

AD 1710–1796

by Dr. Steven Schwarz, PhD

Reid's Life and Place in the History of Philosophy

Reid, founder of the Scottish school of common sense philosophy and its most famous member, was professor of philosophy at King's College, Aberdeen, and later professor of moral philosophy at the University of Glasgow, where he took the position from which Adam Smith had just resigned. His major works are *An Inquiry into the Human Mind on the Principles of Common Sense* (1764), *Essays on the Intellectual Powers of Man* (1785), and *Essays on the Active Powers of Man* (1788). He sent a copy of his *Inquiry* to Hume, who read it and wrote back, commending the work as a serious challenge to his ideas, as it was to the many Scottish philosophers who had accepted Hume's skepticism. Reid was a deeply moral man, committed to the search for truth, patient and persevering, a warm and concerned friend to many, and a deeply devoted husband to his wife, Elizabeth, and father to his five children.

Though born a year before Hume, he really comes after Hume in terms of his place in the history of philosophy. He died twenty years after Hume, and that is where we should place him. He follows the classic British empiricists—Locke, Berkeley, and Hume—and he sees his task as cleaning up the mess they made. That mess is a skepticism that doubts or denies what we all know to be real; what common sense tells us is real. We'll look at this in three key areas.

Reid's Big Idea

Common sense is, or at least should be, the foundation of all philosophical inquiry. Therefore, in any conflict between philosophy and common sense, we should take the side of common sense. Philosophy is not superior to common sense, as Hume apparently thought. It can help us understand better what we already know from common sense. It can go deeper and move beyond common sense; but it can never take away what common sense makes obvious for us. This is because philosophy itself must begin with common sense and must build on it. In daily life, the most skeptical philosopher lives his common sense, not his philosophical theory.

(I) Sense Perception and the Real World

By our five senses we perceive the world. I open my eyes, I see a tree, and so I know it is there. What could be simpler? What could be more obvious? But Reid soon finds out it is not so simple or obvious. How do we perceive things? Locke said it is by having ideas. We have a tree-idea in our mind, and that leads us to believe that there is a tree out there. But how do we get from the idea in our mind to the real tree? In the story from Locke to Hume the answer is as simple as it is devastating: we don't! Here, in brief, is how the story unfolds.

Locke says that nothing is perceived but what is in the mind of the perceiver. We do not really perceive external objects but only ideas representing them in our minds. From these ideas we infer the existence of external objects. Berkeley quickly sees that such an inference can never work. If all we can get to are our own ideas, then that's all we have. We can simply drop the "external objects" Locke claimed are there. Our perceptual experience is the same with or without those Lockean "external objects." Hume agrees, and drops even more things.

And so the story ends in a complete skepticism. As Reid puts it in the dedication to his *Inquiry*, "If my impressions and ideas are the only existences of which I can have any knowledge or conception . . . [then] upon this hypothesis, the whole universe about me . . . sun, moon, stars, and earth, friends and relations, all things without exception, which I imagined to have permanent existence, whether I thought of them or not, vanish at once."

That's the task: rescue the world of common sense; show that in perception we actually reach external objects. Does Reid succeed? Let's see what happens as he examines each of the five senses. In smelling I have a certain sensation; that's in me. There's also a quality in the object. But, Reid tells us, the sensation bears no resemblance to the quality in the object. Taste is the same. As I munch on the steak,

I experience a sensation, what I call the taste of the steak. But that taste quality is not really an objective feature of the steak the way roundness is an objective feature of a basketball. Again there is no resemblance. I hear the sound of a coach and immediately realize there is a coach outside. But of course I don't really hear the coach; what I hear is the sound made by a coach. And that sound is a sensation in me, which has no resemblance to the coach itself. I say the fire is hot, but what I experience is a sensation of heat in my mind. When it is very intense, we say it is a pain. Clearly a pain is not something out there in the world existing independently of me. It's something in me. And the same applies to all the other sensations.

How about the sense of touch? Surely we can reach external objects in this way. I know there is a table here because I can feel it by touching it. Reid examines it carefully. I press my hand against the table. I feel a certain sensation. That's something in me. How do I get from what is in me to the table out there? How are they connected? Reid admits he doesn't know! A sword pierces my skin. I feel a pain. But I also claim that I feel the sword as sharp and pointed. How do I get to these objective qualities of the sword from my sensation, which is in me?

We seem to be back with Locke's view that we perceive only ideas or sensations in us and that these have no resemblance to anything out there in the world. How about vision? We see a color. Reid distinguishes the appearance of the color, which is an idea in us, from the quality of color in the object that is the unknown cause of the color-idea in us. Again we can't reach an objective reality out there; we don't see a real color in objects, but only an idea in us. But Reid has another item: visible figure. By this he seems to mean shape and size. Here he says there is a resemblance; the visible figure is a sign of the real figure, the actual shape that the object has. Is the visible figure we perceive an idea in our minds? Or is it the object itself in its shape and size? Reid doesn't tell us directly. But he seems to mean that the visible figure we perceive is an idea in our minds; else why would he say there is a resemblance? One can't have a resemblance unless there are two distinct things that resemble each other. If in perceiving the visible figure I perceive the object itself, then there is one object of perception; hence no two things, one of which can be said to be a resemblance of the other.

If this is his position—that the visible figure is an idea in my mind and that this idea resembles the real figure (actual shape and size) of the object out there—then we can ask him how he knows that there is this resemblance. He admits he doesn't know. He seems to have fallen back to the very position he set out to criticize: Locke's view that we perceive only our own ideas and sensations, and that we then somehow infer a world of real things existing out there independently of us.

> In a word: perception . . . hath always an object distinct from the act by which it is perceived; an object which may exist whether perceived or

> not. The object may be a tree . . . with trunk and branches. . . . The act is something in my mind of which I am conscious. They are clearly distinct. Why then believe in the real existence of the tree, if all you are really aware of in perception is your own act? That act means having an idea in your mind, one essentially distinct from the real tree out there. . . . I am aware that this belief which I have in perception stands exposed to the strongest batteries of skepticism.

But Reid holds fast to his belief in the existence of the real world out there. "This belief . . . is none of my manufacture; it came from the mint of nature. . . . I even took it upon trust."

That's the basic story. Does Reid succeed in his task of rescuing the world of common sense and showing that in perception we actually reach external objects? On one level he clearly doesn't. He falls back into the "we perceive only our own ideas" trap that he originally wanted to escape from. But the fact that he wanted to escape from this trap, that he was not satisfied in accepting Hume's radically skeptical conclusion, is, I think, highly significant. He sets the philosophy of perception in the right direction. Why didn't he reach the goal? There are, I think, two main factors.

First, he uncritically accepts the language and concepts of his adversaries: that perception starts with ideas and sensations in us, and that these may or may not have a resemblance to what's out there. That is a program for failure. Modern thinkers such as G.J. Warnock and Don Locke have offered us an alternative, which I'm sure Reid would have eagerly embraced. Let me briefly outline what this is.

I press hard on the table. What do I feel? I feel the table itself; I feel its real quality of hardness. True, I feel a sensation; but to feel such a sensation is to feel the table. I feel (and thereby perceive) the table by means of this sensation. Feeling the sensation is not an alternative to feeling the table: the sensation is not what I perceive but what I have when I perceive the table. The old view of Locke, continued by Reid, separated what should have been kept together. The same applies to the pain caused by the sword piercing my skin; that sensation (very painful) is essentially a perception of the real sword and its real quality of sharpness.

The same applies to vision. To see the visible figure of the tree is to see the tree itself. It is to see the tree as it now appears to me. Appearances will vary with distance, perspective, light, and other factors. But appearances are not alternatives to the real thing; they are not ideas in the mind that must somehow be brought back into a relation to the thing itself. An appearance is essentially an appearance of something: the thing we perceive. Distinction does not mean separation. We can distinguish the surface of the chair from the chair itself. Still, to sit on the surface of the chair is to sit on the chair itself, and vice versa. So, too, with appearances: to see the appearance of the tree is to see the tree itself.

And what is true of visible figure applies also to color. As Warnock puts it in his book *Berkeley*, "In seeing the color of the grass we see the grass itself."

Second, perception is really a very difficult topic. It is not all that surprising that Locke, Berkeley, and Hume went off the track. We can retreat back to our own perspective of things and then wonder how that connects to the real thing. How do I get from my bodily sensations when I press against the table to the table itself? How do I get from the visual image I have when I see something to the thing itself? What is that image? It's what the eye doctor tests when he asks me which of two lenses gives me a clearer picture. And how does that image come to exist in my mind as a result of some brain event caused by what happens in my eyes and my optic nerve? All these are causes for wonder! "Philosophy begins in wonder and wonder is the spirit of a philosopher" (Plato, *Theaetetus*).

Reid's contribution is that he set philosophy off in the right direction. He argued strongly that we must get away from the Locke-Berkeley-Hume model. He made a good start, but then lost his way (or dropped the ball). His call was to get back to common sense, and later thinkers such as Warnock, Don Locke, and G.E. Moore have heeded that call; so Reid really belongs with them in the common sense school.* He is their original inspiration.

One more point of the greatest importance needs to be made. The whole discussion of perception in all these thinkers—about distinguishing sensations and ideas and appearances from what is out there in the real world, material objects and their qualities—would not be possible if we did not actually perceive the real things in the world. To take a famous example, the stick that is really straight but looks bent when half immersed in water: we would never notice this discrepancy unless we saw the real object, both when it appears straight and when it appears bent. We see both and so we can compare them. When the stick is in the water, we still see the stick itself, not a mere idea of it (as many philosophers are wont to say). We see the stick as bent.

(2) The Reality of the Self and Personal Identity

A second key area where Reid wants to clean up the skeptical mess is the reality of our own existence. What could be more obvious? Yet, as we saw in the last chapter, Hume claimed that there is no self, no substantial "I," only a bundle of fleeting impressions and ideas. It's hard to imagine a more radical betrayal of common sense!

Reid reminds us of what we all already know by our common sense: I am a person, a self, a substantial being, who has various experiences; and I exist as the

---

* So does Aquinas. See *ST* 1.85.2 (vol. 2, chap. 50, "Epistemology") and G.K. Chesterton, *St. Thomas Aquinas: The Dumb Ox*, for a defense of Aquinas as the philosopher of common sense.

same person over time, what I know as my own personal identity. He points out that the conviction that every man has of his identity, as far back as his memory reaches, needs no aid of philosophy to strengthen it, and no philosophy can weaken it without producing some degree of insanity. This immediate conviction is presupposed every moment of our waking lives. I reason, going from one step to another; at the last step, I must know that it was me, the same person, who took the first step. When I remember a past event in my life, I not only remember the event but also that it was I, the same person I am now, who experienced that event. Without this experienced continuation of myself as the same person, there could be no memory of past events.

My personal identity, therefore, implies the continued existence of that indivisible thing that I call myself. Whatever this self may be, it is something that thinks, and deliberates, and resolves, and acts, and suffers. If there are fleeting impressions and ideas, who has them? Who experiences them? They cannot just float by themselves in empty space; there must be a conscious being who has these impressions and ideas. That being is the self, the substantial self that exists as the same person over time. My thoughts, actions, and feelings change every moment; they have not a continued but a successive existence; but that self or I, to which they belong, is permanent and has the same relation to all the succeeding thoughts, actions, and feelings that I call mine.

(3) The Reality of Causal Connections

A third key area where Reid wants to clean up the skeptical mess is causality: the reality of causal connections in the world. Billiard ball A strikes billiard ball B, and ball B moves. We say ball A caused ball B to move, that it produced the motion in ball B, that there is therefore a real connection between the motion of A and the motion of B. Again, what could be more obvious? Yet, as we saw, Hume denies all this. "All I can see is the motion of the two balls, and that B comes after A, not that it comes because of A. I can't see any real connection, so why suppose there is one? I expect B to move after being struck by A, but that's just a habit in me, not anything out there in the real world. There is no real causality in the world."

Reid finds this incredible. "Of all the paradoxes this author [Hume] has advanced, there is not one more shocking to the human understanding than this, that things may begin to exist without a cause. This would put an end to all speculation, as well as to all the business of life." In his usual manner, Reid appeals to what we all know by common sense.

> A child knows that when one of his toys is missing, somebody took it away; there is a cause. . . . Suppose a man is found dead on a highway . . . his body pierced with deadly wounds. . . . [The matter is investigated,

> and goes to a jury trial.] But we may venture to say, that, if Mr. Hume had been of such a jury, he would have laid aside his philosophical principles, and acted according to the dictates of common prudence. Like all the other members of the jury, Hume would seek to find the most likely cause, based on the firm conviction that there had to be a cause, and that that cause could only be one that was sufficient to actually produce the effect; not some event that merely came before.

Hume denied that we have a conception of causality as an active power that produces its effects. Reid counters that we know this from our immediate experience in bodily actions. I will to move my hand and it moves. I know that my willing causes it to move, and so we have a direct and immediate experience of causal power in ourselves—hence a clear conception of it, contrary to Hume. That is, the very conception or idea of active power, and of efficient causes, is derived from our voluntary exertions in producing effects.

This is what is called today agent causation, in distinction to event causation as we find it in nature. Richard Taylor expresses this difference when he compares two grammatically similar sentences: "This man started that forest fire" and "This match started that forest fire." The first is agent causation, the second is event causation, the striking of the match being part of an event that brought about the fire. The match cannot literally be said to start the fire in the way the man can be said to start it; the match "can only be used to start a fire" (*Action and Purpose*). Reid is important as the forerunner of the modern theory of agent causation, developed by thinkers such as Richard Taylor and Roderick Chisholm.

64

IMMANUEL KANT

AD 1724–1804

Kant's life was remarkably unremarkable. He was born in Königsberg, in East Prussia (later part of the USSR—now called Kaliningrad, Russia), and never, in his eighty years, traveled more than sixty miles away from his hometown. He was raised in a very rigorous Puritanical Lutheran sect, the Pietists, which taught and practiced a lifestyle that was severely moral, thrifty, conscientious, careful, and highly structured. It was individualistic and anti-ecclesiastical but emphasized the fear of hell and divine justice. Kant later abandoned the sect but not the moral seriousness. He later wrote: "People may say what they will of Pietism. Those in whom it was sincere were worthy of honor. They possessed the highest thing that man can have—the quiet, the content, the inner peace, which no suffering can disturb." There are close similarities between Kant's ethics, Pietism, and Stoicism (see vol. 1, chap. 29).

After six years at the University of Königsberg, Kant refused a financially comfortable offer to be a preacher and instead supported himself for nine years with a very small income from private tutoring. In 1755, he was certified by the university as a *privatdozent*, which enabled him to teach at the university "privately," with his salary being paid directly by student tuitions. He was such a good teacher that he attracted many students. He said he always paid the most attention to students of middle ability, since the stupid ones were hopeless and the geniuses could teach themselves.

The university gave him a professorship in 1770 to replace his teacher, Knutzen, who was a disciple of Wolff, who was a disciple of Leibniz. As we shall see below, Kant began as a Leibnizian rationalist but was shaken from his "dogmatic slumber" by Hume and conceived his radically new philosophy as an operation to rescue reason, the foundation of the Enlightenment, from Hume's skeptical critique, by inventing a new epistemology which was neither rationalist nor empiricist.

Kant was the first major philosopher since the Middle Ages to be a professional academic. Not until the twentieth century did this situation become the normal one. (That probably accounts for the dullness of twentieth-century philosophy, outside of the existentialists.)

Study and teaching was his life. It was fascinatingly dull, so regular that it was irregular. One biographer described it as "like the most regular of regular verbs," to which another added: "But this verb was never conjugated: Kant never married." He planned to propose to two women, at different times, but procrastinated so long that both of them got impatient and left. "Live according to reason" and "think before you act" is the philosophy of a lifelong bachelor. Kant described marriage as an agreement between two people "for the reciprocal use of each other's sexual organs." One can imagine the words he would have used had he actually proposed to one of these women—or perhaps one cannot.

He was short (five feet, two inches) and slight (under one hundred pounds), with an unusually narrow chest. One shoulder was higher than the other. His health was delicate. He was a hypochondriac. For instance, he would not converse outdoors, except in summer, because he believed that breathing fresh cold air through the mouth was dangerous.

The poet Heinrich Heine describes his passionately regular life this way:

> I do not believe that the great cathedral clock of this city accomplished its day's work in a less passionate and more regular way than its countryman, Immanuel Kant. Rising from bed [at exactly 4:55 a.m.], coffee-drinking [exactly one cup], writing, lecturing, eating [one full meal a day: a two-hour lunch, at 1:00 p.m., with not less than two nor more than five guests], walking—everything had its fixed time; and the neighbors knew that it must be exactly half past three when they saw Professor Kant, in his gray coat [he had only one], with his cane in his hand, step out of his house door and move toward the little lime tree avenue, which is named after him, the Philosopher's Walk. Eight times he walked up and down that walk at every season of the year, and when the weather was bad, or the gray clouds threatened rain, his servant, old Lampe, was seen anxiously following him with a large umbrella under his arm like an image of Providence.

He missed his walk only once: when he discovered the writings of Rousseau. He did not like music, except for marching bands, and was so indifferent to the visual arts that he had only one object of art in his rooms: a portrait of Rousseau. Yet one of his three most important books, the *Critique of Judgment*, is about aesthetics. His most valued physical possession was his watch. He hated noise and moved twice to avoid noisy neighbors. He once wrote a letter to the police complaining about the hymn-singing of the inmates of a nearby prison.

But he was universally admired as a friend and conversationalist. His public university lectures were so popular that students arrived at 6:00 a.m. to get a seat for the 7:00 a.m. lecture. Everyone knew him as a very kind and generous man. Yet, though he loved and supported his brother and two sisters, he did not exchange a word with them for twenty-five years.

When he was seventy, King Frederick William II of Prussia—a much more repressive ruler than his predecessor, Frederick the Great, who had supported Enlightenment figures like Rousseau and Voltaire—threatened him with "unpleasant consequences" if he continued to publish religiously and politically unorthodox opinions, as he had done in *Religion within the Limits of Reason Alone*. Kant politely promised henceforth to "refrain from all public statements on religion."

There was a political motive behind this warning. (Politicians rarely have religious reasons for caring about religion.) It was Kant's enthusiasm about the French Revolution, which had set all the thrones in Europe quaking. When Kant, then sixty-five, had heard the news of the Revolution, he said, with tears in his eyes, "Now I can say, like Simeon, 'Lord, let now Thy servant depart in peace, for mine eyes have seen Thy salvation.'"

No one expected this mild, personally conservative professor to startle the world even more than Hume had done. But he did, suddenly, in 1781, at the age of fifty-seven, with his masterpiece, the *Critique of Pure Reason*, the single most important book of philosophy in the last seven hundred years. It is so revolutionary that philosophers typically divide all philosophy into "pre-Kantian" and "post-Kantian," as Christians divide history into "BC" and "AD."

The book was at first little read, understood, or appreciated. For it is one of the most difficult books ever written. Philosophy students approach it with dread and boast forever if they read the whole thing. Kant himself called it "dry, obscure, opposed to all ordinary notions, and moreover long-winded." He deliberately avoided all concrete illustrations and examples because, he said, that would make it too long. (It is seven hundred pages as it is.) He sent it to Herz, a professional scholarly friend, who returned it unfinished, with the explanation "If I go on to the end, I fear I shall go insane." For the sake of the reader's sanity, we will oversimplify the book. Even so, it will take many pages.

Kant died peacefully at eighty, after years of gradual mental and physical decline. His last words were "It is good."

Influences

The three main influences behind Kant's work are (1) Newton, (2) Enlightenment rationalism (Descartes; Leibniz; Christian Wolff; and Kant's own teacher, Knutzen), and (3) Hume.

Every philosopher has some nonnegotiable absolute, an "Archimedean point," an unquestioned and unarguable foundation for all argument, even if it is the demand for Cartesian "universal doubt." For Christian, Jewish, and Muslim philosophers of the Middle Ages this was their scriptures, which they believed to be infallible divine revelation. For Kant it was Newtonian science.

Kant's philosophy is essentially a rescue of Newtonian reason, the very foundation for the whole Enlightenment, from Hume's critique. And the bottom-line assumption of his argument is essentially that if Hume is right, Newtonian science is undermined; therefore, Hume cannot be right. Like most Enlightenment thinkers, Kant was simply using a different nonnegotiable starting point (viz., the validity of Newtonian science) than the one used by the clergy who criticized Kant for undermining, altering, or weakening Christianity (viz., the validity of their Scriptures).

Kant will argue that Hume did indeed destroy "dogmatic" metaphysics, though not Newtonian science. Kant famously writes, "I openly confess that my remembering David Hume was the very thing which many years ago first interrupted my dogmatic slumber. . . . Since the origin of metaphysics so far as we know its history, nothing has ever happened which could have been more decisive to its fate than the attack made upon it by David Hume."

Kant believed that Hume's empiricist critique had destroyed forever what Kant called "dogmatic" (i.e., rationalist) metaphysics: e.g., Plato, Descartes, Spinoza, and Leibniz. Why? Because this metaphysics had no *data* from sensory experience to prove or disprove its theories. It meets no resistance. It is not *falsifiable*. Kant makes this point in a famous image: "The light dove, cleaving the air in her free flight, and feeling its resistance, might imagine that its flight would be still easier in empty space. It was thus that Plato left the world of the senses, as setting too narrow limits to the understanding, and ventured out beyond it on the wings of the Ideas, in the empty space of the pure understanding [thinking without sensing]. He did not observe that with all his efforts he made no advance, meeting no resistance."

Like Hume, Kant is going to limit rather than enlarge reason's power. He is going to reverse Plato's image of the cave: his education will move us out of the upper world and down into the lower. But the lower world here is not merely sensation as opposed to thought but appearances as opposed to reality, whether these appearances are sensory or mental. In Kant's terms, this means we can know only "phenomena" and never "noumena" or "things-in-themselves," objective reality as it is independent of our awareness. Even Hume had allowed that we could know "matters of fact" in the real world with probability, though not with certainty, through sensation. That is why Kant is even more skeptical than Hume: he limits reason's ability to know reality even more.

Kant, however, did not consider this to be skepticism at all, but a *justification* of reason. The *Critique of Pure Reason* is not a "critique" in the sense of a criticism, but an investigation that establishes reason's validity by claiming that (a) reason's task is more modest than we used to think—it is not to know "things-in-themselves" but only to structure appearances—but that (b) it succeeds quite well in performing this modified task. Point (a) sounds like skepticism but point (b) is the opposite.

The medievals assumed that "nature makes nothing in vain" and that therefore any universal, innate, natural human desire can be satisfied. Kant disagrees. We innately want to know objective reality, but we cannot ever do it. "Human reason has this peculiar fate that . . . it is burdened by questions which, as prescribed by the very nature of reason itself, it is not able to ignore, but which, as transcending all its powers, it is also not able to answer." What a *koan* puzzle!

What was in question, for Kant, was the very heart and foundation of the "Enlightenment": human reason itself. Descartes had tried to validate reason by redefining it as mathematical, scientific reason, in an attempt to be more critical. The result, Kant thought, was the opposite: "dogmatic" *a priori* systems (remember the "light dove" image). Locke had substituted empiricism, which, against his will, led to Hume's skepticism. Berkeley had responded with a refutation not just of Hume's implicit materialism but of matter itself, from Locke's empiricist premises. But Hume did to mind what Berkeley did to matter. What was left? Only the flames (see chap. 62, "What's Left?").

Another answer was possible: that reason is not the judge but the criminal, not the hero but the villain, not the savior but the sin. Let feeling triumph over reason! That was Rousseau's answer. It was not Kant's. But Rousseau's problem was Kant's problem: he needed a critique of reason—not to dethrone it, as Rousseau had done, but to rethrone it. We had to judge the judge, to certify the certifier. We had to redefine reason in order to rethrone it, but in a different way than Descartes did. This is Kant's "Copernican revolution in philosophy."

The redefining of reason itself had been done twice before: by Socrates and by Descartes. Socrates had redefined reason by separating it from tradition, authority, intuition, and myth and reforming it into syllogistic logic and the intellectual understanding of Platonic Forms (these are the two top quarters of Plato's "divided line"). Descartes had further redefined and narrowed it into scientific method (essentially, the second and third quarters of the line). Kant will redefine it again, into the active, subjective shaping of mental perspectives rather than the receptive knowledge of objective reality ("things-in-themselves").

Kant's "Copernican Revolution in Philosophy"

Kant's *koan* puzzle, four paragraphs above, sounds even more skeptical than Hume. But Kant thinks of it as the *answer* to Hume's skepticism. Why? Because it denies the common, unquestioned assumption of both the dogmatic rationalist and the skeptical empiricist, the assumption that reason's proper task is to know "things-in-themselves," and that if it cannot do that, we must be skeptics. Kant denies that common premise. His *Critique* tries to show that reason performs its task quite adequately, but its task is not to *tell* us what is there but to *make* what is there—not to make its very existence but its essence, its nature, its *logos*, its form, its intelligibility, its knowability. Reason's business is not to discover but to create.*

In other words, reason is like art, not like science—or at least not like what we usually think science is (a way to discover what's "out there"). Reason is active; it is construction work. This is truly revolutionary because it disagrees with every previous philosopher in history. Aristotle typifies traditional, commonsensical philosophy when he defines truth as "knowing and saying of what is that it is and of what is not that it is not." Kant redefines knowledge: not as the conformity of mind to things but of things to mind. We do not abstract form, order, *logos*, or universals from things; we impose them upon things. In other words, in a sense, all our knowledge is subjective, not objective.

However, truth is not subjective in the sense that it is individual or arbitrary, but *universal and necessary*. It is not "my truth" or "your truth." All minds necessarily work in essentially the same way, and Kant will explain and try to justify that way. We live in a work of art we ourselves create, but we create it universally rather than individually, and necessarily rather than arbitrarily, though we do this unconsciously rather than consciously—rather like people looking through colored glasses that they don't notice they have on, and unthinkingly thinking everything they see is colored.

Kant does not mean that the mind *creates* objects, but that it *forms* them. There is indeed a world "out there," though we cannot know it as it is in itself, independent of our knowing. "Things-in-themselves" really exist and influence our thinking; that is why our thinking is receptive. "We must yet be in a position at least to *think* them as things-in-themselves; otherwise we should be landed in the absurd conclusion that there can be appearance without anything that

* We can distinguish "knowledge," "reason," and "truth" here, but the "Copernican revolution" applies to all three: to what knowledge is, to reason as the way to knowing, and to truth as the object of knowledge. The essential point of Kant's "Copernican revolution" can be intuitively grasped by the following three analogies (which are mine, not Kant's): of a sieve, an oven, and three eyeglasses (see diagram on next page). In each case there is (1) the formless "things-in-themselves," or objective reality, (2) our subjective knowing structures that we impose on (1), and (3) the consequent product, all of whose form comes from us (2), not from it (1).

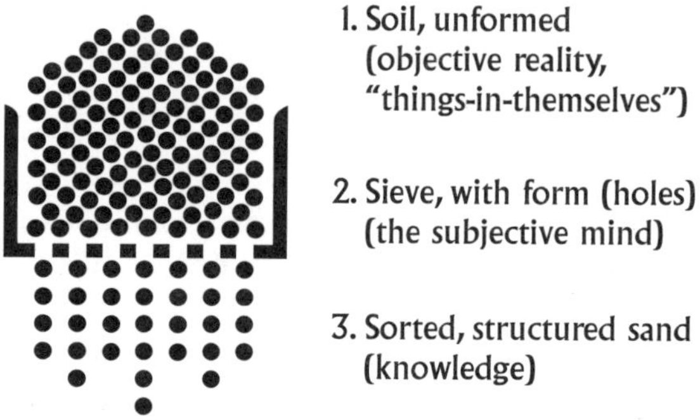
1. Soil, unformed
(objective reality,
"things-in-themselves")
2. Sieve, with form (holes)
(the subjective mind)
3. Sorted, structured sand
(knowledge)

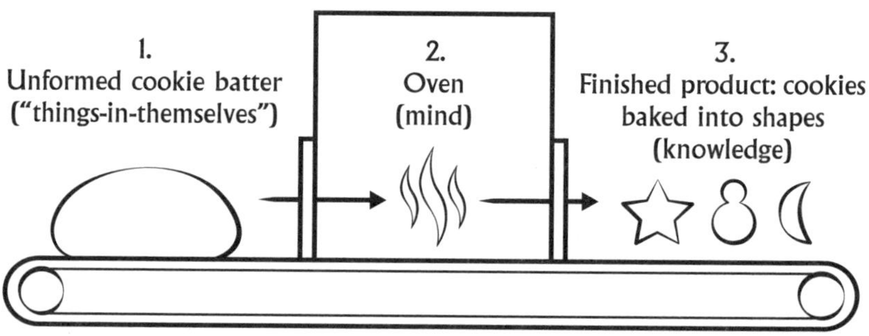
1.
Unformed cookie batter
("things-in-themselves")
2.
Oven
(mind)
3.
Finished product: cookies
baked into shapes
(knowledge)

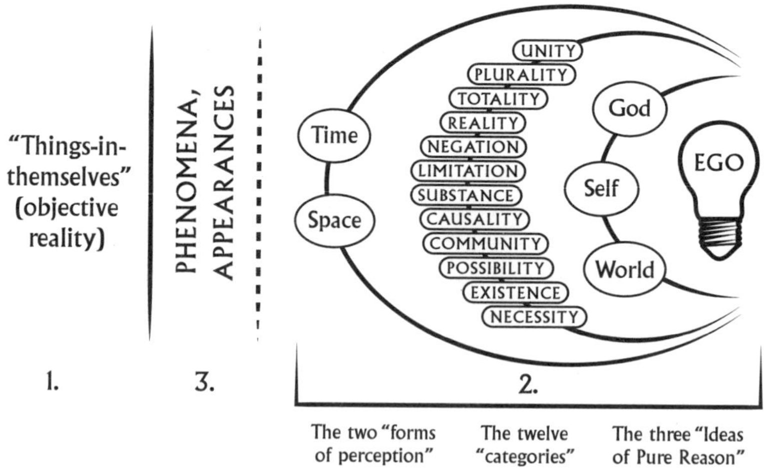
"Things-in-
themselves"
(objective
reality)
PHENOMENA,
APPEARANCES
Time
Space
UNITY
PLURALITY
TOTALITY
REALITY
NEGATION
LIMITATION
SUBSTANCE
CAUSALITY
COMMUNITY
POSSIBILITY
EXISTENCE
NECESSITY
God
Self
World
EGO
1.
3.
2.
The two "forms
of perception"
The twelve
"categories"
The three "Ideas
of Pure Reason"

appears." But we can never know what these things really are in themselves, only how we structure them by thought. We can only know the forms we project onto them, like images onto a movie screen.

Kant will explain that we have three sets of such forms: (1) the forms of sense perception, time and space; (2) the categories of logic; and (3) the ideas of world, self, and God, which he calls the metaphysical "Ideas of Pure Reason." None of these can be known to be real (or, for that matter, unreal). We are limited to the cave and its shadows. But we are projecting all the shadows.

These three sets of forms are not "innate ideas," as in Plato. They are empty forms, structures, ways of thinking rather than thoughts with content.

Socrates and Descartes (and, in a way, Hume) each redefined "reason" as the way to truth, but Kant is even more revolutionary: he redefines "truth" itself. It is conformity of being to thought, not thought to being. Here is the most important paragraph Kant ever wrote, from the preface to the second edition of the *Critique of Pure Reason*:

> Until now it has been assumed that all our knowledge must conform to objects. But all our attempts to extend our knowledge of objects by establishing something in regard to them *a priori* by means of concepts have, on this assumption, ended in failure. We must, therefore make trial whether we may not have more success in the tasks of metaphysics if we suppose that objects must conform to our knowledge. . . . We should then be proceeding precisely on the lines of Copernicus' primary hypothesis. Failing of satisfactory progress in explaining the movements of the heavenly bodies on the supposition that they revolved around the spectator, he tried whether he might not have better success if he made the spectator to revolve and the stars to remain at rest. A similar experiment can be tried in metaphysics.

Somewhere along the way Kant seems to forget that he called this just a thought experiment, and he treats it as a given, as a knowable "thing-in-itself." But if this is anything more than a mere thought experiment, it seems self-contradictory, for it is to claim that we are able to not just construct, as a thought experiment, but know, as an objectively real state of affairs, or "thing-in-itself," the fact that we cannot know "things-in-themselves."

The reader may think that the analogy to Copernicus shows exactly the opposite of what Kant means by his "revolution," since Copernicus made the knowing subject (man on earth and his motion) relative to the object (the sun), while Kant is making the objects of knowledge relative to the (active structuring of the knowing human) subject. But we can also take the analogy the other way: pre-Copernican thought did not know that we on earth are moving, and that

that movement is what makes the stars appear to move; similarly, pre-Kantian thought forgot that our minds and senses are moving and acting to impose form on the world, so that it appears that the forms are "out there" in the world when they are in fact only in the knower, as the motion in the sun and the stars appears to be "out there" when it is really in us.

An old *New Yorker* magazine cartoon gives us the best picture I know of the human situation if Kant's "Copernican revolution" is true. Two lonely castaways on a desert island find a bottle washed up on the beach with a note in it. They see the note as contact with the outside world, but when they read it, their faces fall. The caption reads: "It's only from us." For Kant, all the wonderful form and order and intelligibility and design that we seem to find in the universe is not really there but is only from us.

So Kant has not escaped Hume's solipsism; he has deepened it. He has only made it universal and necessary. This is surely not a happy solution! Do we not long to escape our own skins and relate to the real other, whether divine, human, or natural? If Kant is right, we can never do that. Is that not a philosophy of despair? Is that not, in fact, the psychology of hell, the eternal impossibility of escape from self, whether individual or collective?

Or is it noble humanism that saves rather than condemns reason? There is a story (probably apocryphal) that Kant once responded to an astronomer's argument that "astronomically speaking, man is quite insignificant" by retorting, "But astronomically speaking, man is the astronomer." Kant thought he had *rescued* human reason (and his moral freedom and dignity) from the materialistic worldview that reduced man to a cog in the Newtonian clockwork universe.

A useful way of approaching Kant's "Copernican revolution" might be by asking the question: *Why are the laws of thought also the laws of things?* Why do intelligence and intelligibility coincide? Why is *logos* both objective and subjective? What is the ultimate reason for this "coincidence" that is obviously more than an accident?

There are three possible answers:

1. Things determine thought. This is the answer of empiricists, both "soft" (Aristotle) and "hard" (Hume). It is also the answer of Cartesian and Platonic rationalists, but for them the "things" that determine thought are Ideas or Forms rather than material things.
2. Thought determines things. This is the answer of the Kantian idealist, the answer of the "Copernican revolution."
3. God made the two to correspond, like a man and a woman. (Indeed, the same word, "conception," is used both for the product of sex and for the product of knowledge.) Whether the first or the second answer above is correct—whichever corresponds to which—the ultimate reason for the

correspondence is that God is the source of both. That is why they coincide, like twin children of the same Father. This is the answer of Augustine and Aquinas. Answer (3) could be seen to be compatible with either (1) or (2).

The Idea of a "Critique of Pure Reason"

By a "critique" of reason Kant means a critical investigation of reason—by reason! Descartes tried to do this too. But one can ask: Is this possible? Can the judge of all things be judged? Isn't this "critical problem" an impossible task to fulfill? (See Gilson's rational critique of the critique of reason in *Thomistic Realism and the Critique of Knowledge*.)

A more sympathetic way of framing the question is this: We want to peek under the curtain to see how the Wizard of Oz works the machine, to look underneath conscious reasoning to see the unconscious machinery at work structuring our conscious mental life.

The way Kant expresses this question is that we need to find "the conditions of possibility for experience." We experience sensing, thinking, and understanding. What makes this possible? If the objective world did not have the same structures as our subjective knowing, then knowledge and experience would not be possible at all. It would be like trying to open a lock with a cloud instead of a key or trying to take a photograph of a cloud with a key instead of a camera. And if one of these two poles of our experience, the subject or the object, were unreal—if either the world or the self did not exist—then also experience would not be possible. Kant tries to unravel in more detailed form what the Wizard's machine must be like for it to be able to produce the phenomena we experience, both materially (in sense experience) and immaterially (in reason and understanding).

Kant calls this kind of investigation—into the conditions of possibility for human knowledge *on the part of the knowing subject*—a "*transcendental*" critique rather than a "*transcendent*" one. A "transcendent" critique assumes that we can know the conditions of knowability *on the part of the known object*, or the "thing-in-itself." Kant calls a "transcendental" inquiry "critical" and a "transcendent" one "uncritical" or "dogmatic" because a "transcendent" inquiry simply assumes, without proof, that we can know "things-in-themselves," that we both can and must conform our subjective knowing to the object known rather than vice versa. This is what *all* philosophers assumed before Kant's "Copernican revolution." Even skeptics assumed that we *ought* to do that, even if they held that we *could* not do that.*

---

* One of Kant's ethical principles is that "'ought' implies 'can.'" We can have no obligation to do what is impossible. This apparently commonsensical principle could be used in two ways: (1) to refute skepticism, the idea that we *cannot* know objective truth, on the assumption that we *ought* to know it; or (2) to refute that very assumption that we *ought* to know objective truth, if we begin with the premise that we *cannot* know it.

Kant thinks that if we thus determine both the capacities and the limitations of human reason, both its abilities and its inabilities, we will avoid both extremes of dogmatism and skepticism.

Kant's Four Questions

Kant divides the question about the conditions of possibility for the knowledge that we have into four parts:

1. *How is mathematics possible?*
2. *How is natural science possible?*
3. *How is metaphysics possible?*
4. *How is morality possible?*

However, the fourth question is not, for Kant, about knowledge but about will, which Kant calls "practical reason."

Kant's broader outline of questions, which includes the above but expands it, is as follows:

1. *What can I know?* (theoretical reason)
   a. How can I know mathematics?
   b. How can I know natural science?
   c. How can I know metaphysics?
2. *What should I do?* (morality, "practical reason")
3. *What may I hope?* (religion, God, and immortality)

Kant's Logic: Classifying Judgments*

To answer the first three questions about knowledge, we need to look at the grammar of knowledge, so to speak, the structure of knowledge-claims or truth-claims.

These are expressed in judgments, or propositions, not in concepts or in arguments. Concepts are presupposed by judgments, but they do not by themselves

* To understand this section, the reader must have a clear grasp of the "three acts of the mind" in traditional logic. (1) Conceiving, or "simple apprehension," produces concepts, which are expressed in terms, like "man," which are either clear or unclear but neither true nor false. (2) Judging produces judgments, which are expressed in propositions (declarative sentences), like "all men are mortal," which are either true or false. (3) Reasoning, or inference, whether deductive or inductive, produces arguments, like "all men are mortal, and Socrates is a man, therefore Socrates is mortal," which are either logically valid (when their premises prove their conclusions to be true—either probably true, in induction, or certainly true, in deduction) or logically invalid (when they don't).

constitute knowledge. For instance, "red" is not knowledge, but "Most apples are red" is. "Red" is neither true nor false. "Most apples are red" is true, and "Most apples are not red" is false. Arguments, or reasoning, assume some knowledge as premises, and from them deduce or induce further knowledge as conclusions, either with certainty or only with probability. For instance, if both "all *these* apples are red" and "all *those* apples are red," it is probable that *most* apples are red. And if *all* apples are red and this is an apple, then it is certain that this apple is red.

Judgments (or propositions, or declarative sentences, which claim to know truths) have two parts: the subject term and the predicate term. Hume had divided all true judgments into two classes—"relations of ideas" and "matters of fact"—by the standard of the relation between the predicate and the subject. "Relations of ideas" are tautologies (i.e., they are self-evident simply by the "match" in the content of the subject and the predicate). The predicate merely repeats all or part of the subject. Such propositions are true by the law of noncontradiction alone (e.g., "One-horned horses are one-horned," "Horses are horses," and "*x* is not non-*x*"). In contrast, "matters of fact," since they were not thus logically self-evident, could only be known to be true by experience.

What Hume called "relations of ideas," Kant calls "analytic judgments," because their predicates merely "analyze" out all or part of their subjects. The alternative to these is "synthetic judgments," which "synthesize" or join two different concepts in adding a predicate to a subject. What Hume called "matters of fact," Kant called "synthetic judgments." One way of seeing the difference between synthetic and analytic judgments is this: We can conceive or imagine the alternative to any synthetic judgment, but we cannot conceive or imagine the alternative to an analytic judgment. We can imagine water running uphill, or events popping into existence without causes, or the sky being green, but we cannot even imagine the same water both running uphill and not running uphill at the same time, or causes not being causes, or the same sky both being green and not being green. It's possible to conceive of, and believe in, miracles but not self-contradictions.

But Kant adds a second classification of judgments. Judgments are either "*a priori*" or "*a posteriori*." *A priori* judgments are known to be true prior to experience; *a posteriori* judgments are known to be true only posterior to experience. For instance, "2+2=4," "*x* is not non-*x*," and "I exist" are *a priori* judgments, while "*x*=12," "Caesar crossed the Rubicon," and "I am six feet tall" are *a posteriori* judgments.

Kant gives two criteria for *a priori* judgments: *universality* and *necessity*. They are always, timelessly true and cannot possibly be false. He says: "Experience teaches us that a thing is so and so, but not that it cannot be otherwise. . . . Experience never confers on its judgments true or strict . . . universality . . . but only assumed and comparative [merely probable] universality through induction. . . . Necessity and universality are thus sure criteria of *a priori* knowledge."

Kant thus classifies four possible kinds of judgments:

1. Analytic *a priori* judgments
2. Analytic *a posteriori* judgments (there are no such things according to Kant)*
3. Synthetic *a priori* judgments
4. Synthetic *a posteriori* judgments

Hume said that there were only two kinds of judgments: (1) and (4). Kant says there is also a third kind: synthetic *a priori* judgments. He formulates the question of the *Critique of Pure Reason* this way: "How are synthetic *a priori* judgments possible?" His epistemology is his answer to that question.

Why does Kant think we have any synthetic *a priori* knowledge? He gives four kinds, corresponding to the four questions above ("Kant's Four Questions"):

1. All the judgments of mathematics and geometry.
2. Many of the judgments of natural science, such as "every event has a cause."
3. Some of the judgments of metaphysics, such as "God, soul, and world exist."
4. Some of the principles of morality, especially the "categorical imperative," the "Golden Rule" to treat all persons as you want them to treat you: respected as ends, not used as means.

Kant is convinced that these examples of *a priori* knowledge are all actual and wants to know how they are possible. What are the conditions of possibility for them?

Space and Time and Mathematics

The first kind of synthetic *a priori* proposition Kant explains is mathematical truths. They are all necessary and universal, and thus known *a priori*—we do not need to sense sunrises or colors or apples to know that 2+2=4 necessarily and universally—but Kant maintains they are also synthetic. (Most philosophers today disagree with this and say they are analytic.) Here is Kant's argument:

> It might at first be thought that the proposition 7+5=12 is a mere analytic judgment, following from the concept of the sum of seven and five according to the principle of [non]contradiction. But on closer

* Perhaps Aristotle, confronting Kant's classification, would argue that there are—that self-evident first principles like the law of noncontradiction, "The whole is greater than the part," and "Do good, shun evil" are known only after we first experience examples of them and abstract their common universal form and only then understand it as necessarily true.

> examination it appears that the concept of the sum of 7+5 contains merely their union in a single number, without its being at all thought what the particular number is that unites them.

For a similar reason Kant maintains that truths of geometry are also synthetic:

> That a straight line is the shortest path between two points is a synthetic proposition. For my concept of straight contains nothing of quantity, but only a quality. The concept of the shortest is therefore altogether additional and cannot be obtained by any analysis of the concept of the straight line.
>
> Now the intuitions which pure mathematics lays at the foundation of all its cognitions and judgments . . . are space and time. . . . Geometry is based upon the pure intuition of [absolute Newtonian] space. Arithmetic attains its concept of numbers by the successive addition of units in time.

For Kant, we do not abstract space and time from spatiotemporal things and events, but we project space and time onto them by sensing. That is his explanation for why they are necessary and universal: because all minds (universally) work in the (necessarily) same way. Time and space are not "out there." (Does this mean I didn't really eat my lunch after I ate my breakfast? I just have to think I did?)

The Categories and Physics

Kant's primary concern was to justify Newtonian physical science by his "Copernican revolution." To do this, he begins with a commonsense principle that avoids both rationalism and empiricism, both of which he regards as oversimplifications—the principle that our knowledge of the physical world works like a pair of scissors: it requires the cooperation of two different blades, not just one.

> Our knowledge springs from two fundamental sources of the mind: the first is the capacity of receiving representations (receptivity for [sensory] impressions); the second is the power of knowing an object through . . . concepts. Through the first, an object is *given* to us [passively]; through the second, the object is *thought* [actively]. . . . Neither concepts without [sensory] intuition . . . nor intuition without concepts, can yield knowledge. . . . Without sensibility, no object would be given to us; without [conceptual] understanding, no object would be thought. Thoughts without content are empty, intuitions without concepts are blind. . . . Only through their union can knowledge arise.

But that union does not arise by abstracting forms from experience, as Aristotle and Aquinas said, but by imposing forms upon experience. That is Kant's "Copernican revolution."

This does not mean that Kant thinks there *is* no world "out there," just that we cannot know what it is in itself. The world is not our dream. We do not create its existence; we discover it. We create only its necessary, universal *a priori* forms, its structures, its meanings. It contributes its own existence, which impinges on our minds. In order to have any experience at all, there must be something other than myself that I experience.

We do this experiencing-by-structuring in three dimensions: (1) the "forms of apperception," space and time (the previous section); (2) the "categories" of conceptual thought about the physical world (this section); and (3) the "Ideas of Pure Reason" (i.e., self, world, and God; the next section).

These are all *a priori* concepts, but they are empty of content. Yet, though they are empty, they are "there," or rather "here," in the mind, and they are actively working to structure and classify sensory intuitions. The mind is not a passive *tabula rasa* (blank tablet) on which sense experience writes, as the empiricists claim.

The concepts that are universally necessary for our experiencing a physical world are what Kant calls the "categories." These are not categories of *being*, or "things-in-themselves," as Aristotle thought when he produced his list of ten "categories." Kant's categories are the categories of our *thinking* about the world. In other words, they are not "transcendent" but "transcendental."

For instance, we always think of the world as a world of *things* or entities (what Aristotle called "substances," which we express in language by nouns) having *properties* (which we express in language by adjectives). Kant deduces twelve necessary categories for all thought about the world. That explains why we all seem to live in the same world. The categories are not arbitrary or freely chosen. None of us can choose to see the world in any other way. To prove this, Kant writes the most difficult and controversial section of the *Critique*, "Transition to the Transcendental Deduction of the Categories." It is so difficult that he rewrote the entire section for the second edition of the book and added a whole new section, which he called "Refutation of Idealism," to show that the world thus structured by the categories was not just an idea, as Berkeley's idealism had claimed.*

---

* "Idealism" is a confusing word. It can mean either (1) the metaphysical claim of Berkeley that everything real is idea, not matter; or (2) the metaphysical claim of Plato that there exist "Platonic Ideas" in addition to material things; or (3) the epistemological claim that all we know directly are our own ideas (Locke, Berkeley, and Hume); or (4) the epistemological claim that objects conform to minds rather than minds to objects (Kant's "Copernican revolution"). (This last is often called "Kantian idealism," even though Kant speaks of "the *refutation* of idealism," since he meant "idealism" in sense (1) above.)

The most important of these categories is causation. Hume had argued that causation is the foundation for all our knowledge of the world that goes beyond our immediate experience, yet we never experience causation itself; therefore, causation is merely our own subjective habit or custom of expecting experience to repeat itself—and this can never be certain, only probable. Here is Kant's answer to Hume's skepticism: "The complete solution to Hume's problem rescues, for the pure concepts of the understanding, their *a priori* origin, and, for the universal laws of nature, their validity [but only] as laws of the understanding . . . with a completely reversed mode of connection which never occurred to Hume: they are not derived from experience, but experience is derived from them."

This is also how Kant rescues human free will from physical causal determinism. An act can be both free and causally determined because causality is only a category we use to structure appearances. Free will is an unknowable (but believable) "thing-in-itself," while causality is only a category.

This reduction of causality to a category seems even more skeptical than Hume, rather than less, for Hume at least granted that we could have probable knowledge of "things-in-themselves" by causal reasoning; Kant deprives us of even that. He sacrifices ("real-world") *objectivity* for *necessity* (of concept).

Self, World, and God

Kant's "Copernican revolution" made metaphysics impossible, at least in its traditional, "transcendent" form: we can know only *phenomena* (appearances), never *noumena* ("things-in-themselves"). Yet, Kant says, another kind of metaphysics ("transcendental" metaphysics) is possible. This transcends (sense) experience—not objectively, like traditional metaphysics, but subjectively. It shows us the universality and necessity of three "Ideas of Pure Reason"—self, world, and God—that all minds must use to structure all our experience.

There are three such ideas because reason seeks the ultimate condition of possibility in three directions: back into the knowing subject, out into the world of known objects, and up into the absolute condition for anything at all.

First, the self. Kant says we cannot know the real nature of the self, or mind, or soul. He calls the attempt to do that "rational psychology." He admits that "the 'I' is indeed in all thoughts, but . . . we do not have, and cannot have, any knowledge whatsoever of any such subject." It is a natural illusion, Kant says, to think of yourself as a being, an entity, a substance to which your experienced activities of sensing and feeling and knowing belong. Hume, too, declared this an illusion; since it is not able to be sensed, it is not derived from any sensory "impression." Hume concluded that there really *is* no such thing as a self, or "I," or person, or knowing subject; there are only temporarily together bundles of impressions. Kant avoids this conclusion by avoiding the "transcendent" metaphysical question itself.

Self is a psychologically necessary organizing principle for all experience, not an experienced or experienceable object.

If skepticism means doubting or denying our knowledge of reality, Kant's denial of the possibility of any "rational psychology" may be regarded as making him as skeptical as Hume on this question of the self. On the other hand, Kant may be regarded as teaching a kind of mystical, unknowable reality of the self. He certainly affirms its importance, its dignity, and the necessity of the concept: "The fact that man is aware of an ego-concept raises him infinitely above all other creatures living on earth. Because of this, he is a person; and by virtue of this oneness of consciousness, he remains one and the same person despite all the vicissitudes which may befall him." Kant, unlike Hume, affirms real human dignity and roots it in personhood.

Yet this is purely practical, not theoretical. It is discovered not in speculative but only in practical philosophy, for Kant (i.e., not in metaphysics but in ethics).

The concept of the world is the foundation or condition for our unifying all our experience, for all our experience is in the same "world." And our concept of God is the foundation or condition for our unifying absolutely everything. But these two concepts, like the concept of the self, cannot be verified as objectively, theoretically true. In plainer language, we *cannot* know that there is a real world, God, or self. They are inescapable ways we must think if only we dare to push the envelope and ask ultimate questions. But when we claim that these three things are objective realities, when we claim that we can know them by "pure reason" (i.e., by speculative, theoretical, or contemplative reason rather than merely *believing* them by "practical reason"), we run into difficulties, says Kant. The most famous of these difficulties are the "antinomies of pure reason."

The Antinomies

Kant's most famous attack on traditional metaphysics is that it produces necessary contradictions; our attempt to do it logically results in two opposite, mutually contradictory answers to each of its major questions. Therefore, there must be something wrong with the questions themselves, or with a hidden assumption behind them. (This assumption, Kant thought, was the assumption that reason could know the "transcendent," or "noumena," or "things-in-themselves.")

The four antinomies of pure reason are:

I

Thesis: The world has, as to time and space, a beginning (limit).
Antithesis: The world is, as to time and space, infinite.

2

Thesis: Everything in the world consists of elements that are simple.
Antithesis: There is nothing simple, but everything is composite.

3

Thesis: There are in the world causes through freedom.
Antithesis: There is no freedom, but all is nature [which is necessary].

4

Thesis: In the series of the world causes there is some necessary being.
Antithesis: There is nothing necessary in the world, but all is contingent.

Kant gives what he thinks are equally unanswerable reasons for both thesis and antithesis. For instance, the world must have a beginning in time because otherwise an infinite number of "nows" must have elapsed, but such a "completed infinity" is impossible. (Is it?) But it also must not have a beginning in time, for if it had a beginning, there must have been some reason why it began at that time rather than some other, and that is to assume, absurdly, that a particular time can cause something to be. (Is it?)

These dilemmas, argues Kant, are the result of trying to do metaphysics transcendently, extending reason beyond all possible experience. When we do that, if we only avoid logical self-contradiction, we can get away with *anything*. (Remember "the light dove.") It often seems like that when we argue metaphysics. I once spent three hours arguing with a brilliant logician who maintained that he could not be logically refuted if he believed that everything was really only Jell-O in various disguises. He won the argument.

Kant's Philosophy of God

Transcendent metaphysics usually claims it can prove the existence of God. Kant disagrees. (This is his fourth antinomy: *"some necessary being" = God.*) Like Hume, Kant claims to refute all the arguments for the existence of God, but for a different reason than Hume. Kant is not an atheist but a fideist.

He first divides the arguments into three kinds: the cosmological argument, the design argument, and the ontological argument. (Kant was the first to use that label for the third argument, and it has been used ever since.) Next, he refutes the ontological argument. Then, he tries to show that the other two kinds of argument really presuppose the ontological argument. Thus, he has refuted all arguments that claim to prove the real existence of God.

His refutation of Anselm's ontological argument is similar to, or at least compatible with, Aquinas' objection to this argument. The argument tried to show that atheism ("God does not exist") is logically self-contradictory, since

1. "God" means "that than which nothing greater can be conceived," or "the being that has all conceivable perfections"; and
2. real existence, independent of the mind, is a conceivable perfection, and it is more perfect than merely mental existence, existence that is dependent on a mind;
3. therefore, God must have real existence. Otherwise God is not God, which is self-contradictory.

Kant retorts: "If, in an identical proposition [a tautology, an analytic proposition] I reject the predicate while retaining the subject, contradiction results, and I therefore admit that the former [the predicate] belongs to the latter [the subject] necessarily. But if we reject subject and predicate alike, there is no contradiction." In other words, it is indeed a contradiction to deny the perfection of existence to the Perfect Being—*if* there *is* a wholly Perfect Being! Implicitly, Anselm begs the question, assuming the God he is claiming to prove.

Here is another way to put the same criticism. In his own version of Anselm's argument, Descartes had argued that real existence is logically contained within the concept of God as three angles are contained in the concept of a triangle. But, replies Kant, "to posit a triangle and yet to reject its three angles is indeed self-contradictory; but there is no contradiction in rejecting the triangle together with its three angles. The same holds true of the concept of an absolutely necessary being. If its existence is rejected, we reject the thing itself with all its predicates, and no question of contradiction can then arise."

A second, simpler Kantian criticism of the ontological argument is that "Being" (existence) "is obviously not a real predicate; that is, it is not a concept of something which could be added to the concept of a thing." Existence is judged (affirmed or negated) in a judgment, not conceived in a concept. As Aquinas would say, existence is not an essence. Existence adds nothing conceptual or conceivable. Existence is not conceivable,* only judgable. The concept of "having one horn" adds something conceivable to the concept of "a horse" to make it into the concept of "a unicorn," and "Kentucky Derby winner" adds something conceivable to the concept of "a horse" to narrow it down to just one horse, but

* Wittgenstein therefore calls it "mystical"—see vol. 4, chap. 90.

"existence" adds nothing at all to the concept of "a horse." It merely judges that a horse actually exists. As Kant says, "A hundred real thalers do not contain the least coin more than a hundred possible thalers."

Kant's objection to the ontological argument has convinced not only atheists but also most (but not all) theists, including theists who believe God's existence can be proved in other ways. However, Kant's attempt to prove that the other two arguments necessarily presuppose the ontological argument has been much less universally convincing and is certainly much less clear. It is that the cosmological argument begins with the premise that all the beings in the universe are contingent (i.e., they exist only because of external causes), and therefore their cause, since it cannot be themselves, must be a noncontingent, uncaused Being. This, says Kant, is also to treat existence as a predicate just as Anselm does because it defines a "necessary being" as one whose essence is existence.

However, it is also possible to use cosmological arguments that do not depend on the relationship between essence and existence (e.g., the argument from motion [change] or the argument from design).

Kant also points out that the conclusion of the cosmological argument is still very far from the religious concept of God—a fact that Aquinas quite agreed with.

Kant classified the argument from design as a third argument rather than as one version of the cosmological argument, and his objection to it is essentially the same as the above: its conclusion is weak and proves at most an "architect" of the world rather than a Creator. (Again, Aquinas would have agreed.)

Kant believed in the Christian God, and considered himself a Christian, though his concept of God was not that of either Protestant or Catholic orthodoxy, and he did not believe the Bible was authoritative divine revelation. But he believed, on the basis of reason, that the existence of the God he believed in by faith could not be proved by reason.*

He thought this skepticism of "natural theology," and of its claim that we could prove God's existence, was helpful rather than harmful to faith. He wrote that he "found it necessary to deny *knowledge* in order to make room for *faith*." (Compare Hume's similar but more extreme claim about that in chap. 62, "Hume's Critique of God" and "Hume's Critique of Miracles.") For Kant, it is not "theoretical reason" but "practical reason" (i.e., morality) that proves God, or rather proves the need for God. God is an unknowable "noumenon," but we must live and act "as if" there is a God, whether there is or not, just as we must live and act as if there is a world and a self.

---

* This is no more inconsistent than Catholics believing, as a matter of faith (in what the Church's First Vatican Council authoritatively taught), that the existence of God is not simply a matter of faith but could be proved by reason.

This sounds close to Voltaire's famous "If God did not exist, it would be necessary to invent Him." For Kant, God is not an optional invention but a necessary concept (although the judgment "God exists" cannot be proved), for two reasons: first, God is one of the three "Ideas of Pure Reason" inherent in the structuring activity of the mind itself; and second, belief in a real God is necessary for a complete morality. (We shall see why Kant thought that below.)

The Essential Problem with Kant's Epistemology

The fundamental problem Kant's successors perceived in his fundamental claim, his "Copernican revolution," was the apparent contradiction in affirming that noumena, or "things-in-themselves," were real but unknowable. If they are unknowable, how can we know they are real? They are the limit to thought, a kind of wall that thought cannot get over. But, as Wittgenstein put it, "to draw a limit to thought it is necessary to think both sides of that limit." Thinking the existence of "things-in-themselves" brings them into thought. Thus, Kant's immediate successors, Fichte, Schelling, and Hegel, all avoid this self-contradiction by rejecting the existence of any "things-in-themselves" at all, and turn Kant's "critical idealism" into an "absolute idealism."

We might view this problem as an instance of the problem of all skepticism: that all forms of skepticism seem self-contradictory. If we cannot know how things really are, as Kant says, how can we know that the fact that we cannot know how things really are is a fact, and is how things really are?

The same applies to Kant's concept of causality. If we cannot know it is real, how can we know that this category *really causes* order in nature by being causally imposed by our thought onto *phenomena*? "Imposition" or "forming" is one kind of causality, like cookie cutters forming cookie dough.

There is, in addition to this logical problem, the deep psychological problem of solipsism.

There is also the practical problem for the reader of the difficulty and obscurity of the *Critique of Pure Reason*. Kant recognized this problem, but he did not mitigate it but actually increased it when he attempted (successfully) to abbreviate the book and (unsuccessfully!) to clarify it by the much shorter *Prolegomena to Any Future Metaphysics*.

Reinhold's review of the *Critique*, shortly after it appeared, showed how diverse interpretations of it could be:

> The *Critique of Pure Reason* has been proclaimed by the dogmatists as the attempt of a skeptic who undermines the certainty of all knowledge; by the skeptics as a piece of arrogant presumption that undertakes to erect a new form of dogmatism upon the ruins of previous systems; by

> the supernaturalists as a subtly plotted artifice to displace the historical foundations of religion and to establish naturalism without polemic; by the naturalists as a new prop for the dying philosophy of faith; by the materialists as an idealistic contradiction of the reality of matter; by the spiritualists as an unjustifiable limitation of all reality to the corporal world, concealed under the name of the domain of experience.

Did Kant synthesize truths or errors? The philosophers of the Middle Ages synthesized theological faith and metaphysical reason; for Kant this was a synthesis of two uncritical errors. For a Thomist or an Aristotelian, Kant synthesizes the errors of "innate idea" rationalism and nominalist empiricism, simply forcing the former upon the latter like cookie cutters upon cookie dough. The argument goes on. One thing is agreed: Kant can't be ignored.

Kant in "the Great Conversation"

Since Kant sets himself against the whole tradition, this is a good time to put him into dialogue with that tradition and see what it would say if someone like Aristotle could talk back to him.

From the point of view of nearly all premodern philosophers (Socrates, Plato, Aristotle, Augustine, Aquinas), what is most crucially missing in Kant is the concept of *logos* or real intelligible form, essence, or nature. The three terms refer to the same thing under three different relationships. "Form" means "that which determines matter," or "what makes a potentiality to be actual"; "essence" means "what remains while accidents change"; "nature" means "the source of activity that explains why it is this rather than that kind of activity."

This was the fundamental concept of premodern philosophy. It was the Big Idea of Plato (the Platonic "Ideas" or "Forms"). Aristotle did not reject this key idea but modified it. He rejected only the "separation" (*chorismos*) of Plato's Forms from material substances. Form is also probably the most commonly used, and most commonly misunderstood, concept in Aquinas.

It is misunderstood because, like the history of philosophy itself, it all goes back to Plato, and that is a path into the past that modern philosophers are extremely reluctant to take. Aristotle's "forms" begin with Platonic "Forms" and then "naturalize" them, making them the forms of the things in nature instead of independently existing things. This process, from the top down, so to speak, is easy and clear. To take the contrasting path, i.e., to derive the forms from below, so to speak, rather than from above—empirically rather than rationally—is much more difficult, perhaps impossible. When the typically modern mind, conditioned as it is by empirical science from "below" rather than by revealed theology from "above" as its model, tries to rise to this crucial concept of form or *logos* from empirical experience, all it attains is a materialistic, spatial concept of "form" that means only "shape."

This is because it begins with matter, which the modern mind sees as something concrete and actual, and from that point of view or assumption, "form" is only the abstract geometrical arrangement of material parts. Premodern philosophy, on the other hand, begins with "form" as that which makes a thing actual. Form determines a thing to be "this" rather than "that." It is *matter* that contributes *potentiality* to the thing. An efficient cause (e.g., a carpenter) produces an effect (e.g., a house) by imposing a form (its design) onto its matter (e.g., wood)—that is, by actualizing the potentiality of the wood to be made into a house. Matter is something abstract, not concrete! It is wholly relative to form.

For Aristotle, neither form nor matter are concrete; both are abstract aspects of a concrete individual substance. Platonism concretized abstract forms; modernity concretizes abstract matter. From the point of view of Aristotle, these are opposite but similar examples of what Whitehead called "the fallacy of misplaced concreteness." Of course, from the typically modern point of view it is exactly the opposite: the supreme error of the ancients is this view of *logos* as real, knowable universals. Modern philosophers, especially empiricists, disparagingly call these universals "abstract ideas," because modern philosophers are typically nominalists.

This also explains why real teleology, final causality, end, or purpose is problematic for the modern mind. For final cause depends on formal cause; end depends on form. (To review the four causes, see vol. 1, chap. 25, "The Four Causes.") Without teleology, we are left with the inhuman, chancy, valueless machine-universe: the problem confronting every major modern philosopher.

Kant's Ethics: Its Historical Purpose

Kant famously said that "two things fill the mind with ever new and increasing admiration and awe . . . the starry heavens above and the moral law within." This is the quotation on Kant's gravestone. Kant really had two "Archimedean points," two nonnegotiable absolutes, premises, or starting points, not one: the starry heavens as known (or constructed) by Newtonian science, as the supreme achievement of "pure reason," and the moral law as known (or, rather, willed) by the will, or "practical reason."

Both are forms of "reason" in Kant's new, Copernican-revolutionary sense. For Kant, we actively (though unconsciously) legislate both the order in nature and the order in morality. The first chapter of Genesis (the creation story) and the twentieth chapter of Exodus (the story of God giving the Ten Commandments) are stories of the origin of these two fundamental kinds of order in the world, but in Kant's version it is our unconscious mind, or "transcendental ego," rather than God, that does the ordering.

This answers Hume's radical separation of reason and morality, which reduced morality to sheer feeling. Kant replies that morality is a matter of reason. *Reason and morality are reconciled.*

And more than just "reconciled." Reason is for Kant the whole key to morality. Kant's "Enlightenment" faith in reason was so great that he said that even "a race of devils" could produce a good community if only they were reasonable. This was an extreme version of the faith in reason that the American founding fathers appealed to in constructing the Constitution. But they also took into account man's evil and folly, as the French Revolution did not in its appeal to "liberty, fraternity, and equality"—and it ended in the Reign of Terror and then the dictatorship and imperialism of Napoleon.

At the end of his ethics, Kant thinks, *reason and faith are also reconciled*, since he makes a place for God, not as morality's ultimate origin but as its ultimate ideal.

Kant believed that neither "dogmatic" rationalism nor "skeptical" empiricism could rescue either Newtonian science, or metaphysics, or moral absolutism, or religious faith, while Kant's new epistemology claimed to rescue all four, though at a price. The price was the denial, through the "Copernican revolution," that in any of these four areas we can know the relevant "things-in-themselves."

Hume awakened Kant from his "dogmatic slumber" in ethics as well as metaphysics, and Kant's ethics can best be understood in relation to Hume, as Kant's answer to Hume's ethical skepticism, subjectivism, and relativism. For Kant, moral relativism is not morality at all, for it can give no *moral* meaning to concepts like "ought" or "duty" or "law" or even "right" and "wrong." If Hume is right, nearly the whole human race is wrong, and both sides of any moral argument are wrong when they argue about right and wrong as if they were realities rather than feelings.

Hume's denial of free will forces him to deny real morality. If the determinists are right, if man is essentially only a very complex machine,* then we have no right to be morally outraged when we are treated cruelly or brutally. Even criminals do not believe this philosophy. We cannot help believing in free moral choices, which are to be praised or blamed. And that means that we cannot help believing that some events (our own choices) are not wholly determined by the material forces of Newtonian science, but by our own free will. Kant's ethics tries to justify these two fundamental convictions of moral law and free will.

Kant is a moral absolutist. His most famous ethical work, the *Foundations of the Metaphysics of Morals* (let's call it MM so we don't have to keep repeating that terribly long, dull title) aims to discover and formulate the single *absolute* principle of morality. It is a short and simple book, and much more popular and

---

* The materialist determinist geneticist La Mettrie (1709–1751) had written a famous book with that shocking title: *Man a Machine*.

readable than the much longer and more difficult second "Critique," the *Critique of Practical Reason*.

There are close parallels between Kant's epistemology and his ethics, but they are not *necessary*. The two parts of his philosophy are not related by strict deduction, such that the ethics necessarily depends on the epistemology and the epistemology necessarily entails the ethics. There are philosophers who agree with his ethics but not his epistemology, and there are some who agree with his epistemology but not his ethics, as well as some who agree with both and some who disagree with both.

Kant's essential criticism of Hume's ethics is very simple: Hume, as an empiricist, made the mistake of looking at morality empirically—that is, observationally. He asked how people do in fact make moral judgments (he thought it was by a projection of feeling), and he asked what in fact motivates them to moral behavior (he thought it was essentially the feeling or instinct of sympathy). Kant calls this not ethics at all but "anthropology." Kant asks a different question: not what we *do* do but what we *ought* to do. And he looks to reason, not experience, to answer that question.

The most important parallel between Kant's ethics and his epistemology is that both give primacy to the subject, not the object; both are in that vague sense "subjective." However, "subjective" does not mean "individualistic" or "arbitrary"; in fact, Kant claims to discover ethical principles that are *universal and necessary*, though only in this "subjective" or "transcendental" dimension rather than in the objective or "transcendent" dimension. Just as the essential point of Kant's epistemology is that we actively create all the *logos*, all the intelligibility and order in our knowledge, by the unconscious but active forming operations of our knowing, by what he calls "pure reason," so the essential point of his ethics is that we actively create morality by willing the moral law, and this will is what he calls "practical reason."

Both the structures of "pure reason" and the principle(s) of morality or "practical reason" are synthetic and *a priori*. Because they are *a priori*, they are universal and necessary. In that sense they are surprisingly strong. But although they are "synthetic" rather than "analytic," they are "empty" universal forms, not particular contents. In that sense they are surprisingly weak. For instance, in Kant's epistemology, "space," one of the *a priori* forms of perception, is not the space of any particular, concrete, actual body, which is contingent, but space as such, abstract and universal space, the absolute Newtonian space that all possible bodies necessarily must fit into and conform to. Similarly, the *a priori* law Kant will find at the heart of ethics will not be something like a Ten Commandments that tells us what different kinds of acts to do and what not to do, but a purely formal universal law—essentially the Golden Rule: "Do unto others *whatever* you want them to do to you." It is like the law of noncontradiction in logic.

Kant's Ethics in His Own Words: A Summary of MM

Rather than *explaining* Kant's ethics, we will *present* it, in his own words, by a short summary of his surprisingly readable little classic MM. The numbers are mine, not Kant's. They are there for later reference. The parenthetical additions in brackets and the footnotes are also mine, not Kant's.

1. Purpose: "There is the utmost necessity for working out for once a pure [*a priori*] moral philosophy that is wholly cleared of everything which can only be empirical. . . . The ground of [moral] obligation . . . must . . . be sought not in the nature of man nor in the circumstances of the world in which man is placed, but must be sought *a priori* solely in the concepts of pure reason."

   Kant is trying to fulfill Descartes' program of building a new foundation under philosophy (see chap. 55), one that is more severely rational, one that is based on the new, narrowed, scientific definition of "reason" that is typical of the "Enlightenment." Reason is now sharply distinguished from everything empirical. It is a quasi-mathematical reason, as in Descartes.

   Kant is aiming at a purely "formal" ethics, based on abstract law rather than concrete virtues or values—an ethic that is like purely formal, mathematical logic. That is the new symbolic logic, which begins with what Aristotle called the "second act of the mind"—that is, with the purely formal law of noncontradiction between propositions—rather than the old Aristotelian logic, which begins with "the first act of the mind": intellectual intuition into the contents of universal concepts, terms, "whats," natures, essences, or forms. For Kant is a nominalist and does not believe these things are objectively real or that we possess this power of intellectual intuition into them. It is not a "natural law" ethics because it is not, like Aristotle's, based on human nature and its needs. It would work equally well for angels, or for extraterrestrials.
2. "The present 'Grounding' is . . . intended for nothing more than seeking out and establishing the [single] supreme principle of morality. This constitutes by itself a task which is complete in its purpose and should be kept separate from every other moral inquiry."
3. "There is no possibility of thinking of anything at all in the world, or even out of it, which can be regarded as good without qualification, except a *good will*."

   3a. "Intelligence, wit, judgment, and whatever talents of the mind one might want to name are doubtless in many respects good and desirable, as are such qualities of temperament as courage, resolution, perseverance. But they can also become extremely bad and harmful if the will, which is to make use of these gifts of nature . . . is not good."

   Kant calls things like courage or compassion not "virtues" but "inclinations" and "gifts of nature." Aristotle called them not "gifts of nature" but moral habits or "*second* nature," and he said that these good "habits" of acting morally without having to consciously and rationally think about it (e.g., the courage or compassion that leads you to immediately jump into a pool to save a drowning child) were formed by repeated particular moral acts that began by being conscious and deliberate but became habitual by repetition and practice, so that we are responsible for these moral habits; i.e., we are responsible for what we *are* (our moral character) as well as for what we *do*. For Kant, in contrast, your "character" means not your moral virtues but simply what we would call your "personality," a set of inclinations that are given to you by nature, not by your rational moral choices. (Is this difference only a difference in terminology or a real contradiction between the two philosophers?)

Kant is often criticized for being unrealistic in leaving moral *habits* out of his ethical system. But he is not trying to give us a moral psychology here, with specific content, but only the *logic* of morality, only the single formal law or principle of all morality, the law that is to ethics what the law of noncontradiction is to logic.

3b. "The same holds with gifts of fortune: power, riches, honor, even health, and that complete well-being and contentment with one's condition which is called happiness, make for pride and often even arrogance unless there is a good will to correct their influence on the mind."

Contrast what premodern philosophers like Aristotle meant by "happiness": not mere subjective contentment but objective perfection or completeness. The test that distinguishes the two is suffering: happiness in the sense of contentment excludes suffering, but happiness in the sense of perfection or completeness includes and even requires suffering. (As Rabbi Heschel said, "The man who has not suffered—what could he possibly know, anyway?") The ancients typically identified happiness (in this rich, deep, moral sense) as the greatest good, the *summum bonum*, and the greatest question in their ethics was what it consisted of and how to attain it. The next excerpt shows why Kant disagrees with this long tradition.

3c. "The concept of *happiness* is such an indeterminate one that even though everyone wishes to attain happiness, yet he can never say definitively and consistently what it is that he really wishes and wills. The reason for this is that all the elements belonging to the concept of happiness are unexceptionally empirical, i.e., they must be borrowed from experience."

(Do you agree? Why or why not? What would Augustine say about this? Does his "restless heart" long for something in empirical experience?)

Does he want riches? How much anxiety, envy, and intrigue might he not thereby bring down upon his own head?

> Or knowledge and insight? Perhaps these might only give him an eye that much sharper for revealing, that much more dreadfully, evils which are at present hidden but are yet unavoidable; or such an eye might burden him with still further needs. . . .
>
> Or long life? Who guarantees that it would not be a long misery?
>
> Or health at least? How often has infirmity of the body kept one from excesses into which perfect health would have allowed him to fall, and so on?
>
> In brief, he is not able on any principle to determine with complete certainty what will make him truly happy, because to do so would require omniscience.
>
> Therefore one cannot act according to determinate principles [that are universal and necessary] in order to be happy, but only according to empirical [and therefore non-universal and non-necessary] counsels, e.g., of diet, frugality, politeness, reserve, etc., which are shown by experience to contribute on the average the most to well-being. . . . [These] imperatives of [pragmatic rather than moral] prudence, strictly speaking, cannot command at all. . . . They are to be taken as counsels rather than as commands.

In other words, Kant is saying: Never mind your happiness, just do your duty.

"A good will is good not because of what it effects or accomplishes, nor because of its fitness to attain some proposed end; it is good only through its willing, i.e., it is good in itself."

"For all these effects—even the promotion of the happiness of others—could have been also brought about by other causes, so that for this there would have been no need of the will of a rational being." (His argument here is that since the will to that end is not absolutely *necessary* for that end, it is not absolutely *good*.)

"When it [a good will] is considered in itself, then it is to be esteemed very much higher than anything which it might ever bring about."

In other words, nothing is better than the good will of a good person.

4. "The concept of a will good in itself . . . must now be developed. This concept already dwells in the natural sound understanding and needs not so much to be taught as merely to be elucidated. . . . Therefore we shall take up the concept of [moral, not just social or civic] *duty*."

When we hear the word "duty" we must avoid letting our emotions and imaginations substitute for our reason when they suggest two very misleading associations to us: potty training, and the excuse the Nazi war criminals gave at Nuremberg ("We were doing our duty!"). Duty is respect for moral law.

5. "An action must be done from [the motive of] duty in order to have any moral worth."

   Kant contrasts moral *duty* with psychological *inclination*. Only the first motive has moral worth. (He is assuming that moral worth is determined by motive.)

   He gives three examples:

   5a. "To preserve one's life is a duty; and in addition everyone also has an immediate inclination to do so. But because of that, the maxim [principle] of their action has no moral content. They preserve their lives, to be sure, in accordance with duty [they do the thing duty commands], but not from duty [as their motive]. On the other hand, if adversity and hopeless sorrow have completely taken away the taste for life, if an unfortunate man . . . wishes for death and yet preserves his life without loving it—not from inclination or fear but from duty—then his maxim has indeed a moral content." (Kant is not denying that we act from mixed motives, but he is saying that the only *morally* valuable motive is moral duty, not emotional inclination or feeling.)

   5b. "To be beneficent where one can is a duty; and besides this, there are many persons who are so sympathetically constituted that, without any further motive of vanity or self-interest, they find an inner pleasure in spreading joy around them and can rejoice in the satisfaction of others as their own work. But I maintain that in such a case an action of this kind, however dutiful and amiable it may be, has nevertheless no true moral worth. It is on a level with such actions as arise from other inclinations." (The exact same comment applies to this example as to the previous one.)

   5c. "Undoubtedly in this way also are to be understood those passages of Scripture which command us to love our neighbor and even our enemy. For love as an inclination cannot be commanded; but beneficence [goodwill] from duty, when no inclination impels us and even when a natural and unconquerable aversion opposes such beneficence, is practical [moral] and not pathological [from *pathos*, "passion"] love. Such love resides in the will and not in the propensities of feeling; in principles of action and not in tender sympathy; and only this practical love can be commanded."

   Loving is a free choice of will; liking is a spontaneous inclination of feelings. Scripture commands us to "love," not to "like," our neighbor. Only free choices, not feelings, can be commanded, and can be our moral obligations.

6. "An act done from duty has its moral worth not in the purpose that is to be attained by it, but in the maxim according to which the action is determined. The moral worth depends, therefore, not on the realization of the object of the action, but merely on the principle of volition."

   What makes an act morally good or evil is the principle that motivates the will rather than the end or consequence sought by the act. Kant opposes "teleological" ethics, an ethics based on ends. But Kant does not distinguish two very different kinds of purposes or ends: (a) practical utilitarian gains and (b) moral ideals or values. Thus, there are two very different kinds of teleological ethics: utilitarianism (vol. 4, chaps. 82 and 83) and traditional "natural law" ethics. These two are often misleadingly lumped together in philosophy texts and anthologies, since they are both "teleological" (i.e., based on ends and purposes, rather than on sheer Kantian "duty"). But to confuse them is to confuse Machiavelli with St. Thomas Aquinas!

"Duty is the [moral] necessity [obligation] of an action done out of respect for the [moral] law."

> But what sort of law can that be, the thought of which must determine the will without reference to any expected effect, so that the will can be called absolutely good without qualification? Since I have deprived the will of every impulse that might arise for it from obeying any particular law [that would be "empirical" rather than "pure" morality], there is nothing left to serve the will as principle except the universal conformity of its actions to [moral] law as such, i.e., I should never act except in such a way that I can also will that my maxim should become a universal law.

This is the moral equivalent of the formal logical law of noncontradiction.

7. Kant now answers the natural objection that his absolutist ethic is impossibly idealistic and unlivable.

> We have . . . drawn our concept of duty from . . . reason . . . [and not] experience. On the contrary, when we pay attention to our experience of the way human beings do act [as distinct from how they ought to act], we meet frequent and . . . justified complaints that there cannot be cited a single certain example of the disposition to act from pure duty. . . . Hence there have always been philosophers who have absolutely denied the existence of this disposition in human actions and have ascribed everything to a more or less refined self-love.
>
> Yet in so doing they have not cast doubt upon the rightness of the *concept* of morality. Rather, they have spoken with sincere regret as to the frailty and impurity of human nature, which they think is noble enough to take as its precept an idea so worthy of respect but yet is too weak to follow this idea. . . .
>
> [But] even if there never have been actions springing from such pure sources, the question at issue here is not whether this or that has happened but that reason of itself and independently of all experience commands what ought to happen.

Kant's first answer to the objection, then, is that even if his morality is too high to be subjectively done, it is still objectively right. Even if it does not become real, it is the ideal. Even if no student scores one hundred, one hundred is the only perfectly right score.

His second answer is that this absolutism is also practical:

> The pure thought of duty and of the moral law generally, unmixed with any extraneous addition of empirical inducements, has by the way of reason alone . . . an influence on the human heart . . . much more powerful than all other incentives. . . .
>
> Why is it that moral instruction accomplishes so little, even though it contains so much that is convincing to reason? My answer . . . is . . . that the teachers . . . have not purified their concepts. . . . They try to do too well by looking everywhere for motives for being morally good; they spoil the medicine by trying to make it stronger. For the most ordinary observation shows that when a righteous act is represented as being done with a steadfast soul and sundered from all view to any advantage in this or another world, and even under the greatest temptations of need or allurement, it far surpasses and eclipses any similar action that was in the least affected by any extraneous incentive; it elevates the soul and inspires the wish to be able to act in this way. Even moderately young children feel this impression, and duties should never be represented to them in any other way.

8. In the previous paragraph Kant appealed to experience to show that high, idealistic expectations actually work to motivate people. In the next paragraph he seems to ignore experience when he says that learning morality by personal example (e.g., good parents, or reading the lives of the saints) does *not* work! (But his point here is probably not what will work to practically motivate people but what will work to logically define the moral ideal.)

> Worse service cannot be rendered to morality than that an attempt be made to derive it from examples. For every example of morality presented to me must itself first be judged according to principles . . . in order to see whether it is fit to serve as an original example, i.e., as a model. But in no way can it [an example] authoritatively furnish the *concept* of morality. [This is because the concept of what is moral is a universal, and for Kant no universal can be abstracted from particulars, *à la* Aristotle. For Kant, we can't learn from examples by discovering universal principles in them.]
>
> Even the Holy One of the gospel must first be compared with our ideal of moral perfection before he is recognized as such. Even he says

> of himself, "Why do you call me (whom you see) good? None is good (the archetype of good) except God only (whom you do not see)." But whence have we the concept of God as the highest good? Solely from the idea of moral perfection, which reason frames *a priori.*
>
> Imitation [of examples] has no place at all in moral matters. . . . Examples serve only for encouragement . . . but examples can never justify us in . . . letting ourselves be guided by them.

Kant would say that *The Imitation of Christ* is a bad title and a wrong concept.

> All imperatives are expressed by an *ought* and thereby indicate the relation of an objective law of [moral] reason to a [free] will. . . . Now all imperatives command either *hypothetically* or *categorically*. The former [hypothetical imperatives] represent the . . . action as a *means* for attaining something else that one wants [as an end]. . . . The categorical imperative would be one which represented an action as [morally] necessary in itself, without reference to another end.

"*If* you want to cross the sea, get on this boat" is a hypothetical imperative. "Cross the sea" is a categorical imperative. So is "Get on this boat."

9. "We shall, therefore, have to investigate the possibility of a categorical imperative entirely *a priori*. . . . The categorical imperative is an *a priori* synthetic proposition.* . . . It is not concerned with the *matter* [specific content] of an action . . . but rather with the [ethical] *form* of the action."
10. Kant then gives the first of three formulations of the categorical imperative:

> There is only one categorical imperative and it is this: Act only according to that maxim whereby you can at the same time will that it should become a universal law.
>
> All imperatives of duty can be derived from this one imperative . . . [for] if we . . . attend to ourselves in any transgression of a duty, we find that we actually do not will that our maxim should become a universal law. . . . We only take the liberty of making an exception to the law for ourselves [or just for this one time] to the advantage of our inclination. Consequently, if we weighed up everything from one and the same standpoint, namely, that of reason, we should find

* Technically, imperatives (i.e., imperative *sentences*) are not *propositions* at all, any more than interrogative sentences are. They are neither true nor false. They do not have subjects and predicates. So listing them as one of four kinds of *a priori knowledge* or *judgments* —see "Kant's Logic: Classifying Judgments" above—is not correct.

> a contradiction in our own will, viz. that a certain principle be objectively [morally] necessary as a universal law and yet subjectively should admit of exceptions.

For example, when you tell a lie, you always do so willing that others not lie to you, for then you would not get what you want. The same is true of stealing, killing, and all other morally wrong acts toward others. You always will (a) that everyone should obey the moral law and (b) that you should not (i.e., that *not* everyone should obey). Thus, your will morally contradicts itself.

So Kant's first formulation of the "categorical imperative" is a formula for determining all morally wrong acts: they all contradict themselves in willing two opposite things for two different people. This categorical imperative is a universal negative rule. Whether this is also a universal positive rule (i.e., a formula for all morally right acts) is more questionable, for there seems to be no contradiction in willing some people to be better than others in practicing moral virtues like generosity or mercy. And some actions or choices could be their moral duty for some people but not others (e.g., to become soldiers, or priests, or mothers).

II. The second formulation of the categorical imperative is as follows:

> Now I say that man, and in general every rational being, exists as an end in himself and not merely as a means to be arbitrarily used by this or that will. . . . Rational beings are called *persons* because their nature already marks them out as ends in themselves, i.e., as something which is not to be used merely as means. . . . The practical imperative will therefore* be the following: Act in such a way that you treat humanity, whether in your own person or in the person of another, always at the same time as an end and never simply as a means.

When someone uses us as a means to his own personal ends, he treats us as a thing rather than a person. Persons are to be respected, as ends, and things are to be used, as means, because things have only instrumental worth, while persons have intrinsic worth.

Kant derives this second formulation from the first as follows. The first formulation says that we must treat all men as we want to be treated. But "all men everywhere want to be considered persons instead of things for the

* Note how this "therefore" is deducing ethics from metaphysics (which Kant said was impossible), deriving an "ought" from an "is." Because persons really are ends, we ought to treat them as ends. This certainly sounds like knowledge of "things-in-themselves"! And it uses the concept of a real universal human "*nature*," thus transcending nominalism.

same reason that I do, and [so] this affirmation of the absolute worth of the individual leads to the second formulation of the categorical imperative."

12. Kant then derives the third formulation from the others. It is this: "Always so act that the will could regard itself at the same time as making universal law through its own maxim." This is not just an "as if," a thought experiment, for Kant; the will *does* make universal moral law: "The third formulation of the principle is the idea of the will of every rational being as a will that *legislates* universal law."

    If I am the maker of the moral law, then whenever I violate the law, I violate myself; I morally contradict myself. This is the formula, or formulation, of autonomy: "*Autonomy of the will [is] the supreme principle of morality.* Autonomy of the will is the property that the will has of being a law unto itself."

    "*Heteronomy* [literally, "other-law"] *of the will is the source of all spurious principles of morality.* The will seeks the law that is to determine it . . . and if it goes outside of itself and seeks this law in the character of any of its objects, then heteronomy always results. The will in that case does not give itself the law, but the object does so."

    A heteronomous will is one that is determined either by inclinations or by desire for some object, or by the will of another human being, or even by the will of God. A will that is *influenced* by these things is *partially* heteronomous, or heteronomous to the extent that it is influenced by these things or by any other factors outside itself. Freedom, for Kant, is autonomy, self-determination rather than other-determination.

    If there is a Last Judgment after death, Kant would expect to find himself rather than God on the throne of judgment. And this would make any moral arguments he was prepared to have with God die on his lips. (But if conscience is "God's prophet in the soul," the throne may be occupied by *both*!) Yet Kant seems to leave no room for a *relation* between my will and God's, thus no room for *religion.*

13. Kant then goes on to deduce the traditional concept of free will from this nontraditional concept of autonomy: "*The concept of freedom is the key for an explanation of the autonomy of the will.* . . . If freedom of the will is presupposed, morality . . . follows. *Freedom must be presupposed as a property of the will of all rational beings.* . . . '*I ought*' implies '*I can.*'" This famous maxim means that we never could have had the very idea of duty ("ought") if we had no experience of freedom ("can"). Duty appeals only to free choice. Machines have no duties.

God, Freedom, and Immortality: The Three Postulates of Morality

Kant adds that God, free will, and immortality are three morally necessary presuppositions, assumptions, or "postulates" for morality, though none of them can be proved or known with certainty to be true. We "postulate" them by a rational and moral demand of the will; we do not discover them by the mind. They are not received by the pure or theoretical reason; they are actively legislated into being by the will or practical reason. Although "I ought" *implies* "I can," as a presupposition or assumption, that does not mean that "I ought" (moral duty) *proves* "I can" (free will). Free will, like God and immortality, is a rational belief, not a proof; it is faith, not knowledge. As Kant says, "I found it necessary to deny *knowledge* in order to make room for *faith*."

One may wonder why this is *not* knowledge and proof. It looks like a good *reductio ad absurdum* argument: If we are not free, we cannot be moral; we can be moral; therefore we are free. Aquinas used a similar *reductio* argument to prove free will; why is it not a logical proof leading to our *knowledge* of the truth of the conclusion? Aquinas said, "Man has free will, otherwise all praise, blame, counseling, commanding, rewarding, and punishing are in vain [meaningless]."

Kant argues that immortality is also implied by morality because justice is not complete in this life: good people do not get the happiness they deserve.* Therefore, for justice to be done there must be a next life, and therefore personal immortality.

Immortality is also implied for a second reason: because we are not able to attain *perfect* moral virtue in this life, and only perfect virtue justly deserves perfect happiness. (Kant does not speak of divine grace, which cannot be proved by reason, only of justice, which can.)

And the existence of God is also implied by morality, Kant thinks, because only an omnipotent God could guarantee that moral goodness and personal happiness coincided in the next life. Unlike Plato and Aristotle, Kant does not believe that virtue has any natural, essential connection with happiness, by internal final causality, so that God is required to make that connection, by external efficient causality.

Kant does not mean that atheists or agnostics cannot be truly moral, but that if they explored the requirements for a complete morality, this demand would lead them to the demand for God. It is not a *proof* but a demand of the moral will.

The obvious problem with the idea of "postulating" God by the moral demands of the will is that even if it is true that we need God for a complete ethics, how can we will God into existence by our own moral demands if he does not exist already? If he does not really exist, is it not intellectually dishonest or at least mistaken to insist that he does, to will that he does, and to live as if he does? Isn't it like believing in Santa Claus simply because that belief makes you act morally every Christmastime?

It has been suggested that Kant, like the Jansenists, Puritans, and Pietists, was virtuous but not terribly happy, and that his teaching expresses his personal

* Plato would disagree. His *Republic* claims to prove that even in this life "justice is more profitable ["happifying"] than injustice." Why do Plato and Kant disagree? Do they mean different things by justice, happiness, both, or neither?

experience. Kant led a very *comfortable* life, but not a very *joyful* one—rather like most of us today. The saints, in contrast, are passionately uncomfortable but deeply happy and full of joy. If they and Plato are right, you *can* have virtue and deep happiness (joy) together in this life, but you cannot have both "comfort and joy" together: you can have either much joy but little comfort, like them, or much comfort and little joy, like Kant.

Or is this unfair to Kant?

The Controversial Assumptions Behind Kant's Ethics

There are four reasons for this section. First, every ethical philosophy has assumptions, or presuppositions. You can't avoid at least implicitly "taking sides" in the classical disputes, for instance between nominalists and realists. The second reason is that to compare Kant with other philosophers (mainly Aristotle) about these foundational issues, as well as about the ethical conclusions that issue from them, is the best way to understand Kant himself, because everything is best understood by contrast. The third reason is to motivate you to engage in dialogue and argument with Kant by pointing to controversial points. This has already been done somewhat in the comments on the quotations above; now we go a little deeper. The fourth reason is that ethics is the part of philosophy most people find the most interesting, the most practical, and making the most difference to their lives; and Kant is the most important ethical philosopher of modern times.

Kant's controversial assumptions include the following:

1. *The "Copernican revolution in philosophy."* Although Kant does not *deduce* his ethics from his "Copernican revolution" epistemology, and although one can logically accept either one of these two main parts of his philosophy without the other, nevertheless there is a close connection. Just as the epistemology ascribed to the mind the power to actively *create* the forms it seemingly discovered and received, so the ethics ascribes to the will (which Kant calls the "practical reason") the power to create the moral law that it seems to receive. For Kant it is man, not God, who authors the *logos* in both epistemology and ethics. This is his last main point in MM: the "autonomy" of the will. God for Kant is a deistically distant ideal, not a present, pressing person.

   An obvious objection to this idea that we create the moral law is that the very same self can't be both over and under the moral law. If I tie myself up, I'm not really bound, and I can loose myself by the same power or authority by which I bound myself. Why isn't the same true for moral law as for ropes?

   To answer this question, Kant distinguishes two aspects of the self or ego: "the empirical ego," the self we are conscious of, and "the transcendental ego," the deeper self that we are not conscious of. He says that the empirical ego experiences moral obligation *under* the moral law while the transcendental ego is the active author of that law. Kant also says that the transcendental ego is universal, one and the same for everybody, while the empirical ego is individual. He probably did not mean that the transcendental ego was literally God (though he did identify it as "reason itself"), but his successors (Fichte, Schelling, and Hegel) tended to push him in this direction. But even if he did not mean that the transcendental ego was God, Kant apparently meant by it something more than conscience as God's authoritative representative in the human soul; for our consciences are individual and different and can be mistaken. We have to educate and inform and train our consciences. But the transcendental ego is the teacher, not the one taught; therefore, the transcendental ego is not the same as conscience. But if it's less than God and more than conscience, what is it?

2. *Empiricism.* Another hidden assumption in Kant is the reduction of "experience" to "sense experience." This is ironic, because that is the hallmark of empiricism; yet the point of both Kant's epistemology and his ethics is to go beyond Hume's empiricism to find the *a priori* structures of pure reason independent of experience.

   He *has* to do this—he has to look somewhere other than experience in order to find the moral obligation, or "categorical imperative," that Hume failed to find in experience—because experience does not, for Kant, contain Aristotelian forms that we can discover by intellectual intuition and abstraction (two intellectual powers in Aristotelian epistemology that Kant denies we possess). Therefore, Kant must either (a) agree with Hume's conclusion of skepticism in morality as well as epistemology, as well as his premise of empiricism, or else he must (b) transcend Hume's empiricist premise and find forms *a priori* in pure reason independent of experience—in both epistemology and ethics. Kant cannot get a "natural law ethics" out of experience, as Aristotle can, because what is experienced, for Kant, is not an Aristotelian world full of real substances and actions that contain universal forms that can be abstracted. Experience, for Kant, is only empirical perceptions, just as in Hume. The point is that Kant begins with Humean premises, and you can't get Aristotelian ethical conclusions out of Humean premises.

   In both his epistemology and his ethics, Kant does not *derive* any universals from experience. In both cases, all that experience does is to *trigger* the mind to think using its innate universal categories. For instance, when we experience a baby being born, our minds are triggered to apply the innate *a priori* category of causality to this empirical event to order and structure and explain it: *mother = cause, baby = effect.* And when we experience an evil deed being done, our minds apply the *a priori* "categorical imperative" as a principle to explain why it is evil. Kant agrees with Hume that we do not *experience* causality and we do not *experience* good or evil. Experience is only sensory, only empirical. For Aristotle, by contrast, we find forms or categories like causality and moral values in our experience because our experience is not merely sensory but also intellectual. For Kant, we actively create what for Aristotle we receive and discover, in both epistemology and ethics.

3. *Nominalism.* Nominalism is another presupposition of Kant's, closely related to the empiricist presupposition above (point 2). Kant explicitly says that there is no such thing as intellectual intuition of universals. The medieval Scholastic philosophers called this the "first act of the mind" or *intellectus* as distinct from *ratio* or discursive reasoning. It is the fourth quarter of Plato's "divided line" in the *Republic*, as distinct from the third. For Kant, the human mind's objects do not include universal and necessary forms, either in themselves (as in Plato) or abstracted from experience (as in Aristotle). For Kant, universals are not objectively ("transcendently") real, only subjectively ("transcendentally") real.
4. *No teleology.* In saying that "an act . . . has its moral worth *not in the purpose* that is to be attained by it, but in the maxim according to which the action is determined" (point 6 above), Kant is denying teleology (real purpose, real final causality) in ethics. Another key departure from Aristotle. Final causality had proved worthless in modern physics, and most modern philosophers assume it is also worthless in philosophy. (Does that logically follow? What would make it follow?)
5. *Subjectivism.* In making all of morality dependent on motive, Kant is subjectivizing it. Medieval philosophers (e.g., Augustine and Aquinas) had said there were *three* moral determinants (factors that made a human act morally good or bad): the (objective) nature of the act itself, the (subjective) motive, and the (objective) circumstances or situation. In reducing these three to one only (the motive of duty, or respect for moral law as such), Kant is doing the same thing Peter Abelard did in the twelfth century (see vol. 2, chap. 41, "Ethics"): subjectivizing morality. (To say that morality is subjective does not mean it is arbitrary, irrational, individual, or contingent. It is rational, universal, and necessary. But it comes from inside, not from outside.) And he is doing it for the same reason as Abelard: like Abelard, Kant is a nominalist, so he does not believe that we can *know* universal forms or essences or natures in human acts.

But Kant makes a valid point in *focusing* on motive: even if it is not true that a good motive alone can justify a bad deed, it is certainly true that a bad motive alone spoils a good deed. As St. Thomas Becket says in T.S. Eliot's play *Murder in the Cathedral*, when tempted to be a martyr for the motive of personal glory, "The last temptation is the greatest treason: To do the right thing for the wrong reason [motive]." But to do the opposite, to do the wrong thing for the right reason (motive), is still to do the wrong thing, so that a good motive, however important it is, does not justify a bad deed. All three moral determinants must line up. (This is an unpopular thing to say today, when many people believe that subjective sincerity and good will are the *only* things that count in morality. It is judged to be too "judgmental.")

Kant is trying to answer Hume's moral *relativism* with a moral absolutism. But he is in a sense agreeing with Hume that morality is *subjective*. All moral value comes from the subject, from the self, from within. The difference is that with Kant it comes from "practical reason" (i.e., will), while with Hume it comes from feeling. That gives Kant's morality universality and necessity—absoluteness. The imperative is "categorical."

6. *Voluntarism.* Euthyphro, in Plato's dialogue by that name, and the Ash'arites among the medieval Muslim philosophers, had a similar absolutizing of the will in their ethics. But for them it was the divine will, not the human.
7. *The Stoic opposition between duty and inclination.* Kant said that actions had moral worth only when they proceeded from pure duty and not from inclination. Most ancient and medieval moral philosophers (Socrates, Plato, Aristotle, Augustine, Aquinas) agreed with Kant's distinction between the rational moral will and the feelings, desires, and inclinations, and also agreed with the superiority of reason and will over feelings, but *not* with the idea that the feelings are by nature the enemies of the reason and will in that they always *pollute* moral motives rather than aid them. The Stoics *did* teach that. Kant is often compared with the Stoics.

Kant does not quite say that all fun is bad, that no action is good unless it hurts—his point is rather that we cannot *know* whether our act came from our spontaneous feelings and desires ("inclinations") or from our rational moral will freely choosing to obey duty unless we experienced a contrast between these two forces—in other words, unless it hurt to do the right thing.

That point may be *psychologically* true. But Kant also says that only one of these two forces has any *moral worth* at all: only reason and will, and not at all the feelings, emotions, desires, and inclinations. And this point is highly debatable. (See Hildebrand's critique of this in vol. 4, chap. 92.)

For surely it is morally good when a good man's emotions are educated and "tamed" better than a bad man's, so that when the good man does a good deed, he enjoys doing it, as the bad man does not. The Catholic Church will not canonize a saint unless heroic *joy* is found in his or her life—one of the "gifts of the Holy Spirit." And surely the person who is saintly by habit or "inclination" as well as by the will is a morally better person than one for whom saintly deeds are difficult and unpleasant, for his inclinations have been better tamed and educated. And surely some emotions or inclinations, like a mother's love, or gratitude, or compassion, must count as morally good.

To reduce all morality to duty is like reducing all war to defense. Duty is the last defensive bulwark against evil rather than the first and primary motive for good.

Another difficulty in Kant's reduction of all morality to duty is the notion of heroism, or acts "beyond the call of duty." Logically, it seems Kant must either deny that such acts have any moral worth, since they do not proceed from duty, or he must make heroic acts strict duties, thus depriving these acts of the very thing that makes them heroic: that they go *beyond* the call of duty!

8. *The categorical imperative.* Kant's criterion for a moral act according to the first formulation of the categorical imperative is universalizability. If you can make the maxim (principle) of your act universal (for all), the act is good. But suppose you *want* others to be selfish or warlike. Suppose that makes you happy. Suppose you want universal adultery rather than fidelity, or universal war rather than peace. Kant's rule would not seem to forbid it.
9. *Persons as ends.* Kant's second formulation of the categorical imperative is one of the greatest ethical achievements in the history of human thought. Nearly all contemporary cultures and religions accept it, and it can be the basis for a deep cross-cultural agreement (e.g., the United Nations' Universal Declaration of Human Rights). But it is metaphysical. Its "ought" is based on an "is." Only because each person is an end is it our obligation to treat him as an end. So Kant must admit metaphysics, at least here in the realm of "practical reason."
10. *Freedom.* "What else, then, can freedom of the will be but autonomy, i.e., the property that the will has of being a law unto itself?" Kant confuses two kinds of freedom: autonomy and free choice. But they are different. Autonomy, in Kant, means that I am the author of the moral law rather than under a law I did not make. Free choice means that I, and not just unfree forces outside me (environment) or inside me (heredity), contribute to causing my choices. One can believe in free choice without believing in autonomy. In fact, most people do.

65

JOHANN GOTTLIEB FICHTE

AD 1762–1814

Kant thought he had pronounced a death sentence on traditional, "transcendent" metaphysics with his "critique of pure reason." His philosophy is often labeled "*critical idealism*." But ironically, the fruit of Kant's philosophy was that metaphysics rose from the dead with a vengeance in the form of four systems of "*absolute idealism*" in Fichte, Schelling, Hegel, and Schopenhauer.

Fichte and Schelling are usually treated simply as transitions from Kant to Hegel. Both wrote complete and complex metaphysical systems that were embryonic forms of Hegel's much more formidable, famous, and fruitful one. Both began as disciples of Kant, then branched out into "transcendent" rather than "transcendental" systems.

The lives of four of these five German idealists were academic and unspectacular. Only Schopenhauer was "interesting" personally. It seems to be a rule that the lives of German philosophers are either professorial, academic, and very dull (except, of course, for the drama in the theater of ideas), like Kant, Fichte, Schelling, and Hegel; or else nonacademic, interesting, and very eccentric, like Leibniz, Schopenhauer, Nietzsche, and Marx.

Fichte's Big Idea

Fichte's primary reaction to Kant was to deny the existence of "things-in-themselves" and thus change Kant's "critical idealism" to "absolute idealism." "Absolute idealism" means, essentially, that there is nothing that is not idea, nothing outside of ideas.* This sounds strange, but Fichte argues for it from the premise of Kant's doctrine that noumena, or "things-in-themselves" outside of ideas, are unknowable. If, as Kant claims, we cannot know anything about these "noumena" beyond phenomena, these supposed realities behind appearances, these things beyond ideas, then how could we possibly know that they even exist? "We know that there are unknowables" sounds self-contradictory.

Kant's answer to that question was that even though we could not *know* these noumena, "we must nevertheless be in a position at least to *think* them as things-in-themselves; otherwise we should be landed in the absurd conclusion that there can be appearance without anything that appears." That sounds at least more commonsensical than Fichte's denial of "things-in-themselves" altogether.

In denying "things-in-themselves," Fichte makes the ego (mind-will) creative of not only the *form* of its objects, as in Kant, but also their *matter*, their content, in fact their very existence. The ego thus becomes absolute and all-creative. The most difficult problem in interpreting Fichte is whether to interpret his "ego" as the divine Ego or as the human ego, or to know whether there is even a clear distinction between those two.

The most famous of Fichte's writings was his *Addresses to the German Nation*. This was triggered by Napoleon's invasion of Fichte's native Prussia in 1806. Like most intellectuals, Fichte had supported the French Revolution but not the dictatorship of Napoleon. Fichte idealized the German people in this book, ascribing to them a messianic destiny to educate and save the world. Later, National Socialist propaganda made powerful use of the rabid German nationalism in Fichte's addresses, since Fichte was both a nationalist and a socialist; but of course the Nazi form of National Socialism was a perversion of Fichte's more liberal and humanitarian brand of patriotism, which exalted freedom, not dictatorship.

Like Rousseau, by whom he was strongly influenced, Fichte combined in his political philosophy the notions of the "social contract theory" and the "General Will." He said that even if it originated in the "social contract," once the General Will was embodied in the state it was the supreme and absolute authority. But Fichte was equally strong on personal freedom, arguing that an authoritarian

---

* "Ideas" here includes sensations, feelings, emotions, willing, and desires as well as intellectual concepts and arguments. Absolute idealism says there is nothing outside of consciousness, or that consciousness is not relative to things but things are relative to consciousness.

state and personal freedom did not contradict each other; in fact, they required each other. He did not deify the state, though he idealized it.

His metaphysics centers on the ego, which he virtually *did* deify. No preexisting world stands against the ego, once "things-in-themselves" are omitted; the whole order of nature, in Fichte's system, is created by the ego for its own self-realization. Nature is like a sparring partner for a boxer (the boxer being the ego).

What ego is that? The distinction between the subjective individual human ego and the single universal divine Ego is either not ultimately real or at least not very clear in Fichte.

What *is* clear is that Fichte was a pantheist. God cannot be a person, he argues, because persons are finite (they have limits, as nations have borders) and mutually exclusive (they stand outside each other), but there can be no being outside of the one Absolute, which is infinite. Fichte conceives God's infinity as a kind of all-inclusive spiritual ocean rather than an unlimited quantity of *specific attributes* as in orthodox Christian theology (e.g., infinitely good, not evil; living, not inert; conscious, not unconscious).

Fichte insisted that his philosophy was true to the "spirit" of Kantianism, even though Kant was horrified by it and explicitly repudiated it. Fichte replied that he was truer than Kant was to "the Holy Spirit in Kant"—very much like the "Catholic" theologians of the '60s and '70s who invoked "the spirit of Vatican II" to deny much of what Vatican II literally said.

So now with Fichte there are no "things-in-themselves" but only the all-creative power of the ego. We have absolute idealism. But if there is nothing but ideas, if there are no objective realities, no material objects and no objective truths outside subjective egos, minds, or wills, is objectivity therefore unreal? Is there nothing but ego? No—the ego, Fichte says, creates its own objects, the non-ego. Objectivity is kept, but it is redefined as intersubjectivity.

This is not one-to-one private, personal intersubjectivity; it arises only through something like Rousseau's "General Will." Thus arises the notion of "ideology" as a socially constructed system of "truths" that are correct not because they match objective reality but because they match the creativity of the General Will: they are "*politically* correct." There is a logical connection between epistemological idealism and "political correctness." There is no "objective truth." There is only ideology.

A Confession

I must add a personal note of confession here. Fichte is a very intelligent and clever thinker—indeed, his logic is often daunting, difficult, and demanding—but I have almost certainly failed to do justice to him because I simply cannot work up much sympathy for him at all. I find it easy to admire and learn from great thinkers that I passionately disagree with (e.g., Machiavelli, Hobbes, Hume,

Sartre, Nietzsche, and Marx), but I find it very difficult to learn from thinkers who seem to live in a totally different world than mine, which is mainly that of common sense. What would the world be like if Nietzsche were right? The answer is quite clear and conceivable. What would the world be like if Fichte were right? I cannot even begin to answer that question. To be honest, I'm not sure he could either. To be totally honest, I'm not sure he was even sane.

To this rational objection I must add a moral one. Fichte's philosophy looks to me like intellectual totalitarianism. And that is the very worst kind of totalitarianism because its victims are not just human bodies but human minds. Principled protest is always possible against any other kind of totalitarianism, but this kind makes such protest impossible because it admits no principles except those that arise from within itself. When absolute idealism becomes political, it becomes absolute ideologism.

66

FRIEDRICH WILHELM JOSEPH VON SCHELLING

AD 1775–1854

Shelling many oysters, you can find some pearls. This is also true for Schelling, as it is for many philosophers. For Schelling *is* many philosophers, not just one: his opinions and systems shifted many times, beginning with Fichteanism, passing through various experiments with idealistic systems that centered on the metaphysical status of nature, art, and religion, and ending with a turn toward the history of mythology and religion, which he eventually saw as more essential than abstract metaphysical philosophy.

The problem all these German metaphysicians are struggling with is the problem of the relation between subject ("I," self, ego) and object. They seem to imply each other, for every object I can point to is something *I point to* and therefore is in my consciousness and partakes of the nature of consciousness; on the other hand, every consciousness, if it is really conscious, is *really* conscious and thus partakes of reality or being. (It also seems to be a consciousness *of* some being.) Each is relative to the other, so neither subject nor object can be the Absolute.

Schelling, like Fichte, denied the existence of Kant's "things-in-themselves," but he also disagreed with the primacy of the subject or ego in Fichte. He argued that since ego and non-ego logically imply each other, each absolutely needs the other and defines the other. They have equal primacy. Schelling called his most definitive metaphysical system "the system of absolute identity"—the identity of subject and object, ego and non-ego. Ego implies non-ego, and their otherness implies an identity.

Schelling's primary historical importance is his influence on Hegel. Hegel would erect Schelling's three-step "dialectical" structure—a thesis and an opposing antithesis unified by a higher synthesis—into the structure of all thought and of all reality.

However, Hegel criticized Schelling's notion of the Absolute as a simple *identity* of subject and object as an empty and meaningless idea, "like the night in which all cows are black." It is neither subject nor object, and so it is nothing. Hegel's Absolute, in contrast, is everything; it includes all its particulars rather than abstracting from and excluding them. It is not just identity but identity-in-difference, or difference-in-identity. It is the whole process (of both thought and history) rather than its transcendent goal.

Schelling replied, against Hegel, that Schelling's Absolute seems like nothing only to conceptual thought, but it is everything to intuition. But this is an intuition that cannot be taught. For only what is finite and composite can be taught, by being defined, pointed to, and known by description. In contrast, a kind of intellectual mystical experience is necessary to know the Absolute.

Hegel rejected this as irrational. For Hegel, we know the Absolute by philosophy, not by mysticism. Reason can penetrate its inner essence. For Hegel, "the real is the rational and the rational is the real." Hegel was a philosophy professor, not a mystic.

Schelling, somewhat like Kierkegaard later, criticized Hegel as an essentialist, more interested in the essence of the Absolute than the existence of a God who could be personally encountered in real life, not just abstract thought—a living God who could actually save you from despair and evil. This is done by faith, not reason, for reason does not perceive the personal *need* for God, except to complete a system of ideas. A philosopher seeks a system, but "a person seeks a person."

Schelling criticized not only Hegel's theoretical, impersonal, intellectual pantheism but also Kant's practical, personal, volitional theism; for Kant used God simply as an instrument to unite virtue and happiness in the next life. Thus, argued Schelling, Kant treated God as a means rather than as an end, as Kant argued we should not ever do even to our fellow men.

67

GEORG WILHELM FRIEDRICH HEGEL

AD 1770–1831

Writing this chapter on Hegel was the hardest part of writing this book. It was exhausting, like climbing Mount Everest or falling to the bottom of the sea. And the most puzzling thing is that I'm not sure which of the two it was like.

Hegel's Historical Importance

There have been three ambitiously complete, rationally optimistic metaphysical systems in the history of philosophy, one ancient (Aristotle's), one medieval (Aquinas') and one modern (Hegel's). After each one, the philosophers of that era built no more but instead turned critical and skeptical and subjective. Hegel is to modern philosophy what Aristotle is to ancient philosophy and what Aquinas is to medieval philosophy:

1. He is its culmination, the summit of the mountain. There are no more Hegels after Hegel.
2. He is a synthesis of all the different insights of all philosophers before him.
3. He is the point of departure for all philosophers after him. Almost all subsequent philosophy is a departure from this single summit, a critique of it, a

series of tangents away from this center. "Away from Hegel" in many different directions is the road map of the rest of philosophy.

None of these three historical points means that Hegel was right. As one writer (Henry Aiken) put it, in *The Age of Ideology*: "Concerning no other major philosopher is opinion so divided. Some regard him, as Thomas Aquinas regarded Aristotle, as 'The Philosopher,' in whose commodious system all of the chickens of earlier philosophers have at last come home to roost. Others consider him to be 'the greatest mistake' in the history of philosophy. In a way, this is odd, since . . . as a human being Hegel is uninteresting; he lived, apparently, for no other purpose than that of playing secretary to the Absolute."

Kierkegaard said that if Hegel had only added a single sentence after all his works, he would have been regarded as the greatest philosopher who ever lived; but for lack of this single sentence, he must be regarded as a buffoon, a comic figure. The sentence is "Everything I have ever written is an elaborate joke." (Kierkegaard apparently did not know that that is almost exactly what St. Thomas Aquinas did when he stopped writing before he died, calling all his works "straw.")

Actually, Hegel said something almost as funny as that on his deathbed: "Nobody has understood me except one, and he also misunderstood."

William James wrote that it was only under the influence of the hallucinogenic drug nitrous oxide that he could understand Hegel.

There are at least five reasons why more philosophers regard Hegel as an embarrassment than any other:

1. his exaltation of the state as "the divine Idea on earth," a notion the Nazis conveniently exploited;
2. the arrogance apparent in his claim to have penetrated, by speculative philosophical reason, the inner life and essence of the Absolute;
3. the extremely abstract concepts of his system, which gives the impression of an enormous, elaborate spiderweb of ideas;
4. his habit of qualifying everything and turning every idea inside out, upside down, and backwards; and
5. the difficulty of his terminology. Someone should have translated him—into German.

Yet all this is strangely impressive. Simon Critchley, in *The Book of Dead Philosophers*, says his philosophy resembles the Brooklyn Bridge: "vast, heavy, Gothic, and incredibly solid." Like a bridge, it joins and reconciles two opposite places. There is actually a historical connection here: Hegel's student John Augustus Roebling, who wrote a two-thousand-page thesis on Hegel, invented a new technique for bridge building using wire ropes and was awarded the commission for designing the Brooklyn Bridge.

Hegel's Historicism

The one idea of Hegel's that has been the most widely accepted, both by philosophers and non-philosophers, is also the one that is the most radically new. (This was true of Kant also, remember: his "Copernican revolution in philosophy" was both his most radical and his most influential idea.) In a word, this is Hegel's *historicism*. As Kant made truth relative to the mind, Hegel made it relative to history.

All thinkers before Hegel assumed that at least some truth is unchanging, and—unless they were total skeptics—that we could know at least some of these unchanging truths. Even Hume and Kant assumed that the nature of reason, or mind, or consciousness, and therefore the nature of truth, is the same for everyone and for all times. That is the assumption Hegel denies.

Only four philosophers have influenced human thinking so much that historians use their names to classify all philosophers before or after them: Socrates, Descartes, Kant, and Hegel. Thus, we speak of "pre-Socratic," "pre-Cartesian," "post-Kantian," and "post-Hegelian" philosophy. And historicism is Hegel's lasting legacy. In most intellectual circles today, it is simply taken for granted that to understand a philosophy or an ideology is to understand its history—that not just external events but consciousness itself, or the forms of consciousness, or any given form of consciousness, is historically relative and must be understood in terms of its history.

One good reason for studying the history of philosophy is to discover that the very idea of historicism, or historical relativism, is historically relative. One good reason for studying logic is to learn to ask questions like this: If truth changes with history, does *that* truth also change with history, so that at some time truth does *not* change with history?

The Idea of Progress

The idea of the evolution of thought was not an application or consequence of Darwin's theory of the evolution of biological species; in fact, the idea of evolution was fashionable *before* Darwin. It is closer to the truth to say that Darwin applied Hegelianism to biology than to say that Hegel applied Darwinism to philosophy. (In fact, Hegel *denied* Darwin's theory in biology.) Unlike most other "Enlightenment" philosophers, Hegel was much less interested in science than in politics and history.

The idea of progress—inevitable, long-term, ubiquitous, overall progress—and an optimism about man and his future, had been assumed by nearly all intellectuals since Descartes. (Pascal and Rousseau were the two major exceptions among philosophers.) It was almost unimaginably exciting for Hegel to live in such times. Hegel was a Prussian, yet when Napoleon rode through the Prussian city of Jena in *conquest* of Prussia in the Franco-Prussian war, Hegel wrote, "I saw the World-Spirit on horseback marching through the city of Jena."

Hegel also wrote, "A new epoch has arisen in the world. It seems that the World-Spirit has now succeeded in freeing itself from all alien objective existence and is apprehending itself at last as absolute Spirit." He was writing of his own philosophy here, and by "the World-Spirit" he meant an immanent and evolving God, which had grown throughout the history of consciousness, with its public and self-conscious epiphany culminating in Hegel's own philosophy. Not a bad job for a dull professor: to be the intellectual obstetrician for God's birth.

Hegel sincerely believed in the providential task of Germany to be the instrument of enlightenment and reason for the world. After all, half the geniuses of the eighteenth century were Germanic: Leibniz, Wolff, Kant, Fichte, Schelling, Hegel, Goethe, Schiller, Hölderlin, Novalis, Herder, Beethoven, Mozart, Brahms.

The French Revolution produced tremendous excitement and optimism among almost all European "liberal" intellectuals. Historic change was being made under their eyes. Something had been born that could never again be unborn. Reason had triumphed in history. Hegel wrote,

> It is not difficult to see that ours is a birth-time and a period of transition to a new era. Spirit has broken with the world it has hitherto inhabited. . . . Spirit is indeed never at rest but always engaged in moving forward. But just as the first breath drawn by a child after a long, quiet nourishment breaks the gradualness of merely quantitative growth—there is a qualitative leap, and the child is born—so likewise . . . the gradual crumbling that left unaltered the face of the whole is cut short by a sunburst which, in one flash, illuminates the features of the new world.

The "gradual crumbling" of the ancient regime referred not only to politics but also to religion. It was a nearly unanimous consensus among European "Enlightenment" liberals—in fact, of every major modern philosopher, to some degree, except Pascal and Kierkegaard—that traditional, historic Christianity, Protestant or Catholic, had to be fundamentally changed to adapt to this new world of ideas. Though the philosophers uniformly praised Christian morality (at least until Nietzsche), two features of Christian theology seemed unacceptable to them: supernaturalism and sin. Supernaturalism involved miracles, which the scientifically oriented thinkers thought contradicted modern science; and sin seemed, to the humanistically oriented thinkers, an insulting, pessimistic, and confining notion.

Hegel's New Logic: The Dialectic

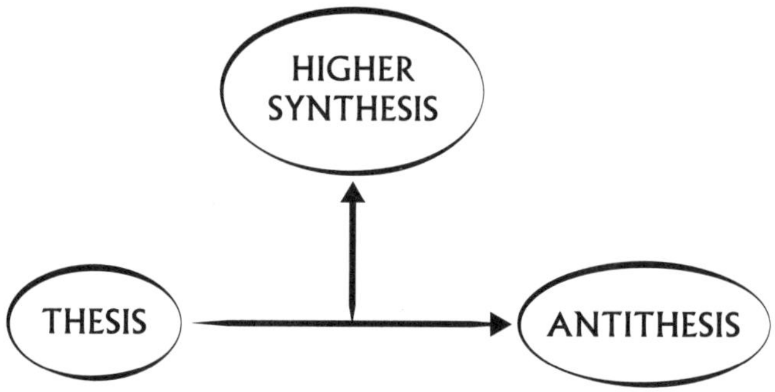

The idea of progress was so dominant in Hegel that it even radically altered logic, the one division of philosophy that had seemed timeless. Where the old logic of Aristotle was the logic of the *logos* (i.e., of the timeless relations among concepts and essences), Hegel's new "dialectical" logic is the logic of progressive change. It is the logic of repeatedly recurring stages of thesis, antithesis, and synthesis on ever higher levels.

It is at the same time the logic (1) of the evolution of God (who, according to Hegel, is in process, not eternal, actual, or complete);* (2) of human consciousness; (3) of human history; (4) of abstract concepts; and (5) of the nature of being, or reality. In other words, it is the logic of what previous thinkers would classify as (1) theology, (2) psychology, (3) history, (4) logic, and (5) metaphysics. Hegel virtually identifies these five things.

God, or "the Absolute," as Hegel prefers to call him (or, rather, it), is Spirit; and Spirit is, for Hegel, always in a *relation* to itself. This relation is dynamic and unstable, always involving conflict between subject and object, self and other. Spirit always overcomes this conflict in a higher synthesis in which both thesis and antithesis are perfected rather than compromised. Then this new synthesis becomes another thesis evoking another antithesis and another synthesis, et cetera, et cetera. Hegel seldom uses the terms "thesis, antithesis, synthesis," but the entirety of his thought is "dialectical." W.T. Stace's summary of Hegel contains a 24-by-24-inch chart, in small print, containing no less than a hundred Hegelian triads, triads of triads, etc. It is a map of absolutely everything, including the Absolute: a map of the Mind of God. And everything is inside.

In this sense Hegel is a pantheist, though unlike pantheists like Parmenides or Shankara he does not deny nature or man or distinctions as illusory but preserves

* For Hegel, God doesn't quite fully exist yet, but he's living in hopes.

them as parts or aspects or stages of the evolution of God's self-consciousness, which, for Hegel, is really the one and only thing that has ever happened.

Take anything—any abstract idea (like "being") or any concrete reality (like "selfishness")—as a thesis. When he examines it, Hegel finds that it necessarily involves its own opposite or antithesis. "Being" is so abstracted from all differences that there is nothing left in it, so that it is really "nothing." It becomes its opposite. Selfishness, or self-interest, requires other people, first to compete against and to conquer, and then, once one realizes that this does *not* fulfill one's own self-interest, to work for and with altruistically. (The only way to be happy is to forget your own happiness and work for others' happiness.) But then comes the higher synthesis. Since "being" passes into "nonbeing" and "nonbeing" passes into "being" (for nonbeing is relative to being), we arrive at the concept of passing-into, or "becoming," which synthesizes being and nonbeing. And both self-interest and altruism are synthesized and perfected by cooperation, community, and identifying with a larger whole: the state.

The Dialectic and Noncontradiction

Kant had said that reason, when it tries to do objective, "transcendent" metaphysics, always lands in contradictions or "antinomies." E.g., reason can both prove and disprove (1) the existence of God; (2) free will; (3) indivisible, simple elements; and (4) an absolute beginning to time, with equally valid arguments. Kant thought these contradictions invalidated metaphysics. But Hegel accepted such contradictions as inherent in and revelatory of the metaphysical nature of things. Kant saw that every thesis in metaphysics generated its own antithesis, but he did not see that they can both be true if seen from the higher and more inclusive standpoint of a synthesis.

Logical critics of Hegel accuse him of denying the logical law of noncontradiction, but this is a misunderstanding, for two reasons.

First of all, Hegel is dealing with concepts here rather than propositions, and thus with contraries rather than true contradictories. You can be both visible (if you are a body) and invisible (if you are a soul), and you can both love and hate the same person at the same time. Those are not contradictions. But having and not having a soul at the same time is a contradiction, and so is loving and not loving the same person at the same time.

Second, Hegel's dialectic does not deny but presupposes and uses the law of noncontradiction. Precisely because we cannot be satisfied with the contradiction between a thesis and an antithesis, we must rise to the higher synthesis, where the lower two moments are no longer in contradiction.

Yet to say, as Hegel does, that being and nonbeing are the same does seem illogical. He admits that "the proposition that Being and Nothing are the same is so paradoxical to the imagination or [ordinary] understanding that it is perhaps taken for a joke." And he calls it "one of the hardest things thought expects itself to do."

Hegel's Metaphysics of Absolute Idealism

For Hegel, logic and metaphysics are identical. The dialectic is a law of thought and a law of being, since for Hegelian idealism thought and being are one thing, not two things. Thus, logic and metaphysics are identical, because on the one hand, logic is not about concepts *as distinct from* realities, and on the other hand, metaphysics is not about realities *as distinct from* concepts, realities understood as the real *objects* of concepts or consciousness, as in epistemological realism; rather, metaphysics is about consciousness itself, which is the very nature of reality according to idealism. Hegel makes this point by his famous equation: "The real is the rational and the rational is the real."

Hegel's argument for this idealism and against realism, which *distinguishes* (1) appearances (or beliefs, or ideas, or consciousness, or reason, or mind, or spirit) and (2) reality, is that it is self-contradictory to speak of a reality that is opposed to appearance, a reality that in no way appears or manifests itself in consciousness; for if reality did not appear to our consciousness, we could not speak of it at all. In other words, the distinction between (1) appearance and (2) reality, or (1) consciousness and (2) its object, appears only *within consciousness* rather than *between* (1) consciousness and (2) reality or "things-in-themselves."

To put the same Hegelian point in still other words, once Kant sets up his distinction between appearances ("phenomena") and reality ("noumena" or "things-in-themselves"), the distinction collapses as self-contradictory, as Fichte showed. And since we cannot deny appearances (for they *do* appear), we must deny "things-in-themselves" and embrace absolute idealism, like Hegel, instead of "critical idealism," like Kant.

(Kant stoutly maintained he was *not* an idealist, but he meant by "idealism" the metaphysical idea that only spirit, and not matter, was real. However, he is often classified as an *epistemological* idealist because he maintained that our ideas [the forms and categories of perception, logic, and pure reason] actively structure reality rather than receptively mirror it and correspond to it: "the Copernican revolution in philosophy.")

Kant's distinction between appearances and realities ("phenomena" and "noumena") was not, however, the same as that of Socrates, Plato, and Aristotle, all of whom were realists. *They* all said we *could* know things in themselves, and only by that standard could we judge some appearances as conforming to these realities and others as failing to conform to them. Only if we know not just ideas but realities can we distinguish true ideas from false ideas.

Hegel's Absolute Idealism as His Solution to the Fundamental Problem of Modern Philosophy, the Critique of Reason

Beginning with Descartes, the primary problem of modern philosophy is the critique of reason, the overcoming of skepticism by examining philosophy's instrument, proving that reason "works." But Hegel points out, "In the case of other instruments, we can try to critique them in other ways than by doing the very work these instruments are designed to do. But the critique of knowledge can only be done by an act of knowledge. To 'examine' this so-called instrument is the same thing as to *know* it. But to seek to know before we know is as absurd as . . . not to venture into the water until you learned to swim." Descartes' critique of reason, of all reason, of reason as such, can only be done by a particular act of reason. Why should that act, the act of the critique of reason, be exempt from the critique? All the prisoners are on trial; why should one of them be the judge?

Premodern philosophers began with metaphysics, with being. Modern philosophers typically begin with epistemology, with consciousness, with Descartes' "cogito" ("I think"). Then they try to find the bridge between this subjective consciousness and objective reality; to get out of the mind and avoid solipsism.* Each one, however, finds himself confined, by his starting point, to his own mental states. Hegel concludes that if all philosophers have been forced to the conclusion that only minds, ideas, or mental states can be known, that must be because that is all that exists. Reality as such is spirit, or mind, or idea. That is the essence of metaphysical idealism.

Kant had posited the existence of unknowable "things-in-themselves" in addition to consciousness, but this was shown to be a self-contradiction by his successors: it was a case of knowing the unknowable. Once the "things-in-themselves" are dropped, only consciousness is left. But *whose* consciousness? Mine? That would be solipsism. The alternative is God, the Absolute, Absolute Spirit, Thought Thinking Itself through nature and man. (And that man is Hegel!)

This Absolute Consciousness is not consciousness *of* anything outside itself (that would be realism) because there *is* nothing outside itself: that is idealism. All finite determinations—nature, time, space, things, man, history, philosophy, the rise of self-consciousness—are "inside" Absolute Consciousness itself.

Therefore, the question of how we know that our thoughts are true, how we know that they correspond to reality, is not solved but dissolved. The presupposition of that commonsense question is realism, the idea that objective reality exists and is the goal and object of our knowledge. Hegel denies that presupposition.

---

* Solipsism is the belief ("ism") that only the self (*solus ipse*) exists. There is a delightfully humorous little science fiction story about this philosophy:

Thought is not true because it corresponds to some objective reality outside it—there is nothing outside it, so it cannot possibly fail to correspond. It can't lose. It's a fixed fight. The two boxers are really the same person. Truth is not the *correspondence* between idea and reality, but the *coherence* of the idea with itself and with other ideas.

(But, one may ask, is *this* situation really objective reality, a "thing-in-itself," and the way things really are? If so, we are back in realism. If not, Hegel's whole philosophy is not *true*, it just *is*, like a dream.)

Idealism is also Hegel's solution to the puzzle that has been called "the gnoseo-ontological circle." *Gnosis* means "knowledge," and *ontological* means "about being," so the "circle" is the problem that all knowledge is being *and* all being is knowledge. On the one hand, knowledge, in order to be real knowledge, has to be real, has to be a case in point of being, surrounded by being, logically subordinate to being. Being must be predicated of it. On the other hand, I cannot deny that being must be known, must be surrounded by knowledge, logically subordinate to knowledge. For as soon as I *think* or *say* that *x* is a being, I assume the *knowledge* of this being that is *x*. Kantian "unknowables" cannot be known. If being is not in knowledge, I cannot know it. But if knowledge is not in being, it cannot be.

Walter B. Jehovah, for whose name I make no apology since it really was his name, had been a solipsist all his life. A solipsist, in case you don't happen to know the word, is one who believes that he himself is the only thing that really exists, that other people and the universe in general exist only in his imagination, and that if he quit imagining them they would cease to exist.

One day Walter B. Jehovah became a practicing solipsist. Within a week his wife had run away with another man, he'd lost his job as a shipping clerk, and he had broken his leg chasing a black cat to keep it from crossing his path.

He decided, in his bed at the hospital, to end it all.

Looking out the window, staring up at the stars, he wished them out of existence, and they weren't there anymore. Then he wished all other people out of existence and the hospital became strangely quiet even for a hospital. Next, the world, and he found himself suspended in a void. He got rid of his body quite as easily and then he took the final step of willing *himself* out of existence.

Nothing happened.

Strange, he thought, can there be a limit to solipsism?

"Yes," a voice said.

"Who are you?" asked Walter B. Jehovah.

"I am the one who created the universe you have now just willed out of existence. And now that you have taken my place—" There was a deep sigh. "—I can finally cease my own existence, find oblivion, and let you take over."

"But—how can *I* cease to exist? That's what I'm trying to do, you know."

"Yes, I know," said the voice. "You must do it the same way I did. Create a universe. Wait till someone in it really believes what you believed and wills it out of existence. Then you can retire and let him take over. Goodbye now."

And the voice was gone.

Walter B. Jehovah was alone in the void and there was only one thing he could do. He created the heaven and the earth.

It took him seven days.

("Solipsist" by Frederick Brown, from *Star Shine* [New York: Bantam, 1956])

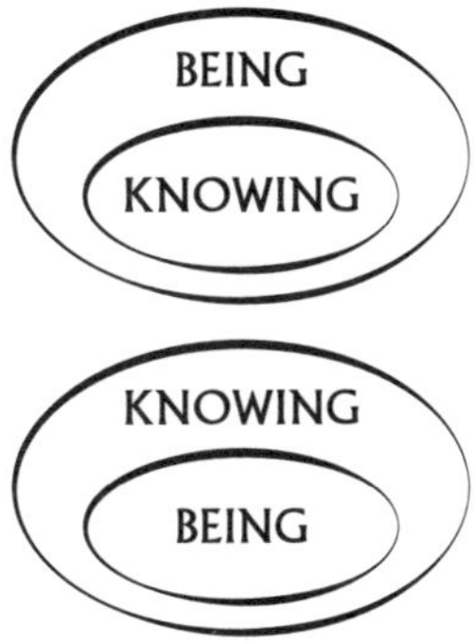

Hegel's solution to this circle is simple: it is the *identification* of being and knowledge. That is the essence of idealism. They are not two things related in a logically paradoxical way; they are the same thing. "The real *is* the rational [knowable] and the rational *is* the real."

Realism distinguishes appearance from reality, the subjective from the objective, thought from being. For instance, the stick appears bent in the water but is really straight; the politician seems to be the people's savior but is really their tyrant. But, Hegel points out, this distinction only arises *within consciousness*. Once consciousness is conscious of itself as well as its object, it becomes divided, and only then can it become aware of any distinction between appearance and reality. Thus reality, the object of consciousness, is created by consciousness. (Does that last sentence logically follow from the ones before it?)

In other words, consciousness is like *Brahman* in Shankara's Hinduism. The universe is not his creation but his dream. And as with Shankara, for Hegel, the Absolute, or Spirit, or Consciousness is not a Person distinct from other persons; you cannot really have any kind of personal relationship with the Absolute as you can with the God of Judaism, Christianity, and Islam. According to Hegel, religion (in the West) uses this pictorial, concrete language of a dualism between God and man, Creator and creature, because the masses cannot understand speculative philosophy in the abstract. Hegel has a gnostic "double truth" theory, like Averroes in the Middle Ages (see vol. 2, chaps. 47–51).

Concrete Universals and Internal Relations

In Aristotelian logic and metaphysics, universals are abstract because they are abstracted from concrete particular substances (e.g., humanity from Socrates and Plato and Xanthippe or blueness from the sky, the sea, and Frank Sinatra's eyes). But for Hegel, concreteness and particularity are opposites. The "bare particular" (like Socrates) is abstract; only the concrete universal (humanity) is fully real. You become a real human being not by your individual uniqueness but by your identification with the Whole, and with the state, which incarnates the Whole. "The true is the Whole."

Apart from its relations to everything else, an individual is merely a "bare" particular and an abstraction from the more-real, concrete Whole. Every particular is defined, essentially, by its relations to everything else. Relations are not extrinsic and accidental but intrinsic and essential. I am not an individual human being first and then, in addition, a son, husband, father, and citizen. I become an individual only by these relations; I am defined by them. In other words, there are no really separate individual substances. Everything is like a leaf of a tree, an organ in a body, a water droplet in a cloud.

And the ultimate reason for this is the master idea of historicism. Everything is part of a single great process.* There are no substances because nothing is static. Nothing stands still and is simply itself. "The seeds of everything are in everything," as Anaxagoras said, because "everything flows," as Heraclitus said (see vol. 1, chaps. 13, 18). There is in you a little bit of your grandmother and a little bit of the chemicals from the sun and a little bit of your enemy and a little bit of the dinosaurs.

For Aristotle there were many substances, made of form and matter, which were related externally and accidentally to each other, like a bat and a ball. For Descartes, there were two kinds of substances, mind and matter, and the relation between the two was problematic (the "mind-body problem"). For Spinoza there was only one substance, God. For Leibniz there was a plurality of independent substances ("windowless monads"). For Hegel, the common mistake of all these previous philosophers was to locate reality in substances rather than relations. Hegel argues that if we locate reality in substances, we cannot do justice to relations, for if reality is primarily substances, and relations are outside substances, then relations are unreal;† but if we locate reality in relations, then substances are also real because substances are within relations, for you cannot have a relation without its two substantial terms. For Hegel, to be is to be related. Substance is relative to relation, not vice versa. Relation is more substantial than substance. Substance is more relative than relation.

Hegel admits that ordinary, practical thought needs to distinguish different substances (e.g., poison and non-poison, friend and enemy, road and ditch) and needs to see each thing as itself and not its opposite. Thus arises the law of noncontradiction. But, he argues, philosophical thought passes beyond this, for it sees that the idea of an isolated, separate substance falls apart when we try to think it out, and so the philosophical, dialectical thinking passes beyond noncon-

* Parmenides and Zeno taught that everything is one and timeless (change is illusory). Democritus taught that everything is many and changing. Hegel taught that everything is one and changing.

† Would Aristotle agree? How would he answer this argument of Hegel's? Is there a third possible position between these two concerning substance and relation?

tradiction and embraces contradiction. (Derrida's deconstructionism inherits and uses this denial of the law of noncontradiction from Hegel. See vol. 4, chap. 95.)

Thus, Hegel is an esoteric, gnostic thinker, distinguishing two very different modes or levels of thought: the ordinary, practical, commonsense consciousness, which is based on what he will call "sense-certainty" (see below, stage one of the "phenomenology of spirit"), versus the philosophical consciousness. For ordinary consciousness, A is not non-A and being is *not* nonbeing. Things stay put. But for philosophical consciousness, being *is* nonbeing, because nothing stays put. Everything turns into its opposite, and thus moves the dialectic onward and upward.

The Phenomenology of Spirit

Hegel does not merely *say* this and *argue* for it: he *shows* it. And that is what he calls "phenomenology." It is not a method of proof but of seeing, in which "all that is left for us to do is simply to look on." *The Phenomenology of Spirit* is like a movie.

Its title could be "The History of Everything." For when we look at Hegel's movie, we will see everything in its historical place and stage. For we will see Spirit, or Consciousness, or God, evolving through dialectical stages.

We could call this "The Odyssey of Consciousness," the long adventure of the wily hero Odysseus (Consciousness) to his proper home and identity. Or we could call it "Following Brahman's Dream." *The Phenomenology of Spirit* is a biography of God, from the most infantile stage, "sense-certainty," which is essentially commonsense realism, to its fully grown stage of "absolute knowledge," which is God knowing and being himself, God finally becoming a Hegelian idealist.

Philosophy's name for the protagonist of this story is "Consciousness" or "Spirit." Myth may name it a semi-divine hero like Odysseus or Hercules. Religion calls it "God" or "Brahman." But the pictorial images used by myth and religion are misleading, for Spirit is not a heroic demigod (Odysseus or Hercules) or an eternally perfect, transcendent, personal creator (God or Allah); nor is it a single, simple, changeless, infinite, mystical reality (*Brahman* or Buddha-consciousness); it is a historical process with an inherent dialectical, finite structure.

Are these stages of consciousness that Hegel traces in his *Phenomenology* stages in *God's* consciousness, in *human* consciousness, or in the logical movement of *ideas*? All three. For these three are, for Hegel, ultimately the same reality looked at from different points of view.

And what is the history of *human* consciousness? Is it the history of a single *individual* from infancy to maturity? Or is it the history of human consciousness *collectively*, from primitive to sophisticated? Or is it the history of the *expressions* of consciousness in world history? Again, it is all three.

1. The first stage of consciousness Hegel calls "sense-certainty." It is the simple and immediate presence of some object to your consciousness, like this book: an object, a "this," presented to a subject, an "I." Sense-certainty makes no judgments about the object; it does not yet use universal concepts or terms like "square" or "long" or "white."

   And here is the shock, the dialectical contradiction that makes consciousness move away from sense-certainty: "Because of its concrete content, sense-certainty immediately appears as the *richest* kind of knowledge [and] . . . the *truest* knowledge; for it has not as yet omitted anything from the object [by abstraction], but has the object before it in its perfect entirety. But . . . this very 'certainty' proves to be the most abstract and poorest 'truth.'"

   Sense-certainty knows nothing. We can't say *what* it is, because we have no universal terms yet. It is preverbal. Sense-certainty utters no judgments because it has no concepts, no universals, no laws, no explanations, no relations, no ordering—no *logos*. It can only point and grunt. Its object is a "bare particular," a "this," abstract and empty. It thus is unstable, and necessarily moves away from what it is and toward that which it is not yet, that which it lacks. It becomes its own opposite. The dialectic of consciousness moves it on to compensate for its inadequacies, like an inherent genetic program in a body that makes it grow into its opposite, into that which it is not (yet).
2. This next, opposite stage Hegel calls "perception." In it, objects are understood by universal concepts (like "white" or "square" or "book").
3. Then, in "understanding," they are understood in terms of *laws*, as in Newtonian physics, which do not merely describe but explain things.
4. Consciousness then realizes that it itself has actively demanded these explanations and created these laws, and it thus becomes "self-consciousness." This is a radically new stage.

   Like Buddha, Hegel sees "desire" as the most basic form of self-consciousness. Why? Because consciousness is divided into its subject and its object, self and other; and when it is self-conscious, it desires objects—food, money, sex, information—because it is aware that it is not everything, that it lacks things. The self by nature subordinates all other things to itself. Desire is a stomach, and its objects are food.

   But then the self finds itself confronted with not just other objects but with another desiring subject, another self, another stomach that desires the same food. The other self is its natural rival. It wants to reduce the other subject to an object, to more food for itself, thus annihilating the other's subjectivity. (Sartre [see vol. 4, chap. 76] famously exposes this "dark side" of the self.)
5. As always in Hegel, the dialectic prods consciousness on. There is a negative hidden in consciousness' positive hope, a defeat in its victory. For it discovers that

a destruction of the other would defeat its own purpose, since what it desires is that the other self should recognize it as a self. I cannot simply "eat" the other, for I do not want to shatter the mirror of the other in which I become myself. In fact, Hegel says (and most psychologists say that this is a profoundly true discovery) it is only in mutual recognition, only in a "we," that "I" consciousness, self-consciousness, is born. "They recognize themselves as mutually recognizing each other." (Compare Levinas on this: vol. 4, chap. 94.) Self-consciousness is necessarily social. The "I" and the "Thou" are born together, as twins.

Before this stage, I could still know objective *facts about* myself, and about another self, such as height or intelligence. But knowledge of self *as subject*, as the person who *has* all these qualities, comes only mutually, when I recognize the same subjectivity in others and recognize that the other recognizes this same subjecthood or personhood in me. This is the Hegelian theoretical basis for Kant's "categorical imperative." (Do you see why?) But in practice it is not easy. It is a struggle—against egotism.

6. Out of the struggle between egotism and altruism emerges a compromise, "the master-slave relationship." The stronger self makes the weaker one its slave, thus apparently achieving both of its goals: control of the other and recognition by the other.

   But this, too, is negative and unstable. For recognition by a mere slave is not what the self wants. (It's like Groucho Marx's famous line: "I wouldn't want to join any club that would have somebody like me as a member.") Only a free self's recognition of my own free selfhood can count. Thus, enslaving the other is as counterproductive as killing or eating the other.

7. Ironically, the next stage in the evolution of consciousness, "self-realization through labor," emerges not in the master but in the slave. The slave does the master's menial, physical work, and in so doing achieves something the master does not: in putting himself into his work, into the products of his labor, he puts his work into himself, so to speak. He synthesizes self and world, humanizes his world, turns mere things into *his* things: his farm, his shack, his shoes.

   A little later, Karl Marx emphasized this part of Hegel's dialectic, though in a purely materialistic way, saying that if the slave, or the proletariat, cannot own the products of his labor that give him his identity, he is alienated from himself; and this is his deepest critique of capitalism.

8. The next stage Hegel calls "Stoic consciousness." Both masters (Emperor Marcus Aurelius) and slaves (Epictetus) can be Stoics, because Stoics identify themselves only with their own interiority, interior freedom, and self-sufficiency. Epictetus says, "You are not made miserable by things [most of which you cannot control] but by the view you take of things [which is under your control]." Whether your world makes you a master or a slave, you can always control your own attitudes,

beliefs, and desires, and thus your own freedom and happiness, by disidentifying with the outside world. If it gives you lemons, you make lemonade.

This, says Hegel, is also both positive and negative. It is a positive stage in self-consciousness and freedom, but it is only freedom in thought, not life. The Stoic has to abstract himself from his external life, and disvalue external life in order to value himself. He is not free *in* life but free *from* life.

9. "Skeptical consciousness" is the next stage, reached when everything external is doubted (as in Descartes) while self alone is affirmed. Hegel says that "skepticism is the realization of that of which Stoicism was only the notion"—namely, the negation of the world.

   But skepticism, too, is unstable. Skeptics cannot live in the world, because they cannot make judgments; they cannot distinguish appearances and reality. But they need to, in order to live. As Pascal says, "Nature backs up helpless reason."

10. The contradiction inherent in skepticism evolves into "the unhappy consciousness," which is a divided consciousness. It identifies with its own ideal self—wise and good—but knows that its real self is unwise and bad. It is the master-slave relationship come back, this time within the same self.

    The ideal self is then projected outward into a God-figure, considered as an independently existing being, a perfect self. (This *seems* to make Hegel an atheist. Instead of God creating us, we created him.) The "unhappy consciousness" is essentially the religious consciousness. St. Paul's complaint in Romans 7 is the classic expression of it: "The good that I will, I do not do; the evil that I abhor, I do."

11. Hegel called Christianity "the absolute religion" because he interpreted it as a primitive, mythic, pictorial version of his own philosophy. He interpreted Christ as *overcoming* the Jewish objectification of God as an infinitely perfect being distinct from finite and imperfect human beings (Hegel called this "the bad infinite"), and not as God become man but as a man who discovered the Infinite as immanent within himself (which is "the good infinite"). He praised Christ's love ethic and life of love as the lived synthesis of the infinite and the finite, the divine and the human, which was his reinterpretation of the central Christian dogma of the Incarnation. He called Christ divine, but not *uniquely* divine ("the *only-begotten* Son of God," as the Nicene Creed says), for the Absolute lives in all of us. Thus, Christianity is a stage of progress, but only a stage, in the evolution of Spirit. It overcomes "the unhappy consciousness." (Poor unhappy St. Paul seems to have been not quite a Christian. If only he had had Hegel to teach him!)

12. So far there have been two basic stages of consciousness: three before self-consciousness (1–3) and eight within it (4–11). We now enter the third and final basic stage, in which we transcend even self-consciousness. Here the

cosmic odyssey of Spirit, God, or Consciousness is completed. It now sees everything in its own past as its own work, from initial "sense-certainty," through all the other stages, to its projection of itself into a God-figure and its overcoming of this self-created alienation. Everywhere it looks it sees nothing but itself. There *is* only itself, under many names: being, becoming, consciousness, Mind, Spirit, God, and the Absolute.

Hegel realizes that this pantheism seems shocking to ordinary people, but he explains the shock as the residue of "sense-certainty" (epistemological realism) in us. On the level of sensation, it does not *seem* that we ourselves create what appears when we open our eyes; and we therefore also think of God, or Absolute Consciousness, as being just as objective, just as *other*, as the material universe. But this is an illusion. Though Hegel does not put it so baldly, we *are* God. (Does this mean that the snake in the garden was right when he said, "You shall be as God"? Was the apple Hegelianism?)

Hegel's ultimate realization is thus very similar to that of Hinduism: *tat tvam asi*, "thou art that" (see vol. 1, chap. 3). But "enlightenment" for Hegel comes not through arduous yoga and mystical experience but through philosophical reason. "Reason is the certainty of consciousness that it [consciousness] is all reality."

Simple religious believers, in every religion, think and live by faith. Believers who are also philosophers, like St. Thomas Aquinas, join faith and reason. Kant limited reason, he said, to make room for faith. But for Hegel there is no need for faith. Faith relies on an *other*, but there is no other to Consciousness. In its final stage, Consciousness finally realizes this: that all the details, all the stages, all the finitude, and all the negativity—all of which was quite real, and not an illusion, as it is said to be in most other pantheisms—was only within itself. Even nature was its own objectification. (Sounds pretty flattering: my true self is not only Einstein but the designer of Einstein's universe! Imagine how shocked Hegel would be if he met God after death and God said to him what he said to St. Catherine, summing up all divine revelation in four words: "I'm God. You're not.")

Hegel's Philosophy of History

The philosophical recognition on the part of Consciousness that it is all of reality is not yet the end of Hegel's dialectic, for Consciousness must also actually *make* itself real by actualizing itself in history, rather like a singer singing the music he has made up in his head.

When he speaks of history, Hegel calls this Consciousness, or Spirit, "the World-Spirit." This is Consciousness manifesting itself in the world of history; it is God (not the biblical God, of course) coming to self-realization through human minds and human history. In other words, we are God's obstetrics ward.

Therefore, to the philosophical mind there are no dark corners, no mysteries, to history. For there is no *other*, no "things-in-themselves"; there is only Consciousness, which is Reason. ("The real is the rational and the rational is the real.") Thus, Hegel says in the introduction to his *Philosophy of History*,

> The only Thought which Philosophy brings with it to the contemplation of History, is the simple conception of *Reason*; that Reason is the Sovereign of the World, that the history of the world, therefore, presents us with a rational process. . . . On the one hand, Reason is the *substance* of the Universe; viz., that by which and in which all reality has its being and subsistence. On the other hand, it is the *Infinite Energy* of the Universe; since Reason is not so powerless as to be incapable of producing anything but a mere ideal, a mere intention, having its place outside reality, nobody knows where, something separate and abstract, in the heads of certain human beings. It is *the infinite complex of things*, their entire Essence and Truth. . . . That this "Idea" or "Reason" is the *True*, the *Eternal*, the absolutely *powerful* essence; that it reveals itself in the World, and that in that World nothing else is revealed but this and its honor and glory—is the thesis which, as we have said, has been proved in Philosophy, and is here regarded as demonstrated.

The reader might want to turn to the last section of this chapter and read the satirical words of Kierkegaard at this point, as a kind of mental *rinse*. Then again, he might want to listen to Hegel's answer to the charge that this is a ridiculously optimistic picture of history:

> Nothing great in the world has been accomplished without passion. . . . Passions, private aims, and the satisfaction of selfish desires are . . . tremendous springs of action. Their power lies in the fact that they respect none of the limitations which law and morality would impose on them; and that these natural impulses are closer to the core of human nature than the artificial and troublesome discipline that tends toward order, self-restraint, law, and morality. [Contrast all classical philosophers, from Socrates through Aquinas, on this point. Hegel is here siding with Rousseau against Kant. He is a Romantic as well as a rationalist.]
>
> When we contemplate the display of passions and the consequences of their violence, the unreason which is associated not only with them, but even—rather we might say *especially*—with *good* designs and righteous aims, when we see arising therefrom the evil, the vice, the ruin that has befallen the most flourishing kingdoms which the mind of man ever created, we can hardly avoid being filled with sorrow at this universal

> taint of corruption. And since this decay is not the work of mere nature, but of human will, our reflections may well lead us to a moral sadness, a revolt of the good will. . . . Without rhetorical exaggeration, a simple, truthful account of the miseries that have overwhelmed the noblest of nations and polities and the finest exemplars of private virtue forms a most fearful picture and excites emotions of the profoundest and most hopeless sadness, counterbalanced by no consoling result. . . .
>
> But even regarding History as the slaughter bench at which the happiness, wisdom, and virtue of peoples have been sacrificed, the question naturally arises: To what principle, to what final purpose, have these monstrous sacrifices been offered?

It is all for the self-realization of Spirit, of course. And this is supposed to be an explanation that satisfies us! Inquisitors burned heretics and crusaders slaughtered Jews and Muslims "for the greater glory of God"; Hegel's Spirit seems to practice a similar morality and a similar justification.

Hegel says we should be reconciled to this system and accept the world as it is: "The insight to which . . . philosophy should lead us is that the actual world is as it ought to be, that the truly good, the universal divine Reason is the power capable of actualizing itself. This good, this Reason, in its most concrete representation, is God."

One cannot help wondering how this philosophy would have sounded to a Jew in Auschwitz.

The only ancient people that produced prophets who dared to challenge unjust tyrants in the name of a higher power were the Jews, whose God, unlike Hegel's, was the transcendent personal Creator, a particular person with a character and a will who demanded justice of his creatures. This God was not the immanent, impersonal universal Consciousness of Hegel, which is not a person with a moral will, and which is the agent of everything in history, of its injustices and its justices alike, using men as mere instruments.

The previous paragraph is not ideology or opinion. It is historical fact.

Hegel's Three Stages of History

History moves through three basic stages for Hegel: the stages of "objective spirit, subjective spirit, and absolute spirit."

"Objective spirit" is the world of culture, especially art, religion, law, morality, and the family. In this first stage (whose pinnacle, Hegel says, was reached by ancient Greece), society's and the individual's mores were identical. There was an instinctive identification with the society. In the stage of "subjective spirit," typified by the Sophists and Socrates, self-consciousness and critique emerge and social mores are questioned. This stage of doubt continues through the Protestant Reformation, Descartes, and Kant. The third phase of "absolute spirit," the synthesis, begins with (surprise!) Hegel's absolute idealism.

The very same dialectical process works (a) in history, (b) in logic (or metaphysics), and (c) in the phenomenology of consciousness, both for universal consciousness itself and for an individual's consciousness.

The process moves because Spirit is always in relation to itself. That is why there is always contradiction and negativity and instability in it. The subject and object stand in opposition to each other as thesis and antithesis; then they are synthesized by the subject recognizing itself in the object and the object in (and as) itself, the subject.

Spirit is free by its own essential nature, but that freedom is only gradually realized in history. Oriental societies, says Hegel, knew only that "one was free" (the despot). Greece and Rome realized that "some were free" (citizens, not slaves). Modernity, beginning especially with the French Revolution, realizes that "all are free."

Hegel believed what has been called "the Great Man theory of history": that to accomplish its purposes, Spirit uses certain remarkable individuals as its unconscious instruments. Even though their own conscious aims are merely to increase their own power, these "great men" serve the larger purpose of Reason in history. Hegel calls these "world-historical individuals." Alexander, Caesar, and Napoleon are examples. (Would Hegel have included Hitler?)

Conservative or Liberal?

After Hegel's death, his disciples split into the conservative "Hegelian Right" and the liberal "Hegelian Left," which eventually supported Marxism. There is a tension and a polarity in Hegel that gives rise to these two poles. On the one hand, he said that freedom is the ultimate aim of all the evolution of Spirit. On the other hand, he preached an acceptance of the existing order of history and a worship of the state as "the divine Idea as it exists on earth." All existing orders are stages in the Absolute's rational and necessary self-development; it is therefore impossible and foolish to try to interfere with it. This seems to be typical of German intellectuals—the combination of outward subservience with inner freedom, of political servility with spiritual thoughtfulness.

There is both a "conservative" and a "liberal" aspect inherent in Hegel's dialectic. Each stage of history both affirms and negates its predecessor. Each stage carries history forward, taking up, conserving, and perfecting whatever in it is valid in its past for the later integration or synthesis with its antithesis into a higher, richer stage. This is its "conservative" aspect. But the price paid for this "conserving" and affirming positivity is an equal negativity and revolutionary critique. This is its "liberal" or "radical" aspect. Thus, each generation, or regime, or stage, can regard itself as (a) the preserver, (b) the destroyer, and (c) the transformer of what it has inherited. The third stage unites and reconciles the contradiction between the first two (the "conservative" and the "liberal" or "progressive").

Freedom

Many readers think that Hegel "makes freedom walk the plank" (as one commentator put it, with a pirate's "aaaarrgh!" implied). Judge for yourself.

The common conception of freedom is either (a) the shallow notion of the power to do what I please and get what I want or (b) the deeper notion of not being wholly determined by other, external causes, both within (heredity) and without (environment), even though influenced and conditioned by them.

Concept (a) is pretty much the concept of liberty in "liberal" thinkers like Hume and John Stuart Mill, but it breaks down when we consider spoiled brats and drug addicts, who fit the definition but are certainly not free.

But the more traditional concept of indetermination (b) also breaks down, according to Hegel, for the freedom exists not in human individuals but only in God, or Spirit; and *nothing* can determine the movements of Spirit, since there is nothing else outside it to determine it, and everything that happens is one of its movements. So there is no freedom of *indetermination* in Hegel, as there is in (b).

But, Hegel says, there is (c) freedom of *self-determination.* This self-determination is not the kind of external and political power over others that masters possess and slaves do not. It is *self-realization* for man. It means realizing, both in thought and reality, your true self as a predestined instrument of Spirit. It is somewhat similar to Spinoza's notion of freedom. It is (supposedly) compatible with determinism.

What Hegel means by self-determination is in a way similar to what Kant meant by "autonomy": it is not only rational and *conscious* will but active and *creative* will. It is *not* free will in the common sense of (b) the power to choose between alternatives—alternative possibilities that are not yet determined until you choose one of them.

The fact that Hegel's notion of freedom is far from the ordinary one can be seen in the fact that, for Hegel, freedom culminates in the German state of Prussia.

The State: Hegel's Political Philosophy

Hegel did not think of himself as a totalitarian, nor did he think any state, even Prussia, was perfect and infallible. But he did say that the state was the highest manifestation of Spirit, or God. (You heard right. Not the Church, not the individual, not the family, not lovers, but the state.) "The State is the divine Idea as it exists upon earth. . . . The State is the march of God through the world."

Hegel was also an extreme German nationalist and racist (though a spiritual and cultural rather than biological racist). He wrote, "The German spirit is the spirit of the new world. Its aim is the realization of Absolute Truth."

He did not think of himself as a totalitarian because he believed that the perfect, fully developed state manifested itself through each individual's freedom. The relation between the individual and the community is organic, like the relation between a leg and a body. Individual and community, as thesis and antithesis, are *both* perfected in their synthesis in the fully developed community, in which individuals are fulfilled by their relationships to the community and the community is fulfilled by each individual's self-realization and "freedom."

This sounds a little like heaven. But then Hegel goes on to identify the highest form of this community as the political state—something no religion and few philosophers in history have ever done. (Marx is the most notable exception.)

Hegel also politicized ethics. As Hegel identified logic and metaphysics, he also identified ethics and politics. He criticized Kant's ethics for being too abstract and individualistic and apolitical. Higher than the individual moral saint, he thought, is the objective realization of morality in concrete institutions: first in interpersonal contracts, then in the family, and finally in the State.

What kind of State? Hegel was not in favor of democracy. He said that the monarchical constitution "is the constitution of developed reason, and all other constitutions belong to lower grades." He also wrote that "it is false to maintain that the foundation of the state is something at the option of all its members." We do not make it; it makes us.

But, to be fair, this is clearly *not* a defense of totalitarianism, either ancient tyranny or modern fascism or communism. The unanimity Hegel preaches is neither the ancient unthinking "cake of custom" or tradition (that would be a thesis), nor its opposite, a rational abstraction from tradition by individuals, as in Kant (that would be its antithesis), but a higher communal harmony *and* a higher individual self-realization, *together*. That is the higher synthesis. The individual sees his identity and freedom in his role in the community, and therefore the community is not external and restrictive, as in tyranny or totalitarianism.

The *principle* seems profoundly right, especially as an alternative to both the unthinking traditionalism of radical conservatism and the anti-traditional abstractions of radical liberalism. But when Hegel applies this principle by calling the State "this actual God" and identifying "the Kingdom of God on earth" with the Prussian state, one suspects that philosophers tend to political naïveté, to put it mildly, and one breathes a sigh of relief that Marcus Aurelius was the last philosopher to attain supreme political power. Plato and Machiavelli both failed in their personal political ambitions. Heidegger, whom many called the profoundest philosopher of the century, called Hitler "the new god" who had "altered every aspect of human existence." Jesus was wiser: when they wanted to make him king, he fled. Judas Iscariot did not. Lesson: When you see a philosopher run for office, run the other way.

If Hegel had been truer to his dialectic here, he would have emphasized equally both (a) the wisdom of Mr. Spock's words in *Star Trek III* justifying his self-sacrifice to save the rest of the crew of the *Enterprise*, viz., that "the needs of the many outweigh the needs of the few," *and* (b) the wisdom of Captain Kirk's words in *Star Trek IV* justifying the whole crew risking their lives to bring Spock back, viz., that "the needs of the one outweigh the needs of the many." In other words, "all for one" as well as "one for all": the slogan of the Three Musketeers is more Hegelian than Hegel.

War

Hegel not only justified but glorified war. One reason was that "war has the deep meaning that by it the ethical health of the nations is preserved." He meant by this not just that the perils and sufferings of war offer opportunities for individual courage and heroism, but that war *itself* is good. In evaluating this opinion, it is certainly a significant fact that Hegel was a university professor who never experienced war, except intellectually, as an abstract idea.

Another reason for his glorification of war was that "a single person is something subordinate, and as such he must dedicate himself to the ethical whole. Hence if the State claims life, the individual must surrender it."

War is *necessary*, Hegel argues, because the nation-state is the supreme authority on earth. There is no universal natural law, no higher standard, to judge nations; therefore, war is inevitable when two sovereign nations disagree. It is like a conflict between two gods: there is nothing higher to adjudicate the conflict.*

Another justification for war is Hegel's concept of Spirit as progressing only through negation, contradiction, and conflict. The dialectic proceeds only by wars between concepts, and history necessarily reflects this in wars between nations.

Hegel disbelieved in Kant's hope for "perpetual peace" and also in any kind of league of nations or international organization. Though he underemphasized the individual person in relation to the state, he overemphasized the individual state in relation to the world. He was a nationalist, not an individualist *or* a globalist.

Among nations he saw the German nation-state as superior and supreme in his time. He wrote of it that "this people is the dominant people in world-history for this epoch—*and it is only once that it can make its hour strike.*" Certainly Hegel did not foresee or justify the Nazis, but it is not hard to see some of the origins and justifications of their ideology in the seeds he planted, and in the German national anthem, "Deutschland, Deutschland über alles!"

* Since for Hegel the state is God, Hegel is really a polytheist.

Hegel and Christianity

Hegel thought of himself as a Christian and called Christianity "the absolute religion." But by the standards of historic, traditional, orthodox Christianity, Hegel is a classic example of the modernist heresy, in at least thirteen ways. The first three characterized his early development and were later modified, though not totally rejected.

1. Hegel saw Christianity as an alien religion imported from Israel and not an element of German culture, not a *Volksreligion* (folk religion). It did not spring from the soil, the culture, the *Volk* (people), but was imposed from without by a book (the Bible) that was the product of an alien race.
2. He also saw Christianity as negative, pessimistic, and unprogressive because of its notion of sin. He thought it was hostile to human happiness, natural pleasure, and beauty.
3. He saw Christ as a philosophical human moralist, not a divine Savior, and his message as essentially Kantian ethics. Christ was forced to call himself the promised Messiah and a prophet from God in order to accommodate himself to the primitive Jewish belief that authentic religion had to be divinely revealed.
4. He saw creeds and dogmas as impositions from without that threatened freedom of thought.
5. He saw the idea of a moral law (the Commandments) coming from God as "heteronomous" rather than "autonomous," just as Kant did, and as destructive of human freedom.
6. He saw Judaism not as divinely ordained and revealed but as unenlightened legalism, with God as a master and man as his slave.
7. He saw Christ as rising above the Jewish morality of obedience to law and teaching a more Rousseauean morality of spontaneous self-expression of love and of universal human participation in divine life.
8. He criticized the Jewish notion of God as eternal and already existing. For Hegel, God is in process. God is ever changing, ever evolving.
9. Hegel's God is not a person with a will. You cannot meet him or obey or disobey him. He is not a he but an it, an impersonal Mind.
10. Hegel is a pantheist. There is nothing outside God. God did not create a world distinct from himself. The world is a projection of divine consciousness, a moment in God's gradual self-realization.
11. Hegel is a humanist, in the theological sense. God is dependent on man for his self-realization. For Hegel, God is not an objective and independent reality outside man. The Jews produced this idea of God by objectifying him, projecting their own consciousness onto an "other." Rather, for Hegel, God is immanent in man and nature and realizes himself only through human

consciousness. Even nature is necessary for both human and divine consciousness, as the "other" that is needed to generate the concept of a "self."

12. For Hegel, philosophy is higher than religion. It must judge religion, not vice versa. For it is philosophy, not religion, that is the actual life of God. The task of philosophy is not just to *reveal* but to actually *construct* the progressing life of the Absolute. The history of philosophy is the process by which "self-thinking thought" comes to think itself. Religion is mythic, pictorial thinking, necessary only for primitive stages and peoples. That is why religion produces its picture of a concrete, personal, individual God freely choosing to create a world and mankind, giving a law, and redeeming man. None of that is literally, but only mythically, true. Thus, religion is not a revelation of eternal truths, as philosophy is, but is relative to culture and history.
13. Hegel thus interpreted the central Christian doctrine of the Incarnation of God in Christ as a mythic version of his own philosophy of the oneness of the human and the divine.

Kierkegaard's Critique of Hegel

Although Kierkegaard, with the other existentialists, is not covered until Volume IV, his critique of Hegel shows the striking contrast between two opposite kinds of philosophy, in both style and content. It is parallel to Pascal's criticism of Descartes.

The following passage focuses on Kierkegaard's *philosophical* criticism of Hegel. Religiously, he is even more severe: essentially, he sees Hegel as an apostate posing as an apostle, a Judas Iscariot betraying his Lord, a Dracula sucking the lifeblood of Christianity and leaving only its bloodless, abstract corpse.

As a sample and an appetizer, here are some of Kierkegaard's satirical remarks about Hegel's rationalistic system, from his *Concluding Unscientific Postscript*. (That modest title is also satirical and harks back to Pascal's *Pensées* [thoughts].) It and Voltaire's *Candide* are probably the two most memorable and powerful (and funny) satires in the history of philosophy.

> Lessing has said: "If God held concealed in His right hand all truth, and in His left hand the single-minded, serious striving after truth, and, warning me against eternal error, said: 'Choose!' I would fall before His left hand and say, 'Father, give me this; the pure truth is for You alone.'"
>
> When Lessing wrote these words the System [of Hegel] was presumably not finished; alas! And now Lessing is dead. Were he living in these times, now that the System is almost finished, or at least under construction, and will be finished by next Sunday, believe me, Lessing would have stretched out both his hands to lay hold of it. . . . But, then, the System

also has more to offer than God had in both hands. This very moment it has more, to say nothing of next Sunday, when it is quite certain to be finished. . . .

I shall be as willing as the next man to fall down in worship before the System, if only I can manage to set eyes on it. Hitherto I have had no success; and though I have young legs, I am almost weary from running back and forth between Herod and Pilate. Once or twice I have been on the verge of bending the knee. But at the last moment, when I already had my handkerchief spread on the ground, to avoid soiling my trousers, and I made a trusting appeal to one of the initiated who stood by: "Tell me now sincerely, is it entirely finished? For if so I will kneel down before it, even at the risk of ruining a pair of trousers (for on account of the heavy traffic to and from the System, the road has become quite muddy),"—I always received the same answer: "No, it is not yet quite finished." And so there was another postponement—of the System and of my homage.

System and finality are pretty much one and the same, so much so that if the System is not finished, there is no System. . . .

The System, so it is said, begins with the immediate, and hence without any presuppositions, and hence absolutely. . . . But . . . *how* does the System begin with the immediate? . . . Only when reflection comes to a halt can a beginning be made, and reflection can be halted only by something else, and this something else is something quite different from the logical, being a resolution of the will. . . . [So] there is no absolute beginning. "How so," I think I hear someone say, "when we have abstracted from everything, is there then not, etc., etc.?" Aye, to be sure—*when we* have abstracted from everything. Why can we not remember to be human beings?

With what do I begin, now that I have abstracted from everything? Ah, here an Hegelian will perhaps fall on my breast, overcome by deep emotion, blissfully stammering the answer: "with nothing!" And it is indeed true, as the System says, that it begins with nothing. Very well, but now I must offer my second question: *How* do I begin with nothing?

What if instead of talking or dreaming about an absolute beginning, we talked about a leap? . . .

Let us then ask quite simply, as a Greek youth might have asked his teacher (and if the superlative wisdom can explain everything but cannot answer a simple question, it is clear that the world is out of joint): "Who is to write or complete such a system?" Surely a human being, unless we propose again to begin using the strange mode of speech which assumes that a human being becomes speculative philosophy in the abstract, or becomes the identity of subject and object. So then, a human being—and surely a living human being, i.e., an existing individual. . . . Two ways, in

> general, are open for an existing individual: Either he can do his utmost to forget that he is an existing individual, by which he becomes a comic figure, since existence has the remarkable trait of compelling an existing individual to exist whether he wills it or not. . . . Or he can concentrate his entire energy upon the fact that he is an existing individual. . . .
>
> Every system must be pantheistic precisely on account of its finality. Existence must be revoked in the eternal before the system can round itself out; there must be no existing remainder, not even such a little minikin as the existing Herr Professor who writes the system. . . .
>
> If a dancer could leap very high, we should admire him. But if he tried to give the impression that he could fly, let laughter single him out for suitable punishment, even though it might be true that he could leap as high as any dancer had ever done. Leaping is the accomplishment of a being essentially earthly, one who respects the earth's gravitational force, since the leaping is only momentary. But flying carries a suggestion of being emancipated from earthly conditions, a privilege reserved for winged creatures, and perhaps also shared by the inhabitants of the moon—and there perhaps the System will first find its true readers. . . .
>
> A logical system is possible. . . . An existential system is impossible. . . . Existence [i.e., human existence] itself is a system—for God; but it cannot be a system for any existing spirit. System and finality correspond to each other, but existence is precisely the opposite of finality. . . .
>
> If the concept of existence is really to be stressed, this cannot be given a direct expression as a paragraph in a system. . . . In view of the elusiveness of existence, such a form of expression will have to be an indirect form, namely, the absence of a system. . . .
>
> The systematic idea is the identity of subject and object, the unity of thought and being. Existence, on the other hand, is their separation.

To end with a purely personal interjection: There are three kinds of philosophers, in terms of one's reading experience. There are philosophers who are sparkling and delightful and profound on first reading and on every subsequent reading too. Plato and Augustine are examples. There are others who seem dry and difficult at first yet become clearer and wiser with every re-reading. Aristotle and Aquinas are examples. And there are still others who seem exhilarating and profound on first reading, but on every subsequent reading fall apart and become more and more absurd and ridiculous. Hegel and Heidegger fit this pattern—to me, at any rate. And I am not alone.

68

ARTHUR SCHOPENHAUER

AD 1788—1860

The Hegelian tradition continued for about a century in the English-speaking world with F.H. Bradley, T.H. Green, Bernard Bosanquet, Josiah Royce, and Brand Blanshard.* But Schopenhauer is the last of the original German absolute idealists. He was Hegel's contemporary but also his polar opposite in every way: eccentric, pessimistic, cynical, sarcastic, and utterly *non*-edifying.

Why is he called an "idealist"? Because idealism should really be called "idea-ism." The "l" is misleading. Not all philosophical idealists are idealistic in the popular sense (i.e., optimistic). In fact, Schopenhauer is the classic pessimist.

His Miserable Life

His family was of Dutch origin and settled in Danzig, in east Germany. His father, a merchant, was not pleased that his genius son Arthur chose to be a poor philosopher rather than a rich businessman. He committed suicide when Arthur was a teenager, and Arthur blamed his mother, a glamorous and influential so-

* Blanshard's *The Nature of Thought* is such a brilliant *tour de force* that in one of his seminars in epistemology at Yale, by its sheer logic he converted (at least for the duration of the semester) every one of twenty-four very bright and aggressive graduate students to absolute idealism, all of whom were at first absolutely convinced that absolute idealism was absolutely unjustifiable. The author was one of them.

cialite. Arthur had many affairs during his life, and two illegitimate daughters, who died in infancy.

Once, he was so annoyed by an elderly woman who was talking loudly to her friend outside his apartment door that he threw her down the stairs, causing permanent injury. A court judged that he had to pay her a monthly allowance for the rest of her life. When she died, twenty years later, he wrote, "Obit anus, abit onus." (The old crone dies, the burden departs.)

Schopenhauer deliberately scheduled his lectures at the University of Berlin at the same hour as the great, world-famous Hegel. His classroom was usually empty.

His published doctoral dissertation, *On the Fourfold Root of the Principle of Sufficient Reason*, remained unread and unsold, even though Goethe praised it highly.

His masterpiece, *The World as Will and Idea*, fared not much better. This was his reaction: "Whoever has accomplished an immortal work will be as little hurt by its reception from the public, or the opinions of critics, as a sane man in a madhouse is affected by the upbraidings of the insane."

When the Royal Danish Academy announced an essay competition for a prize, he submitted one. He did not win the prize, even though his was the only essay anyone submitted.

His Miserable Personality

The one word that summarizes Schopenhauer's personality *and* philosophy is "pessimism." It is a mysticism of evil, not good. Bertrand Russell, in *A History of Western Philosophy*, describes its "bottom line" this way: "When we pierce the veil we behold not God but Satan, the wicked omnipotent will, perpetually . . . weaving a web of suffering for the torture of its creatures." Schopenhauer summarized life this way: "Life is an expiation of the crime of being born. . . . We begin in the madness of carnal desire and the transport of voluptuousness, we end in the dissolution of all our parts and the musty stench of corpses."

Not surprisingly, he never married. You could deduce that fact from the first line in his most famous book, *The World as Will and Idea*: "The world is my idea." (No married man ever was allowed to believe that.) He defined marriage this way: "Marrying means to grasp blindfold into a sack hoping to find an eel in an assembly of snakes."

Life, for Schopenhauer, is purposive; but its purpose is to seduce us to procreate more of those meaningless living things to perpetuate the cycle of misery. No other reason, no positive purpose, lies behind it.

To answer the question "What is man?" Schopenhauer loved to point to examples in the animal kingdom like the Australian ant: decapitated, it turns into two insects, one all head and the other all thorax. The head tries to bite the thorax to death and the thorax tries to sting the head to death.

His Miserable Evaluation of Hegel

Common sense usually thinks that some things are good, rational, and meaningful while others are evil, irrational, or meaningless (random chance). For Hegel, *everything* is in the first category: "The real is the rational and the rational is the real." For Schopenhauer, *nothing* is.

Schopenhauer's opinion of Hegel, and of himself, can best be summarized by the following quotations:

> There is no philosophy between Kant and myself, only University charlatanism.
>
> Out of every page of Hume there is more to be learned than out of all the philosophical works of Hegel.
>
> Installed from above, by the powers that be, as the certified Great Philosopher, [Hegel] was a flat-headed, insipid, nauseating, illiterate charlatan who reached the pinnacle of audacity in scribbling together and dishing up the craziest mystifying nonsense.
>
> I should like to see the man who could boast of a more miserable set of contemporaries than mine. [Beethoven, Goethe, Kant, Hegel . . .]
>
> I have lifted the veil of truth higher than any mortal before me.

The Miserable World as Idea and Will

Pessimism was not just a personal feeling but a reasoned philosophy for Schopenhauer. This philosophy, as summarized in *The World as Will and Idea*, has two basic parts, corresponding to the last two nouns in the title.

1. "The World as Idea" begins with the premise of epistemological idealism: "All that exists for knowledge, and therefore this whole world, is only object in relation to subject, perception of a perceiver, in a word, idea. . . . What he knows is not a sun and an earth but only an eye that sees a sun, a hand that feels an earth. . . . The world which surrounds him is there only as idea" (i.e., as an object of and in consciousness, relative to consciousness, a representation of consciousness, a *Vorstellung*). This is what unifies all *phenomena*.
2. The point of the other word in the title is that what holds together all *noumena*, all "things-in-themselves," is *will*.

We might think that ideas are impersonal while wills are personal; but Schopenhauer thinks exactly the opposite. "Idea" means "my idea." But "will" does not mean "my will" but cosmic will, a cosmic, impersonal necessity. Will is a blind, irrational force, a cosmic cyclops, a kind of mad and evil monster-god. It is "a blind, incessant impulse . . . the will to live . . . endless striving . . . without knowledge."

There is no *logos*, no cosmic reason that our human reason can participate in; but there is a cosmic will, and our individual wills are (unfree) participations in this cosmic will. So "will is . . . the closest and most distinct manifestation of the thing-in-itself. . . . The inner nature of everything is will."

Man is not superior to animals by his reason, (1) because our reason is the slave of will, passion, and instinct, and (2) because reason is dependent on the body—in fact a *function* of the body—just as in animals. In fact, (3) reason, or intellect, is only a part or attribute or accident of will rather than a distinct and independent power.

We *seem* to be moved by formal and final causes, by our knowledge of the true and our choice of the understood good (i.e., by reason), but we are really moved only by material and efficient causes, like the rest of the universe.

There are three possible philosophical options on this issue of causality:

1. Ancient and medieval philosophers claimed that the entire universe was moved by formal and final causes, from above and from ahead, teleologically.
2. Classical modern philosophers, beginning with Descartes, sharply divided man, who could be moved in this formal and final way, from the rest of the universe, which (as pictured by modern science) is not. The universe is a blind, unfree machine, moved from behind and below. Descartes' dualism gives us two opposite worlds.
3. Schopenhauer returns from dualism to monism but by unifying down rather than up, so to speak: "Men are only apparently drawn from in front; really, they are pushed from behind." We are like nature not in having but in lacking formal and final causality. (Hobbes had said pretty much the same thing.)

This would be one of Freud's key premises: that we do not freely and rationally will but are moved (*willed*, Schopenhauer would say) by unconscious forces over which we have no power. For Freud this was the impersonal animal instincts (the "id") within us; for Schopenhauer it was the impersonal cosmic will that enclosed us.

The aim of nature, Schopenhauer says, is to produce life; and the aim of life is simply to continue the cycle; and for this to happen one thing has to kill and eat another. All human progress is either war or peace, and "in peace, industry and trade are active, inventions work miracles, seas are navigated . . . But what is the aim of all this striving? To sustain ephemeral and tormented individuals through a short span of time." It's simply not worth the effort. It is exactly the philosophy of Ecclesiastes (see vol. 1, chap. 1): "All is vanity."

In other words, life is will, will is desire, desire causes pain, and pleasure is only a temporary respite from pain. Life sucks, then you die; that's all, folks.

Buddhism vs. Misery

Since Schopenhauer's *diagnosis* of will and desire as the cause of pain and suffering is the same as Buddha's, it is not surprising that his *prognosis* is also similar to Buddha's: we can stop the effect (pain), at least temporarily, by stopping the cause (desire).

We can do this in two ways: (1) by aesthetic contemplation, during which the will is temporarily outwitted by this shift of attention from objects that excite passion to objects that do not; and (2) by an ethic of pity, of compassion instead of passion, in which passions and desires are ignored and denied. The first is a nonmystical, Western version of Buddha's mystical transformation of consciousness, of the *prajna* (wisdom) that is emphasized in Theravada Buddhism; the second is a Western version of Buddha's ethic of *karuna* (universal impersonal compassion) that is emphasized in Mahayana Buddhism.

But this victory, even if achieved, is only temporary; for there is no *nirvana*, no hope for any final success in the end for Schopenhauer, as there is for Buddhism. Nothingness is the best bargain we can get; the only alternative is "continual desire without satisfaction." In other words, Mick Jagger's most famous line.

Schopenhauer learned this philosophy from reading the Hindu Upanishads. He was the first Western philosopher to learn from the East. (He named his dog Atman.)

Schopenhauer's influence was much greater after his death than before. He was greatly admired by Nietzsche, Goethe, Wagner, and Freud.

His most readable works are his short essays (e.g., "On Women," "On Religion," "On Ethics," "On Suicide," "On the Vanity of Existence"). Each of these ideas is treated as a balloon and Schopenhauer's mind is a sharp and brilliant pin. (Does that make him a pinhead?)

II

THE POLITICAL PHILOSOPHERS

Introduction to the Political Philosophers

To preserve the logical rather than chronological continuity of "the great conversation," I have kept the practical political philosophers separate from the theoretical philosophers (the epistemologists and metaphysicians), because each group has its own distinctive set of questions.

I have omitted many important political philosophers entirely (e.g., Edmund Burke, Adam Smith, Montesquieu, and Alexis de Tocqueville) because they are *only* political philosophers (i.e., practical and not theoretical philosophers). The two exceptions to this rule are Machiavelli and Rousseau, whose influence was immense even though neither wrote any speculative, theoretical philosophy (metaphysics or epistemology). However, in both cases definite anthropologies—in fact, two very new and radical anthropologies—can be extracted by logical deduction from their remarks about practical psychology and politics, explicitly for Rousseau and implicitly for Machiavelli. It would certainly be unthinkable to omit the founder of the whole stream of modern political philosophy. For it was Machiavelli who turned the political conversation around more than anyone else in history.

Locke is not here because I have classified him primarily as an epistemologist, even though he is also a very popular and influential political philosopher. To keep the continuity of "the great conversation" in this section, Locke's political philosophy should be studied after that of Hobbes. It can be found in the last section of chapter 60.

Hobbes is a very important philosopher in all areas, not just politics, but I have included him here because his masterpiece, *Leviathan*, is primarily about politics, though it is based on a complete system of metaphysics, epistemology, anthropology, and ethics.

I must offer some apology to those who would have preferred a strictly chronological order—but only a slight apology, since it should be easy for them to simply read the chapters of this book in the order of the philosophers' births or deaths.

69

NICCOLÒ MACHIAVELLI

AD 1469–1527

Niccolò Machiavelli is the only philosopher whose essential point is so distinctive and so well known that he has an adjective named after him in popular thought. For a policy, person, or act to be "Machiavellian" is to be amoral, shrewd, calculating, and totally pragmatic, to believe that the end justifies the means. That is a formula Machiavelli never exactly wrote, but it is an accurate description.

He is also the only philosopher whose name instantly conjures up something negative, in fact something wicked, even demonic: the English nickname for the devil, "Old Nick," was derived from Machiavelli's first name, Niccolò (Nicholas). His enemies called him "the devil's son."

So his philosophy is much more *interesting* than most. (Why do we find evil more interesting than good? Is it, really?)

His Life

His life was also much more interesting than that of most philosophers. He aspired to political power but failed. His masterpiece, *The Prince*, is a long and unsuccessful job application for the position of advisor to the ruler of Florence, Lorenzo de' Medici, "Lorenzo the Magnificent," whom Machiavelli shamelessly flattered in the introduction to his book—the very book that has a chapter (23) entitled "How Princes Should Avoid Flatterers." (Was it Machiavelli or Lorenzo who forgot the law of noncontradiction? Probably Machiavelli was just toying with the Magnificent's less-than-magnificent mind.)

The most important events in Machiavelli's life were:

1. His study of the classics, especially the history of Rome, the most successful political entity in Western history.
2. His stormy love-hate relationship with his native Florence and its rulers, who were repeatedly at war with other Italian city-states.
3. His experience of humiliation when the French King Charles VIII marched through the streets of Florence in conquest.
4. His observation of the state of piety (or rather impiety) in the Catholic Church in his day, which was typified by the "Pazzi conspiracy." In 1478, the Pazzi family, who bankrolled the papacy, attempted to murder Lorenzo the Magnificent, grandson of the nationalist hero Cosimo de' Medici, during the Easter Mass in the cathedral, on the signal of the priest's elevation of the consecrated Host. To avenge this sacrilege, the parishioners captured the archbishop who organized this conspiracy and threw him and his co-conspirator out the window with a rope around their necks. They cheered while the two dangling men bit into each other's flesh, and the crowd tore the limbs off the other conspirators. An edifying spectacle.
5. His observation of the burning at the stake of the pious Franciscan reformer Savonarola by the same people who had adored and obeyed him earlier but now had tired of his moral reforms.
6. His acquaintance with the spectacularly successful tyrant Cesare Borgia, whose father had become pope by *buying* the office and publicly had many mistresses and illegitimate children.
7. His imprisonment and excruciating torture by *strappado* (you don't want to know) because he was accused by turncoat friends of plotting an assassination. He was stripped of his job of international diplomat and banished to a beautiful country estate, where he wrote his most famous works amid natural beauties that he found unendurably boring.

It does not take an expert in psychology to guess that this man is not going to have an optimistic philosophy of human nature and politics.

His Importance: His Radicalism

Leo Strauss nicely sums up Machiavelli's importance in *What Is Political Philosophy?*:

> The founder of modern political philosophy is Machiavelli. He tried to effect, and did effect, a break with the whole tradition. . . . [For]

> all classical political philosophers the goal of political life is virtue. . . . Machiavelli consciously lowers the standards. . . . His lowering of the standards is meant to lead to a higher probability of actualization. . . . Thus the dependence on chance is reduced: chance will be conquered. . . .
>
> Let us then cease to take our bearings by virtue, the highest objective which a society might choose; let us begin to take our bearings by the objectives which are actually pursued by all societies. . . . One cannot define the good of society, the common good, in terms of virtue, but one must define virtue in terms of the common good. By the common good we must understand the objectives actually pursued by all societies. . . .
>
> Virtue in the effectual sense of the word is the sum of habits which are required for or conducive to this end. It is this end, and this end alone, which makes our actions virtuous. Everything done effectively for the sake of this end is good. This end justifies every means. Virtue is nothing but civic virtue, patriotism, or devotion to collective selfishness. . . .
>
> [But] patriotism is not natural. Just as man is not by nature directed toward virtue, he is not by nature directed toward society. By nature man is radically selfish.
>
> Yet while men are by nature selfish, and nothing but selfish, hence bad, they can become social, public spirited, or good.
>
> This transformation requires compulsion.

Machiavelli's radically new political philosophy is implicitly based on a radically new philosophy of human nature. In the quotation above, Strauss focuses on four major points that sharply distinguish Machiavelli from all previous political philosophers:

1. The end of politics is success, not virtue.
2. "Virtue" is simply social acceptance. Societies cannot be judged by any higher standard as being good or evil; "good" is simply whatever society wants. Society *invents* and thus judges morality, not vice versa.
3. Whatever produces what society wants (which is always material success: freedom, order, wealth, and conquest) is good. The end justifies the means.
4. These means are essentially force—arms, or the threat of arms. For men are selfish and can act cooperatively not by nature but only by violence, by being forced or threatened.

This philosophy, though radically new for medieval Christendom, is not radically new in history. It is essentially the philosophy of the ancient Greek Sophists, applied to politics.

Aristotle had defined man as "a political animal," which meant that civil society is as natural to man as the family; that "the body politic" is as much a part of human nature as the body physical; that the state is natural and organic, not artificial and mechanical. Machiavelli denies this assumption, and in this denial he is followed by nearly all the most influential modern political philosophers right up to the present, except Hegel, Burke, and Tocqueville. Machiavelli's denial that the *polis* is natural and innate to human nature leads to the "social contract theory" of the origin of the state, which philosophers as opposite as Hobbes and Rousseau both embrace.

His Implicit Metaphysics

Even a pure pragmatist cannot avoid theory, for all practice implies a theory. And within theory, no one can avoid metaphysics, for no one can avoid the verb "is." We can see Machiavelli's implicit metaphysics at work in some of the most famous passages in *The Prince.*

Machiavelli's most obvious philosophical opponent is Plato and the *Republic.* This is evident especially when he writes,

> Our next task is to consider the policies and principles a ruler ought to follow in dealing with his subjects or with his friends. Since I know many people have written on this subject, I am concerned it may be thought presumptuous for me to write on it as well, especially since what I have to say, as regards this question in particular, will differ greatly from the recommendation of others. But my hope is to write a book that will be useful, at least to those who read it intelligently, and so I thought it sensible to go straight to a discussion of how things are in real life and not waste time with a discussion of an imaginary world. For many authors have constructed imaginary republics and principalities that have never existed in practice and never could.

"Principles" for Machiavelli are purely practical, not moral. *The ideal and the real do not overlap at all; ideals are not real; reality does not include ideals.* Ideals, Platonic Forms, and the Good do not exist; they are imaginary, subjective. The only world is the world of competitive matter and competitive men. Matter is competitive because two bodies cannot share the same place at the same time without loss of mass, and men are competitive because two men cannot share the same material good at the same time without loss either. The more money, land, or power I share with you, the less I have left for myself. For Machiavelli, there are no such things as invisible goods, or spiritual goods like wisdom, love, or beauty that multiply when shared. Machiavelli is implicitly but clearly a materialist and atheist, like Hobbes and Hume.

Of course, he has to *say* pious-sounding things about God, and about moral virtue, or else he would be punished by the powers that be, which in his day were religious. But he does not believe what he says—and by Machiavellian reasoning, so what? If there is no God, there is no sin, including hypocrisy.

Machiavelli's metaphysics is the ultimate foundation for his ethics. There *is* no other world, no God, no Platonic Forms, no natural moral law, no eternal soul, no heaven or hell; that is why there is no appeal to a higher world and no judgment or condemnation of moral evil in this world, which is the only world, except from some men (your enemies). *Morality is simply some men's opinions about other men's behavior.*

Machiavelli uses the word "virtue" (*virtù* in Italian) in a deliberately ambiguous way. The old meaning was *moral goodness*. The new, Machiavellian meaning is *successful power*.

This ambiguity gave him an "escape clause" or "credible deniability" for the censors or inquisitors. He can pose as the champion of virtue! And Machiavelli's "God-talk" is a bone cleverly thrown to the naïve inquisitor dogs. It is like a cover for a spy, or a mask. You can choose to read him either cleverly or uncleverly, from within either his mindset or that of his victims.

Virtù (power) and *fortuna* (chance) are the only two forces in the world. This metaphysical assumption enables Machiavelli to treat politics as a practical *science*, like engineering. Success now has a formula. And that formula is even quantifiable, though Machiavelli does not pursue that aspect: success equals the maximization of *virtù* and the minimization of *fortuna*. It is the exact opposite of Stoicism, which argued for the passionless acceptance of all things (*apatheia*), since all things in the world are fated and only our own subjective reactions to the world are under our power.

This formula for success—*virtù* conquering *fortuna*—is always assumed and operative even when Machiavelli is mapping and outlining details. For instance, in the very first chapter of *The Prince* he asks how a prince can acquire new territories, and his first step is to classify all answers as "either through fortune or through strength [*virtù*]."

Machiavelli is radical because a new *summum bonum* is the most radical cultural change possible for the human race. Machiavelli's new *summum bonum* is the same as Francis Bacon's: "man's conquest of nature" (i.e., power). The main difference between the two is that for Machiavelli "nature" is not the world of physics, the subhuman world, but the world of human affairs, politics. As Bacon gives us the inductive rules for a science and technology to control matter, Machiavelli gives us the inductive rules for a science and technology to control men.

When Christianity came into the world, it added many categories to pagan Greek thinking (such as an infinite God and the act of creation), but it subtracted one pagan category: chance, or fortune. Nothing escaped divine providence; nothing was left to chance, except to the mind of ignorant mankind. But chance was an ultimate reality for the pagan Greeks. They considered Fate (*Moira*) superior to gods as well as men. (Fate and chance are not quite the same, but both are outside our control.) Machiavelli returns to pagan categories in (1) omitting the Christian God entirely from his reckoning and (2) restoring *fortuna* to the important place it had had in the pagan worldview. More exactly, he offers a new option: the Baconian, Faustian, Promethean one in which man can learn to *conquer fortuna* by *virtù*.

There are two kinds of *virtù* for Machiavelli: physical arms and mental cleverness. Use of the second is more efficient than the first. (This is a very practical and very old principle: it is even in the Tao Te Ching, of all places!) Speaking of the Romans, his ideal rulers, he says: "The Romans did in such matters what all wise rulers ought to do. It is necessary not only to pay attention to immediate crises but to foresee those that will come. . . . In this matter it is as doctors say of consumption: in the beginning the disease is easy to cure and difficult to diagnose, but after a while, if it has not been diagnosed and treated early, it becomes easy to diagnose and hard to cure." Machiavelli is quite right here: time management, planning, and foresight are essential practical needs in every field, from winning wars to getting good grades.

His Epistemology

Machiavelli is an empiricist. Whereas past political philosophers deduced their conclusions from abstract general principles of metaphysics, anthropology, and general ethics, Machiavelli's method is strictly inductive. He offers *The Prince* as an *empirical science* of politics, based on observation, both indirect (his study of history) and direct (his personal experience of contemporary affairs). Politics becomes "the art of the possible," and the possible is defined by observation of the actual.

His Anthropology

Although his metaphysics and epistemology are implicit, his anthropology, or philosophy of man, is explicit: all men are selfish animals.

In arguing that "it is better to be feared than to be loved,"* he gives this as his reason:

> For of men one can, in general, say this: They are ungrateful, fickle, deceptive and deceiving, avoiders of danger, eager to gain. As long as you serve their interests, they are devoted to you. They promise you their blood, their possessions, their lives, and their children, as I said before, so long

---

* The movie *A Bronx Tale* centered on this famous Machiavellian quotation.

> as you seem to have no need of them. But as soon as you need help, they turn against you. Any ruler who relies simply on their promises . . . will be destroyed. . . . Men are less nervous of offending someone who makes himself lovable than someone who makes himself frightening.

There are three possible philosophical anthropologies:

1. that man is by nature selfish and wicked (Machiavelli and Hobbes), so he must be compelled by others, by society or government, by force and fear, to be good, contrary to his nature;
2. that man is by nature unselfish and good (Rousseau), so that it is the artifices of society and governments, not human nature, that are to blame for wickedness; or
3. that men are free to choose between good or evil, both of which are to be found in their nature and behavior (traditional Aristotelian and religious common sense).

For (1), there is no real virtue; for (2) there is no real sin; for (3) there is both. In light of these options, one must ask in critique: Is Machiavelli really a "realist"?

The criterion of this critique is practice: Does his advice work? Here is an example. He advises that after a conquest "the new ruler should go and live in his new territories . . . [because] if you are there in person, the territory will not be plundered by your officials." He calls the following principle "a general conclusion that will never (or hardly ever) be proved wrong: He who is the cause of someone else's becoming powerful is the agent of his own destruction." So you must micromanage. Trust no one.

Is this efficiency? Is this practicality? Is this realism?

The assumption is that there is no such thing as a real, natural "we" or social consciousness, either among private friends or among public citizens; that all individual human beings, like individual material things (e.g., rocks), are essentially in competition. If one gives another some money, land, or power, the giver loses whatever he gives away. Since this is true of all material things, but not of immaterial things like truth, love, moral example, beauty, and happiness, Machiavelli's practical advice reveals his implicit anthropological and metaphysical assumption of materialism.

The assumption is also that there is no such thing as what the Chinese call *te*, moral power, the power of moral example to influence others for good, or of moral ideals or obligations to influence man by the power of conscience. Thus, there is no natural solidarity and loyalty that leads men to risk their lives for their friends. Machiavelli speaks as if this simply does not exist when he advises a new ruler to treat his conquered people as follows: "You will only offend those from whom you seize fields and houses to give to your settlers, and they will be only a tiny minority. . . . All the rest will remain uninjured, and so ought to remain quiet."

Machiavelli simply cannot account for the fact that spiritual power, moral or religious, exists. When dealing with the effective rule of the Church over its then-considerable lands, facts compel him to admit that "only ecclesiastical rulers have states but no need to defend them; subjects, but no need to govern them. Their states, though they do not defend them, are not taken from them; their subjects, though they do not govern them, do not resent them, and they neither think of replacing their rulers nor are they in a position to do so. So these are the only rulers who are secure and happy." How does he explain this fact, if there is no such thing in man as *te*, or moral and religious conscience? He can't. But he uses a very useful piece of hypocrisy—a pretended piety—to justify his ignorance: "But because they are ruled by a higher power, which human intelligence cannot grasp, I will say no more about them; for since they have been built up and maintained by God, only a presumptuous and rash person would debate about them."

His Practical Psychology

It is Machiavelli's cynical anthropology plus his metaphysics of *virtù* versus *fortuna* that justifies his practical psychology of appealing to fear rather than love:

> Is it better to be loved than feared, or vice versa? My reply is that one ought to be both loved and feared; but, since it is difficult to accomplish both at the same time, I maintain it is much safer to be feared than loved, if you have to do without one of the two. . . . For love attaches men by ties of obligation which, since men are wicked, they break whenever their interests are at stake. But fear restrains men because they are afraid of punishment, and this fear never leaves them. . . . Since men decide for themselves whom they love, and rulers decide whom they fear, a wise ruler should rely on the emotion he can control, not on the one he cannot.

Since others' love comes under *fortuna* and their fear under *virtù*, and since success demands maximizing and relying on *virtù* rather than *fortuna*, the key to success is to rely on fear, not love.

Classical philosophy in general, especially Socrates and Plato, distinguished appearance and reality, and questioned appearances to find reality, which was deemed much more important. It was deemed more important to *be* than to *seem*; to *be* good than to *seem* good. But Machiavelli reverses this: appearances are more important, for his practical purposes, because they have more power over foolish mankind. In the words of modern advertising, "Image is everything." "One cannot have all the good qualities, nor always act in a praiseworthy fashion, for we do not live in an ideal world. You have to be astute enough to avoid being *thought* to have those evil qualities that would make it impossible for you to retain power. . . . So a ruler need not have all the positive qualities I listed earlier, but he must seem to have them. [For] everyone sees what you seem to be; few have direct experience of who you really are." It is *virtù* versus *fortuna* again: you can control appearances more than reality, so they are more important than reality.

Machiavelli explicitly denies the central point and fundamental conclusion of Plato's *Republic*, that "justice [virtue] is more profitable ["happifying"] than injustice [vice]." That is why Machiavelli's claim in *The Prince* is not to teach you how to be good but how to be bad. For evil, not good, is often the road to happiness; and goodness, not evil, the road to destruction: "Anyone who wants to act the part of a good man in all circumstances will bring about his own ruin. . . . So it is necessary for a ruler, if he wants to hold on to power, to learn how not to be good."

His Ethics

Yes, Machiavelli has an ethics. Good and evil are important terms for him. Look at the last sentence of the quotation above: it's not just that he will *not* teach you how to be good but that he will teach you *how not* to be good (in the traditional way). He does not ignore good and evil but gives a radically new content to the words.

The new, Machiavellian meaning of "good" is now simply "successful." What you ought to do depends on what works. The "ought" does not judge the "is," but the "is" judges the "ought"; that is, principles do not judge human actions, but they are to be judged by human actions, by which ones succeed in attaining military, political, personal, or other nonmoral ends. Morality is wholly instrumental: whatever means succeeds in practice is what the wise man "ought" to do. For instance, he says that "if the King of France had the military capacity to attack Naples, he should have done so."

Machiavelli's immoralism has a historical argument behind it. He argues that in historical fact morality causally depends on immorality. For (1) morality is dependent on society, not vice versa; it is an artifact. Man is not moral by nature but must be educated, habituated, or trained to act in socially acceptable ways. (2) But the original founders of society, and thus of morality, were neither moral by nature (no one is) nor were they educated to morality by society (for at first there was no society). For instance, the founder of history's most successful society, Rome, was Romulus, who murdered his brother, Remus. (That's why it's called Rome, not Reme.) All of human history began with Cain's murder of his brother Abel. Cain survived and built cities—and morality. *So morality is created by immorality.* Justice rests on injustice. The existence of the laws of America depended on killing enough English soldiers to win the Revolutionary War.

Machiavelli's argument for his first premise, above, that man is not by nature virtuous, is the simple observation that man fears pain more than wickedness; that the pains of moral conscience are far less fearful than the pains of physical punishment. It is an observation that had plenty of data to support it in his life's experience.

Three particular virtues come in for special criticism by Machiavelli: kindness, generosity, and honesty.

For Machiavelli cruelty is often better than kindness. E.g., the Greek tyrant Agathocles was cruel but successful: "Perhaps you are wondering how Agathocles and others like him, despite their habitual faithlessness and cruelty, have been able to live safely in their homelands year after year. . . . I think here we have to distinguish between cruelty well used and cruelty abused. . . . Those who use cruelty well may indeed find both God and their subjects are prepared to let bygones be bygones, as was the case with Agathocles." In other words, most men are wimps. (And so is God. The prophets are wrong about him.)

Generosity is self-destructive, because of the materialist principle above: material goods diminish when generously shared. If there *were* spiritual goods, they could multiply when shared; but there are none. Thus, "there is nothing so self-defeating as generosity, for the more generous you are, the less you are able to be generous. Generosity leads to poverty and disgrace, or, if you try to escape that, to rapacity and hostility" (to recoup your losses).

Honesty can also be self-defeating for Machiavelli. In chapter 18, "How Far Rulers Should Keep Their Word," Machiavelli says that "those rulers who have not thought it important to keep their word have achieved great things, and have known how to employ cunning to confuse and disorientate other men. In the end, they have been able to overcome those who have placed store in integrity."

But to say this seems to be self-contradictory in practice. The problem with listening to a teacher like Machiavelli who tells you to lie is: Why should you believe him, if he is practicing what he preaches, and therefore lying? And why should you believe him if he *isn't* practicing what he is preaching?

His Social and Political Philosophy

Machiavelli is a social relativist: morality, being an invention of society rather than an innate component of human nature, is relative to society. Thus, while all previous political philosophers (except the Sophists) defined the common good, or the good of society, in terms of moral virtue and as a means to the end of moral virtue, Machiavelli defines virtue in terms of the common social-national good, and as a means to it.

He is also a pure pragmatist or utilitarian: the end justifies the means. Moral good is "what works," whatever is most efficient in attaining your end. There is no such thing as a natural end of human nature or human life, according to Machiavelli, so we can set any end we want.

But although he is thus a social relativist, he lists a few goals that all societies seek. They are the same goals that all individuals seek, and power is the key to all of them: (1) freedom from being conquered, controlled, or bullied by others (this freedom comes by power or force of arms); (2) wealth (which gives you another kind of power); (3) glory or conquest (the fruit of power); and (4) law and order, predictability, safety—which also come only through power and control.

Virtue is defined in terms of these ends: whatever attains these (nonmoral) ends is a virtuous or good (moral) means.

And since man is not by nature social or cooperative, he must be compelled to act against his nature by force, by a wise prince using the force of arms and the threat of punishment.

Justice is simply a propaganda term to justify obedience to laws, a term invented by those who have seized power and made the laws for their own advantage. (This is exactly the philosophy of Thrasymachus in Plato's *Republic* and Callicles in his *Gorgias*.)

This is why Machiavelli says that "since there cannot be good laws where there are not good armies, and since where there are good armies, there must be good laws, I will omit any discussion of laws and will talk about armies. A ruler, then, should have no other concern, no other thought, should pay attention to nothing aside from war, military institutions, and the training of his soldiers. For this is the only field in which a ruler has to excel." (Is that "realistic" and "practical"?)

It is instructive to compare the title of Machiavelli's primary work with Plato's. *The Prince* is written to a single individual who wants to rule and control the people. *The Republic* (*res publica*, "public things") is written to bring about a just regime that (supposedly) makes everyone virtuous and therefore happy.

Critique

Two lines of critique are possible. (1) The usual one, that Machiavelli's thoughts are wicked, is not a critique at all from his point of view, for he does not claim to teach any rules of moral virtue, only rules for political success. (2) The telling critique is as pragmatic as the philosophy itself: that it does not work. It is unrealistic. It ignores half of human nature and half of human history.

But it succeeds in getting everyone's attention. Strauss asks the disturbing question: Why did it seem so persuasive?

"In Machiavelli's teaching we have the first example of a spectacle which has renewed itself in almost every generation since. A fearless thinker seems to have opened up a depth from which the classics, in their noble simplicity, recoiled. As a matter of fact, there is in the whole work of Machiavelli not a single true observation regarding the nature of man and of human affairs with which the classics were not thoroughly familiar. An amazing contraction of the horizon presents itself as an amazing enlargement of the horizon. How can we account for this delusion?"

A suggested answer: the lust for power corrupts minds as well as morals.

Machiavelli's *summum bonum*, like Bacon's, is power, or the conquest of *fortuna* by *virtù*, and any means is good if it attains this end. In fact, the image Machiavelli uses at the end of his book for this "good," this conquest, is *abuse*: "Fortune is a lady. It is necessary, if you want to master her, to beat and strike her."

Something in "macho" man naturally seeks power. But power treated as the end turns into weakness! At the end of the book, Machiavelli admits that in order to be successful and powerful, you have to turn yourself into a personal sycophant and wimp, and "suck up to" fickle Dame Fortune. Instead of coercing her, you have to conform to her: "A ruler will flourish if he adjusts his policies as the character of the times changes. . . . The sort of behavior that is successful changes from one time to another. . . . If one knew how to change one's character [*virtù*] as times and circumstances [*fortuna*] change, one's luck [success] would never change. . . . I conclude, then, that since fortune changes . . . men flourish when their behavior suits the times and fail when they are out of step." So the conquest of *fortuna* by *virtù* paradoxically turns into the conquest of *virtù* by *fortuna*!

A Machiavellian adjusts his *virtù* to the demands of *fortuna*, to the *Zeitgeist*, like a cold-blooded reptile conforming its body temperature to the air outside. He is spineless, not macho, as the image of "mastering" fortune by "beating and striking her" suggests.

Machiavelli wrote that "all armed prophets have succeeded. All unarmed prophets have failed." But it looks as if the "unarmed prophets" who "failed" because they were martyred were the real men after all. Fortune did not change them. Socrates did not change his character even in the presence of death, fortune's trump card; rather, death changed its character in the presence of Socrates. When you read his death scene at the end of the *Phaedo*, when the idea of death and the idea of Socrates thus meet in your mind, the idea of death does not change the idea of Socrates, but the idea of Socrates changes the idea of death.

Thus, Socrates refutes Machiavelli, as he refuted Thrasymachus, (1) by logical argument (*Republic*, Book I), (2) by a positive alternative (the rest of the *Republic*), and (3) by practice (the end of the *Phaedo*). Jesus was also an unarmed prophet. Did he fail?

70

THOMAS HOBBES

AD 1588–1679

Like most philosophers, Thomas Hobbes was a child prodigy and a nonconformist. He had a stormy relationship with his father, himself a stormy character who was so hot-tempered that he once had a fist fight with the parson at the church door, after which he and his family had to run away and hide. Thomas was sent away to school at the age of four to live with his rich uncle. In school, he learned to hate everything Aristotelian, especially syllogistic logic.

The most influential environmental influence on his philosophy was the trauma of civil war. This provoked him to try to find a permanent cure for war by first finding its cause. For both the Bible (James 4:1–3) and Aristotle this cause was moral vice, the sin or greed and selfishness inherent in human nature, and it could be effectively treated only from within, by cultivating habits of virtue such as moderation (reason controlling the passions) and the practice of unselfish charity and generosity. For Hobbes the materialist, like Machiavelli, it was not the weak "inner cop" of conscience but the strong "outer cop" of the state that was the only effective counter to chaos.

Hobbes offered not a more *just* order in the *soul*, like Plato, but a more *powerful* order in the *state*, one that ruled by fear rather than love. Machiavelli had said that "it is better to be feared than to be loved" *for the prince*; Hobbes says it is also better *for the people* to fear the prince than to love him. For law and order can be maintained only by force, and a totalitarian force is the most effective.

Thus, Hobbes offers us his ideal state as a "Leviathan," named after the formidable sea monster in the book of Job.

Leviathan is in many ways the exact opposite to Plato's *Republic*. Perhaps the most basic psychological difference is that where the political system of the *Republic* depended on reason, Leviathan depends on fear. It begins and ends in fear. Its diagnosis of the fundamental human problem is fear—the fear of violent death in a lawless society. And its fundamental solution is another kind of fear—the fear of the state that enforces its laws with an iron hand. Hobbes' account of the basic motive that led men to create states (or "civil society") in the first place is fear—fear of violent death—and the thing that in his eyes justifies absolute monarchy as the best kind of state is its solution to the problem of this fear, which is another kind of fear, the fear of the state. Instead of love casting out fear (1 John 4:18), it is civilized fear that casts out uncivilized fear: it is the fear of the "monster" state (Leviathan) that casts out the fear of violent death, the fear that reigned in the "state of nature" that preceded the state of civil society.

Hobbes famously described life in this state of nature as "solitary, poor, nasty, brutish, and short." A student once began an essay, "Thomas Hobbes was solitary, poor, nasty, brutish, and short." I replied, in the margin, "He was not poor, solitary, or short. But two out of five ain't bad."

Hobbes admits that fear is central to his personality. "Fear and I were born twins," he wrote, for his mother panicked and gave premature birth to him when she heard that the Spanish Armada was about to invade England.

To escape the fears of England's civil war, Hobbes moved to France, where he antagonized the French by attacking Catholicism, especially the power of the pope, as well as attacking Descartes, especially his mind-body dualism (Hobbes was a materialist). He returned to England to work for Cromwell once his power was safely established. He wrote, "So I returned to my native land, not well assured of safety, but because there was nowhere else I could be safer. It was cold, the snow was deep, I was old, the wind was biting and fierce, my horse restive, and the road full of potholes." This was not a cheery philosopher!

Politics was his love. Religion, metaphysics, and logic were to be endured or used in the service of politics. He was actively involved in politics all his life, in a pragmatic, semi-Machiavellian way, working both for Cromwell and, when the monarchy was restored, for the king, who gave him a generous pension of one hundred pounds a year for defending the monarchy, but who also prohibited him from publishing any more philosophical works because nearly everyone (except himself) identified him as an atheist. He contented himself with writing a verse translation of the *Iliad* into English in his old age.

Like Freud, he says that religion originates in fear. Out of our fear of the unknown and of death, we invent comforting doctrines and protecting gods.

Though almost certainly an atheist, Hobbes carefully and prudently posed as a Christian theologian to save his life and reputation. The last half of his magnum opus, *Leviathan*, is about theology—even though he was a materialist! (This contradiction is quite understandable if only we remember that he passionately disliked logic, and that he taught that reason was a slave of passion.)

His Relationship to His Contemporaries and His Times

Like most intellectuals of his day, Hobbes deeply loved the new scientific method. That was probably his main motive for being a materialist: he saw the scientific method as the most certain road to truth and saw *reductionism* (Ockham's Razor) as central to that method. Thus, he reduced spirit to matter, mind to body, man to a machine, and thinking to calculating. He discovered and fell in love with geometry at the age of forty and conceived the goal of explaining *everything*, without remainder or mystery, by reducing everything to mathematics. This is one reason for his rejection of all explanations by teleology (design, purpose, or final causality), and also his rejection of Platonic or Aristotelian forms (essences, natures, or universals).

His metaphysical materialism is the logical key to all his philosophy, for it is the foundation on which all his conclusions are based. His is a more modernized version of the philosophy of Democritus, the pre-Socratic philosopher who was the first materialist, and of Lucretius, Democritus' Roman disciple who authored the classic materialist manifesto *The Nature of Things*. For materialists, nothing exists except matter, space ("the void"), and physical motion. Motion has no final cause, goal, purpose, or end. It is blind force, "pushing" from behind; there is no end or design "pulling" from ahead. Formal and final causes are eliminated; only efficient causes exist. Even the notion of *potentiality* (which is what Aristotle meant by "matter" and "material cause") is rejected because it is invisible. Only the actual, concrete, physical universe exists. The so-called "new" scientific atheists are essentially only elaborators of this very old worldview.

Hobbes tried to explain man himself and everything in human experience by this simple materialistic machine model, more completely than anyone had ever done before him, including La Mettrie, who had written a book entitled *Man a Machine*. If the new science explains the world better, Hobbes thought, it must also explain man better. (Does that logically follow? Why or why not?)

Hobbes thought of himself as totally radical (which he was) and original (which he was not) *and* successful: he thought that his philosophy alone should and would be taught in future schools. (Philosophy and prophecy are different talents.) He thought the entire history of human thought had totally failed, both in theory, to explain man and the universe, and in practice, to lead man to peace and happiness. Like Machiavelli, Hobbes was convinced that the ancients had failed because they had aimed too high.

He met many famous people of his time, including Bacon and Descartes, but was most impressed by Galileo and his new physics. Hobbes applied this not only to the external universe but to man himself. He wanted to be the Galileo of anthropology.

One of the most important things that made the new physics new was that in Aristotle's physics, matter is passive and its motion is only accidental and temporary, until it finds its rest and end; but in the new physics, matter is in motion by its very nature and is restless energy. Similarly, for Hobbes, man (who is only matter) is essentially desire, restless and dissatisfied until death; life is an endless, never-successful attempt to fill his desires with satisfactions, like trying to fill up a barrel that is full of holes (the image comes from Plato's *Gorgias*). To use a more contemporary image, we are Gollum, and we are not happy until we are Sauron, the Lord of the Rings, and can control the ring that gives us all power on earth. (But is Sauron happy?)

Like Bacon (whom he met and did not admire), Hobbes' *summum bonum* was power, "man's conquest of nature" by science and technology. Machiavelli had prepared for this revolution by a more purely scientific account of history and politics, free from morality and religion, and by a formula for the conquest, not of nature, but of other people. (The formula was the maximization of *virtù*, military or intellectual power, and the minimization of *fortuna*, chance or luck.) Hobbes' version was more respectable than Machiavelli's, for he spoke of natural rights and even of religion (though he put a purely materialistic meaning into these traditional terms), and because he sought peace rather than war, pedestrian power and hedonism rather than military conquest and glory.

Hobbes' primary target was Aristotle, especially in his Christianized form in Catholic, Thomistic, Scholastic theology and philosophy. Every time he mentions Aristotle's name, he speaks with vituperation and insult. Yet he was astonishingly ignorant of the actual teachings of his archenemy: in attacking the theory of separately existing Forms or essences, Hobbes ascribes this teaching to Aristotle! In fact, of course, this was the primary disagreement between Aristotle and Plato. Such a mistake would merit an F on a freshman philosophy exam.

This is not atypical. Nearly all great modern philosophers are surprisingly ignorant of the past (pre-Cartesian) history of philosophy. Yet Hobbes says we should study the ancients: he writes of "how necessary it is for any man that aspires to true knowledge to examine the definitions of former authors." Either he had in mind only a very narrow and select group of "former authors," viz., those that agreed with him (like so many purportedly "multicultural" programs today), or he is simply preaching what he does not practice.

Hobbes vs. Descartes: the "Meaningless Language" Argument

The easiest way to understand Hobbes is to (1) begin with Descartes' dualistic "clear and distinct ideas" of mind versus matter, thought versus extension, and then (2) reject Descartes' dualism, accepting half of it (the mechanical universe) but not the other half (mind).

In his published debate with Descartes, Hobbes never gives any *premises, evidence, reasons,* or *arguments* for his rejection of "thinking substances" or immaterial minds, but only *explains and accounts for* Descartes' (and common sense's) belief in it (i.e., in anything more than matter). He explains it as the result of linguistic confusion—a ploy many twentieth-century analytic philosophers would also use.

The debate centered on whether we have any concepts that are not derived from sense experience (Descartes said yes and Hobbes said no), and Hobbes' arguments are about the *language* we use to express our experience rather than about our actual experience directly. The debate never got anywhere because Hobbes assumed rather than proved his materialism.

Of course, *if* that assumption is true, there can be no other substance than material substance, and "linguistic confusion" is a reasonable explanation of the illusion that there are also immaterial minds. But *is* the assumption of materialism true? That's the fundamental question. All that Hobbes' arguments do is explain how someone like Descartes, and most of the rest of us, could come to believe in "mental substances" that aren't there ("souls" or "minds")—and that explanation is linguistic.

Hobbes' explanation is epistemological as well as linguistic. The reason Hobbes dismissed all language about immaterial things as "absurd speeches . . . without any significance at all" is because, as a materialist, and therefore an empiricist, he assumed that all genuine knowledge is empirical (sensory) and *therefore* that words have meaning only when they copy sensations or feelings, which are produced by the motion of material bodies. Thus, his linguistics depends on his epistemology, and his epistemology depends on his metaphysics, not vice versa. In his arguments with Descartes, he assumed the opposite order. He never refuted Descartes' metaphysical or epistemological premises as false or his arguments as illogical, only criticized his terms as meaningless.

Hobbes says that all "words whereby we conceive nothing but the sound, we [rightly] call *Absurd, Insignificant,* and *Nonsense,*" and gives as two examples "*immaterial Substances*" and "*a free-Will.*" Of anyone who believes in any such things that transcend his materialistic limits, he says, "I should not say he were in an Error, but that his words were without meaning, that is to say, absurd."

Nonmaterialists use material images, metaphors, or analogies for immaterial things (e.g., we say an idea "entered" our mind or that we "see" the truth). But Hobbes does not accept the meaningfulness of analogical or metaphorical language. He criticizes those "that say, *Faith is infused*, or *inspired*, when nothing can be *poured*, or *breathed* into anything but body." Matter is very literal, and so are most materialists. Materialists make poor poets.

Whenever Hobbes finds a term that ordinary language, tradition, and common sense use to mean anything nonmaterial, he either denies that it has any meaning at all (as in the above examples) or, if there is any personal or political gain in professing belief in it, or danger in professing unbelief in it (the two main examples of this are "God" and "spirits"), he claims that he *does* believe in it, but interprets that belief in a radically different way than everyone else does, thus making his materialism sound like traditional common sense: "Nor does it follow from hence that spirits are *nothing*; for they have dimensions, and are therefore really *bodies*, though that name in common speech be given to such bodies only as are visible or palpable; that is, that have some degree of opacity: but for spirits, they call them incorporeal [immaterial], which is a name of more honour, and may therefore with more piety be attributed to God himself, in whom we consider not what attribute expresseth best his nature, which is incomprehensible, but what best expresseth our desire to honour him."

In other words, God-talk is reduced to subjective psychology. God-talk is invented by our desire, not discovered by our intellect. There is no intelligible object "out there," just a desire "in here" to honor it.

There are a number of problems here. First of all, if he says that "God" is really unintelligible or meaningless, how can Hobbes be anything but an atheist? He says that there is no objective truth or falsehood at all in language about God or souls, only the subjective emotion or desire to give honor. Honor *to what*?

Second, there is a logical problem when a materialist says that language about immaterial things lacks meaning. Meaning is not material, not visible. (It has no size, shape, mass, or color.) So how can it exist, even in Hobbes' language about material things?

Third, Hobbes is avoiding argument in taking refuge in the "meaning of language" gambit—I call it "the linguistic dodge"—in claiming that language that means something to most other people is meaningless because it doesn't mean anything to *Hobbes*. This is not an argument. It is a personal psychological confession.

Fourth, there is also a psychological problem here. How can *the desire to honor* "God" have any meaning if "*God*" has no meaning? How does it differ from a desire to honor the void, or the devil? A desire gets its meaning from its object. That is why hunger is not the same as thirst.

Hobbes' "Political Correctness"

Though Hobbes never offered any proofs of his fundamental point, materialism, his *motives* (as distinct from *reasons* or *proofs*) for accepting materialism are clear.

Those motives were the consequences of this belief rather than its *premises*: its (purported) ability to explain all of experience more simply and scientifically—that was the main *theoretical* motive—and, even more fundamentally for Hobbes, the *practical* motive of its ability to generate a successful political program for peace through a scientific analysis of the causes of war. In other words, "It works." Hobbes, like Machiavelli, was less interested in theory than in practice. He seems to have implicitly assumed that practice justified theory rather than theory justifying practice—that "if it works, it's true" rather than that "if it's true, it will work."

This pragmatism is very clear when it comes to politics. Politics is for Hobbes what God is for a theologian or a saint: the ultimate reason for everything else. Here is Hobbes' justification for including metaphysics in his most famous book, *Leviathan*, which is about politics, and for his "refutation" of the philosophical idea that there are universals, or essences. It is a political, rather than a metaphysical, argument that he gives for metaphysical nominalism:

> But to what purpose (may some men say) is such subtlety (viz. metaphysics) in a work of this nature, where I pretend to nothing but what is necessary to the doctrine of government and obedience? It is to this purpose, that men may no longer suffer themselves to be abused by them, that this doctrine of *separated essences*, built on the vain philosophy of Aristotle [*sic*], would fright them from obeying the laws of their country, with empty names. . . . [So "political correctness" determines metaphysics! As in the totalitarian systems of the twentieth century.]
>
> For it is upon this ground that when a man is dead and buried, they say his soul (that is his life) can walk separated from his body. . . . Upon the same ground they [Catholics] say that the figure and colour and taste of a piece of bread has a being, there [the Eucharist], where they say there is no bread; and upon the same ground they say that faith and wisdom and other virtues are sometimes *poured* into a man, sometimes *blown* into him from Heaven . . . and a great many other things that serve to lessen the dependence of subjects on the sovereign power of their country. For who will endeavor to obey the laws if he expect obedience to be poured or blown into him? . . . Or who that is in fear of ghosts will not bear great respect to those that can make the holy water, that drives them from him? . . . Or who will not obey a priest, that can make God [by transubstantiation], rather than his sovereign?

We've finally found Hobbes' bottom line: political correctness decides whether or not (not!) there is life after death, divine grace, and transubstantiation.

Hobbes saves his bitterest ire for the last, long section of his major work, where he identifies his primary enemy. It is called "The Kingdom of Darkness," and it is the Catholic Church. This is not physical science; it is spiritual warfare.

Hobbes' Metaphysics

Perhaps Hobbes' basic premise is (1) his empiricist epistemology, for he rejects everything that does not fit into that. Perhaps it is (2) his reductionistic methodology, which was working so well in the new science. Perhaps it is (3) the end and goal of both the scientific methodology and the epistemology—namely, the technological "conquest of nature" proclaimed by Bacon as the new, modern *summum bonum*. But logically, it is (4) his materialistic and mechanistic metaphysics. For everything logically depends on metaphysics; whatever you say about what anything *is* (i.e., about what kind of reality it has) depends on what you believe about what kinds of reality there *are*. Even if metaphysics is not prior motivationally, it is prior logically.

Hobbes' metaphysics is extremely simple: *being = matter*, and *matter = being*. He writes, "Every part of the Universe, is Body; and that which is not Body, is no part of the Universe; and because the Universe is All, that which is no part of it is nothing."

Scholars wonder whether this entails atheism. Non-scholars do not. It is easier to fool scholars than non-scholars. Hobbes succeeded amazingly well in fooling the intellectuals of his day by using pious God-talk and devoting half of *Leviathan* to religion, claiming that God exists but is not an immaterial being. He thus cleverly avoided persecution. But if the quotation in the preceding paragraph is true, then the only God that could possibly exist must live on some other planet in the universe, or some unexplored place on this one, and must be detectable by sense observation. Although Hobbes prefers the newer science, he apparently prefers the older religion; it is pagan polytheism minus all the other gods except one.

Only three things exist for Hobbes: matter, space, and motion (and thus time). Only one thing ever happens: atoms bump into other atoms. There is no room for anything else to exist.

Certainly not universals, of any kind whatsoever. (Not all nominalists are materialists—Ockham was not—but all materialists are nominalists, because universals are not concrete material things but the qualities or forms or kinds or species or essences or natures or relationships of things.) Hobbes is an extreme nominalist. Even general *material* qualities, like redness—or materiality itself!—are unreal: "What have all the things that fall under a general term in common? What binds the indefinitely large class of such things together? Nothing, except the possession of the common name which we attach to them."

Unlike the nominalists of the Middle Ages (like Ockham), Hobbes offers no reason for this position. It is his premise, not his conclusion. He also offers no explanation for how general terms can be linguistically useful if they have no basis whatsoever in reality. Nor does he raise and answer any objections against this position. The position did not come from critical analysis or argument; it is an ideological posit, a "politically correct" dogma.

The ultimate consequence of Hobbes' nominalism is that there is no being. For being is a universal. "As we use the word is, so the Latins use their verb *est*, and the Greeks their *esti*, through all its declinations. Whether all other nations of the world have in their several languages a word that answereth to it, or not, I cannot tell; but I am sure they have not need of it. . . . But what then would become of these terms, of *entity, essence, essential* . . . that are derived from it? . . . They are no names of things." So *is* isn't. "Being" is a meaningless word.

Free Will

And there is no such thing as *free will.* Hobbes knows that most people believe there is, but he rejects the idea as logically inconsistent with materialism. His argument is, ironically, syllogistic: (1) No material body can move itself; its motion must be caused by other moving bodies. (More irony: this is the old Aristotelian physics, which Hobbes supposedly rejected.) But (2) free will means that a person is not merely determined by other things but moves himself to choose and act. Ergo, (3) there is no free will.

For Hobbes, what happens when we make a choice is merely a power struggle between passions: whichever one is stronger must win. He calls this "liberty" simply because the winning passion wins and succeeds in moving us to action, without being physically impeded, as the weaker passion was. "Liberty, or Freedom, signifieth properly the absence of opposition (by opposition I mean external impediments of motion) and may be applied no less to irrational and inanimate creatures than to rational." This is a very strange use of "liberty," but it is similar to his use of "God" to mean something no one ever meant by it before in order to avoid the inconvenience of being denounced as an unbeliever. It is not an act of reason but an act of will, a dictate, a ploy, a *power* play. In doing this, he is simply practicing what he preaches! It is a kind of linguistic terrorism.

The moral and ethical consequence of determinism (i.e., the denial of free will) is radical: How can we ever rightly praise, blame, reward, or punish anyone if every act is as necessitated as a machine? When the Coke machine fails to deliver a Coke, we do not call it a wicked sinner and tell it to go to confession; we kick it. (And that is essentially Hobbes' response to human evil: a stronger force, the "Leviathan" of the state, is needed to restrain the weaker ones.)

When confronted with the objection that determinism makes meaningful moral discourse impossible, Hobbes did not answer it, but accused the believer in free will of using words in a meaningless way—that is, in a nonmaterialistic way: "I should not say he [the believer in free will] were in an Error, but that his words were without meaning, that is to say, absurd." This ploy may feel maddening to one who believes in both free will and logic, but once again, it is consistent. For if everything is matter, then everything is simply a power struggle, *including how we use words.*

To the argument that we have free will because our will can overcome our desires (e.g., resisting a temptation), Hobbes replies that it cannot. And again he uses the linguistic ploy: he asks what we can possibly *mean* by "will" other than the strongest desire, or "the last appetite in deliberating." So will cannot overcome desire or appetite because it *is* nothing but an appetite or desire. Will is merely effective desire, the one that wins. Any other meaning to "will" is simply declared meaningless, as are universals, souls, spirits, minds, etc. Thus moderation, self-control, or temperance, the cardinal virtue that is most obviously the prerequisite for all civilization, social or individual, is declared meaningless, nonexistent, and impossible.

A logical consequence of the notion that passion controls everything in us is egotism and hedonism. Hobbes embraces this consequence. He reduces good and evil to pleasure and pain, and these are always private, individual, and egotistic. It is always my own good (which is nothing but my own pleasure) that I seek; I cannot seek yours. Altruism is impossible. Love is simply a disguised egotistic passion.

Note how similar to Machiavelli this is, and how this reductionism elicits the same fundamental objection to both thinkers. They both claim to be more "realistic" than traditional common sense, which allows also for "idealistic" dimensions of human life like altruism (and universals, and souls). Ordinary human experience, as reflected in both common sense and all the wisdom traditions of the world that have stood the test of time, sees this simpleminded egotism (Machiavelli's or Hobbes') as *unrealistic* (i.e., untrue to the concrete fullness of human experience) and as the imposition of an unproved abstract ideological idea—a very simple and reductionistic one—upon a much more complex reality (human nature, human life, and human motivations). So-called "realists" can be just as "unrealistic" as so-called "idealists."

For instance, how does Hobbes account for the experiential fact that apparently immaterial things like wisdom, love, and beauty, when shared with others, do not diminish in the giver, as do material things like money, power, and fame? The answer is that he simply denies the data, denies the experience.

At least he is consistently, in fact shockingly, egotistical. All pleasures of mind, he says, are caused by "glorying," by which he means one's own good opinions that one has of one's own power. These good opinions are themselves always competitive, based on comparison with others. To raise the opinion of my own value, I must lower the opinion of the value of others, in my own mind and in theirs. Hobbes reduces everything to power. He defines "honor" as nothing but the acknowledging of another's superior power to help or harm you. And he defines "reverence" as the concept that another person does not will to use the power that he has to harm us. Power and fear are everything; there is no room for anything like love. The fact that many people found Hobbes charming was apparently due to his one redeeming grace: he did not really practice, or probably even believe, what he preached.

Hobbes' Anthropology

The consequences of Hobbes' metaphysical materialism are a ubiquitous reductionism. The word "only" describes his position in every single dimension of philosophy.

1. For one thing, reason is reduced to sensation plus calculation: man is only an animal plus a computer. Reasoning is literally calculating. *Calculus* is Latin for "pebble," and reasoning is only rearranging the pebbles of sensations and their faded images, which are memories. (The Greeks used to do math by arranging pebbles along strings, rather like an abacus.)
2. For another thing, man is reduced to a complex machine. Hobbes is what we today call a behaviorist. There are no *persons* behind actions. I am not an "I" but only an "it."
3. Reality is only matter.
4. Man is only body.
5. Body is only a machine made of passions.
6. Passions only push us from behind and below, as power or efficient causality; they never pull us from ahead or above, as ideals, by final causality.
7. Reason is only calculation. Minds are only computers.
8. Reason is only the slave of the passions. There is no such thing as the control of the passions by reason. Thoughts are passion's slaves. "The Thoughts are to the Desires as Scouts and Spies, to range abroad and find the way to the Things Desired."
9. Will is only desire. There is no free will.
10. Desire is only power.
11. Good is only a matter of desire, only subjective, only pleasure, and only egotistic. "There is no common Rule of Good and Evil to be taken from the nature of the objects themselves." Good and evil are man-made, relative, and subjective. What we mean when we say "That is good" is nothing more than "That pleases me."
12. Love is only disguised egotism. All men are selfish and competitive. Only force and fear can make them cooperative. Men associate only for gain and glory. (Hobbes never married. Duh!)
13. Laughter is only a sudden gust of physical convulsion caused by something that pleases us by making us think we are superior to another person by demeaning him. There is no such thing as happy, hearty, healthy, human humor. Laughter is a verbal stab in the back.
14. Politics is only artificial, not natural. Man is not by nature a political animal, as Aristotle and all the premoderns except the Sophists said.
15. Politics works only when it is based on force and fear.

16. Power is the only good. Power is not a neutral means to further ends, either good or evil. There are no other ends. Power is good in and of and for itself. Power is the greatest good. Power is God.
17. Happiness is only a dream. It is unattainable. It is not an end.
18. There are no ends, therefore no peace, only endless motion. Therefore, the only human happiness is a continual increase of power, a continual increase of success in getting whatever we desire, an endless, restless, always-dissatisfied movement. "In the first place I put for a general inclination of all mankind, a perpetual and restless desire of power after power, that ceaseth only in death." It is Callicles' "leaky cask" in Plato's *Gorgias*. ("It's all in Plato, all in Plato. . . . What *do* they teach them at these schools!" [C.S. Lewis, *The Last Battle*])
19. The only laws are human laws. What people call moral law does not exist; there are only man-made laws, artificial laws, civil laws, contracts. Therefore, there can be no such thing as a bad human law, a bad ruler, or a bad state. The state is the absolute, the state is God, and God cannot be wrong. And no higher standard can judge him (it).

Hobbes' Epistemology

Epistemology is not the center of Hobbes' philosophy, as it is the center of Hume's. But he has a definite epistemology: like Bacon and Hume, Hobbes is a "hard empiricist." (In fact, there is an almost perfect match, point by point, between Hobbes' and Hume's epistemologies, except that Hobbes did not draw the skeptical consequences that Hume did.) Aristotle, in contrast, is a "soft empiricist": he believed that all human knowledge began with sense experience (thus he is an empiricist) but that knowledge can go beyond sense experience (thus he is a "soft empiricist") by causal reasoning and by abstracting universal forms from individual material things. "Hard empiricists" like Bacon, Hobbes, and Hume do not believe this because they do not believe there *are* universals: they are nominalists. (Once again, we see that everything depends on your metaphysics.)

Hobbes maintains that it is simply impossible for us to think of anything we have not experienced. All we can do is recombine the elements of sense experience, e.g., by imagining a unicorn, or a man with a mule's head (or a mule's heart that is nasty, poor, solitary, brutish, and short).

Therefore, for Hobbes, we can have no positive concept of God at all. There are two reasons for this. One is that Hobbes does not admit any meaning to analogical concepts, so there are no analogical bridges from our worldly experience to God. (Contrast Aquinas.) The other reason is that for Hobbes all concepts are directly derived from outer or inner sensation (imagination). He says, "Whatever we imagine is *finite*. Therefore there is no idea or conception of anything we call *infinite*." This assumes that intellectual conception cannot transcend sensory imagination. Hobbes, as a lover of geometry, should have known better: we can clearly conceive the difference between a circle and a one-hundred-sided enclosed figure, even though we cannot imagine it.

The only way Hobbes allows reason to transcend sensation is *not* by understanding concepts but by rearranging sensations, like checkers on a checkerboard, moving around the atoms of consciousness, the separate data, which are sensations. In other words, Hobbes reduces human intelligence to "artificial intelligence," the thing computers do. It is mechanical. Mathematics is the model for all human knowledge for Hobbes. He defines reasoning as "nothing else but the addition and subtraction of names. . . . True propositions [are] not about the nature of things but about the names of things."

On this basis no rational *argument* is possible, in principle. It is merely a contest of wills: I want to use one word and you want to use another, or I want to make A mean B and you want to make A mean C. Whoever has the most power will win. And this is quite consistent with Hobbes' worship of power. This is the essence of the theory of language in contemporary deconstructionism. Not only does might make right; it also makes truth. Mao Zedong and Hitler both believed that.

Hobbes believed that all qualities that could not be quantified, like color (these would later be labeled "secondary qualities"), and all qualities that involve values (these would later be labeled "tertiary qualities") are subjective, and that only what is quantifiable (which would later be called "primary qualities") is objectively real. The real world is colorless, odorless, and tasteless, and has no beauty or goodness. It is a gray machine. Hobbes' universe is the inside of an office, and the workers are cyborgs.

The problem with this is the law of causality: How can more come from less? If the only real things are quantities, how can something more than these quantities ever arise? They do arise somehow; even Hobbes has to admit that they exist in our consciousness. Where do we get them from? How can something come from nothing? How can there be more in the effect than in the cause? Is that a "scientific" principle?

There may be no apparent *logical reason* for Hobbes' reductionistic epistemology, but there is a very apparent *psychological motive*: the Baconian love of power, "man's conquest of nature." The connection is this: in order for the conquest of nature to happen, we must first reduce nature to what we can conquer by science (theoretically) and technology (practically); we must reduce reality to what can be manipulated, in thought and practice, by the scientific method. The justification for reductionism is practical rather than logical.

There is also another logical problem with Hobbes' materialistic metaphysics when it comes to its application to epistemology. For a materialist, knowledge must be a purely physical process, in which atoms from the tree that we see are carried by light to the eye and along the optic nerve to the occipital lobe of the brain. The mind is merely the brain, and the only thing that is present to the brain is the electrical impulse carried by the nerves. But this is not the tree! So we do not really contact the tree "out there" but only electrical impulses "in here." The outside world, which according to the materialist is merely physical, cannot physically fit into our mind; for the mind, according to the materialist, is merely the brain, which is far too small to hold a tree. The logical conclusion of a materialist epistemology (though Hobbes did not draw this conclusion) is skepticism: no one can ever know the outside world as it is in itself.

But if this is so—if we cannot know objective reality, or "objective truth," if you will—then we cannot know that *that* is an objective truth. So if Hobbes' epistemology is true, it cannot be known to be true (nor can anything else); and only if it is not true, can it (or anything else) be known to be true.

Hobbes' Ethics

Hobbes' ethics is as Humean (or Hume's is as Hobbesian) as his epistemology is.

"Good" is the fundamental term in ethics. Hobbes defines "good" as "that which is desired." It is obviously true that we desire what we think is good in some way, not what we think is bad or less good, but Hobbes means something more than that. He means that *whatever* we desire, by the mere fact of our desiring it, is good; we make it good by desiring it. In other words, "good" is subjective and relative: subjective to the desiring person and relative to his desires. Hobbes is a moral subjectivist and a moral relativist.

Aristotle also defined the good as the object of desire, but he distinguished between the desired and the desirable, between wants and needs. He did not think that our desire was the efficient cause of the goodness of its object, as Hobbes did, but that the good object was the final cause of our desire for it; it was the end or ideal or value that caused our desire by a "pull" rather than a "push," so to speak—like a beautiful woman attracting a man simply by being beautiful (by final causality) rather than like a bouncer throwing a drunk out of a bar (by efficient causality). In other words, Aristotle said that goodness caused our desire as a final cause (ideal, end, purpose), while Hobbes said that our desire caused goodness, brought it into existence, as its efficient cause. For Hobbes there *is* no final causality. It does not fit into the quantitative scientific method. Final causes are not empirical or mathematically measurable. Therefore, they are not real.

For Hobbes, "good" is simply a word we use to refer to "what we desire" and "evil" to refer to "what we fear." These, in turn, are purely material: pleasure and pain. Whatever gives us pleasure, we call "good"; and whatever gives us pain, we call "evil." Hobbes is a hedonist. Hedonism says that *good = pleasure* and *evil = pain*. It is as simple as that. And since pleasure and pain are subjective and relative to the individual, so are good and evil. Good and evil are not properties of anything objectively real; they "are ever used with relation to the person that used them, there being nothing simply and absolutely so, nor any common rule of good and evil to be taken from the nature of the objects themselves, but from the person" who uses these two words to express his subjective desires.

So Hobbes cannot logically distinguish what is subjectively desired from what is objectively desirable. Therefore, no errors are possible in ethics, for errors are subjective mistakes measured by objective reality. Thus, for Hobbes, the questions "Should I desire this or not? Is this good or evil?" are literally, totally *meaningless*. Moral reasoning, moral argument, is impossible.

However, Hobbes is not a simple egotist. Though "good" means merely "good for me," never "good in itself," yet there is also "good for us" as well as "good for me." This is possible when many *me's* create an *us*, or a society in which individuals give up their natural, physical rights to the state, which they create for the sake of protection from each other, as Hobbes explains in his "social contract" theory (see the next section). This political dimension allows Hobbes to judge *individual* choices and acts as good or evil by the man-made laws of the state. This is his only escape from moral relativism: that in the state, good and evil are not relative to individuals. But they *are* relative—to the state. And in the "state of nature" before civil society is invented, there simply is no morality, no moral judgments; we are only animals. In fact, even when socialized, we are still animals, just socialized animals. We act out of fear of punishment, not out of moral conscience.

If "good" equals "whatever we desire," what is desire? How does it work? Not surprisingly, Hobbes' answer is "not by final causality but by efficient causality." For Aristotle, we move morally by being drawn and attracted by our final cause, our good, our end, our perfection, our improvement, the actualization of our natural potentialities. For Hobbes, there are no such things; desires simply push us around physically, like bullies. Or, rather, since there is really no "us" in the sense of a soul or self, stronger desires push around *weaker desires*, and thereby move our bodies to act as they do. For desires, too, are merely physical forces. It is like a larger, stronger animal pushing a smaller one around.

If what we desire is not an ideal, what is it? What we desire is not a future value but a present fact: it is simply self-preservation. We are like everything else in the universe, from animals to bubbles. Everything resists destruction, even bubbles; for when you touch a bubble, it will bend, but when you release your finger, it returns to its round shape. We, and plants, and animals, are just more complex bubbles. The supreme good is survival, and power: the power to survive and act. However low this may be as a theory of good and evil, you have to admire Hobbes for being logically consistent: even his ethics conforms to his materialistic metaphysical premise.

Hobbes' Political Philosophy

Hobbes' political philosophy can be seen as a partial mitigation of Machiavelli. For one thing, he took the common good more seriously than Machiavelli did. Where Machiavelli wrote a book entitled *The Prince*, Hobbes wrote one entitled *On the Citizen*. For another thing, Hobbes, unlike Machiavelli, spoke of a "natural right" and a "natural justice," though this meaning was purely materialistic and not at all the traditional notion of "natural law." "Natural right" for Hobbes is simply the liberty that we have to use our power in any way we think necessary to preserve our life. In calling this "natural *right*," Hobbes is once again using words in a new and uncommon sense, a purely materialistic sense, as he did when speaking of "God" or "mind." He means simply the fact that we desire to avoid death and will try to overcome all obstacles to this goal if we can. So "natural right" means simply the universal desire for self-preservation. Hobbes derives our "rights" not from our end but from our beginning, from the primitive urges that push us to live, not from the aspiration to moral goods or ends that move us by inspiring or calling us to something better (i.e., some *reason* to live).

Two other apparently idealistic words Hobbes uses that seem to raise him above Machiavelli but really do not are "liberty" and "the laws of nature." As we have seen in our discussion of free will, "liberty" means for him merely the absence of physical obstacles to obtaining whatever we desire. And "the laws of nature" means not natural *moral* laws about moral values or duties, but simply the physical fact that physical restrictions are placed on our physical "liberty." "Rights" are merely what we can do, "liberty" is merely the power to do it, and "natural laws" define what we cannot do, at least not without punishment, inflicted either by man (e.g., imprisonment for theft) or by nature (e.g., broken bones from jumping off a cliff). "Natural laws," for Hobbes as for Machiavelli, have nothing to do with man's perfection, or final cause. And they come not from reason but from the passions, which for Hobbes determine everything in us, as efficient causes. Hobbes defines all law in terms of will and passion, not reason, and in terms of egotism, not altruism. The object of everyone's will is his own good; therefore, every law aims at the good of the lawgiver(s). (Hobbes was never a parent—thank God.)

The three most distinctive ideas in Hobbes' political philosophy are "the state of nature," "the social contract," and "the Leviathan."

The "state of nature" before the invention of the artifice of civil society is a state of perpetual war, "such a war as is of every man against every man." In this state, life is "solitary, poor, nasty, brutish, and short." The only thing good about the state of nature (i.e., about *human* nature in its natural state) is that it can be escaped, by the invention of civil society through the "social contract."

This "state of nature" may or may not have actually occurred at a specific time in history before the rise of civil society. Hobbes' argument does not depend on its literal historical facticity. It is a picture of what life without states would be or could be, not necessarily what it actually was. However, it is not a mere abstract "thought experiment" but a real possibility: we civilized men can descend into this state in practice; Hobbes gives two examples of this: (1) civil war and (2) the life of the "savages" ("Indians") in America (*sic!*).

In the state of nature there is no kind of morality at all. For all morality comes from the conventions of society, and these have not yet been set up. Only society, not God or human nature, creates morality. In the state of nature, "the notions of right and wrong, justice and injustice, have there no place. [For] where there is no common power, there is no law; where no law, no injustice." (Law is based on power, not reason; justice is based on human law, not any "natural law.") The state of nature is war, and "force and fraud are in war the two cardinal virtues." In this state, the only "laws of nature" are pragmatic strategies for survival, not morally binding commands.

Hobbes' metaphysical materialism necessitates the conclusion that we are essentially competitive by nature, since our good is simply power, and my power over you necessarily diminishes your power over me. And since power is happiness, it follows that the happier I am, the more unhappy I must make you (though Hobbes does not pursue this consequence to all its dreadful logical conclusions).

But the most important power we have makes us essentially equal: the power to kill each other. Even "the weakest has strength enough to kill the strongest." We are equally vulnerable to murder. And this gives each of us good reason to fear all others. Fear is the strongest of all passions, and fear of violent death is the strongest of all fears.

There is no *society* in the state of nature, because man is not by nature social or political, as the ancients thought. And since all morality is a social invention, there is no *morality*, thus no appeal to justice. But we do have *reason* (i.e., cleverness), even in the state of nature. And we can calculate the means that will work to attain the end of our self-preservation. These means are the only things Hobbes means by "natural law," "laws of nature," "the dictates of reason," and "the moral law."

These are very different meanings than the meanings these terms have in ordinary usage. For instance, "law" in Hobbes is not a dictate of reason but of will, based on desire. It could not be a dictate of reason because there is nothing really there for reason to know: there is no real moral good or justice or natural moral law. Morality is wholly artificial, like the rules of a game. And reason is merely "the scout for the senses" and the servant of desire. It sees no ends (for there are no real ends); it only calculates the most effective means to whatever end is subjectively desired.

Again Hobbes plays the linguistic game of willfully changing the meaning of words. This is the same Hobbes who criticized Descartes for using words in a meaningless way when Descartes, like everyone else except materialists, spoke of "minds" or "spiritual substances" (nonmaterial things). Hobbes abandons his empiricism in his language: he does not begin empirically, by observing ordinary usage; he begins rationalistically, by an *a priori fiat*, by his own "linguistically correct" ideology. He begins not with his premises but his conclusions.

This pessimistic view of human nature is Hobbes' "bad news." Now comes the "good news." There is a way out. Parallel to Bacon's conquest of nature by scientific reason creating technology, Hobbes offers a conquest of *human* nature (in its natural state, the "state of nature") by practical reason creating civil, public society by a "social contract."

It is reason that comes to our rescue from the state of nature. Since reason is the servant of the passions, reason serves the greatest passion, the fear of violent death, by inventing law itself, and thus creates morality—creates it out of nothing moral, for there is absolutely nothing moral there to begin with. So this is another instance of there being more in the effect than in the cause.

Here is how reason rescues us. Imagine two cavemen, Og and Glog, bashing each other's brains out with their clubs because they hadn't invented boxing, hockey, or football yet. Og has more reason than Glog and says, "Hey, Glog, I figured out a way we could both be happier: if we agreed to stop beating each other up." Glog objects: "But it feels really good when I bash you." Og replies, "But how does it feel when I bash you back?" "Bad." "How bad?" "Really, really bad." "Well, don't you see? The pain is worse than the pleasure. So we could both get less pain if we stopped beating each other up." "Gee, Og, you're smart." "So let's make that agreement. Let's call it 'the social contract.'" "Wait a minute. That's not going to work, because the rest of the tribe will see us throw away our clubs, and they'll bash us and we won't be able to bash back." "Well, then, we'll have to convince them to stop bashing too. It's got to be public, not private." "But even if we do convince them, one of us could still bash the other when he was asleep. Why would anybody keep that agreement if they could get away with breaking it?" "Because we'll make it impossible to get away with it. We'll make cops." "What's cops?" "We'll give the three strongest guys in the tribe the biggest clubs, and tell them to kill anybody they see beating up their neighbors. Then we'll all be happy. We'll be protected by the cops from being bashed to death and they'll have the power of being the protectors." "But what if all three cops are asleep? What's to stop somebody from stealing their big clubs and killing somebody else?" "We'll have to invent something else: religion." "What's that?" "Invisible cops in the sky with such big clubs that they can beat you forever after you die if you don't obey the law." "Do you think they'll actually believe that?" "Let's try it and see if it works." Well, it did, and that's the tribe we all descended from, by natural selection, while the others killed each other off.

See how attractively simplistic a reductionistic explanation can be?

The problem is: *why not* kill, steal, lie, cheat, rape, etc. if you can get away with it? Traditional moralists like Plato and Aristotle answer: because vice makes you miserable and virtue makes you happy, because human nature is teleologically ordered toward virtue. Obviously Hobbes can't say that. What can he say? Only one thing. Hobbes has absolutely no answer to the "Why not, if I can get away with it?" question, except: let's make sure nobody gets away with it. That's why he demands an absolute monarchy, a fearsome monster (the Leviathan, from Job 41:33–34).

If I *can* get away with murder—and in every society in human history, some people can—the only thing Hobbes could say to me is: Go for it then. It's not evil for you, only for your victim. Really, there is no such thing as moral evil, only physical evil. Use the ring of power if you can. Be Sauron.

The reason why Hobbes logically must come to this shocking conclusion is that he has reduced reason to a mere pragmatic calculation of means. Reason is not at all the understanding of ends, or goods. So he can appeal only to fear of pain, not love of good—very much like Machiavelli, who says it is better to be feared than to be loved. He can appeal only to cops, not conscience. He can only say that the Leviathan will make it unprofitable for you to disobey the laws by catching you and punishing you. But *if not*, there is absolutely no reason why you should act contrary to your egotistic nature and be moral instead of immoral, just instead of unjust, altruistic instead of egotistic, social instead of antisocial.

Hobbes could point out that if *some* do not yield their rights to the Leviathan, then *all* will have more pain, and profit less. But why should *I* be one of the ones to do that if I can profit more by refusing the contract and violating the law, if I can get away with it? Why should I be social if it's not personally profitable to me? Why not be the "superman" of Thrasymachus, Callicles, Sauron, Ivan Karamazov, and Raskolnikov if there is no "crime and punishment" by conscience, only by Leviathan (the state), and you can escape that? Hobbes' only possible answer is to make it impossible to escape that—as impossible as escaping God. Thus, Hobbes has to make the state into something godlike, something omnipotent.

Leviathan

Leviathan (the state) can take any structural form—rule by one, a few, or all—but absolute monarchy is the best because it is the most effective and powerful form of control. The most effective and powerful control is through fear, because fear is the most effective and powerful passion. Fear of death then turns into fear of the monarch.

This must be an absolute monarchy, not a constitutional monarchy, because the sovereign did not contract to give up any of his natural rights to anyone; everyone else did that to him. Therefore, he is bound by no contract.

He therefore works only for selfish motives, like Machiavelli's prince, not for the *res publica*, the public things. The ideal state is not a "republic," much less a democracy. The ideal state is totalitarian because the sovereign has total power, unlimited by contract.

Aristotle's definition of a good state was one in which the sovereign, whether one, few, or many, worked for the good of the whole rather than for his own good. For Hobbes that is literally impossible, and Aristotle's distinction is literally meaningless.

According to Hobbes there are no duties or obligations in the state of nature, because all duties arise from contracts or covenants, and there are none yet in the state of nature. The problem with this is that all covenants depend on trust in the other to keep the promises made in the covenant, and there is no trust in the state of nature, because there is no trust where there is fear of the other violating the covenant. The only thing that can compel us to keep our promises is not love or trust or morality but force, compulsion, power: the Leviathan. Enforcement is not the last requirement for law; it is the first. Therefore, all law (and thus all morality, which is created only by law) depends on this sovereign, who is the enforcer. But he himself is outside the law. Therefore, morality depends on immorality, legality on illegality, as it does in Machiavelli. (Remember Romulus and Remus.)

Hobbes admits that the sovereign usually gets power by force, fraud, conquest, blood, and murder. It makes no difference. The sovereign is the sovereign. It is a meaningless question whether the war he fought to acquire his conquest was just or unjust, for justice exists only after the sovereign is in power to enforce the law, not before. Logically, then, there can be no difference between the rightful, legitimate ruler and a wrong, illegitimate one. There is no law for him who makes the law. In three words, might makes right. Literally. The sovereign is God. He is infallible. He cannot be criticized.

He must also have legislative and judicial as well as executive powers. There can be no division of powers, for that would weaken enforcement and, consequently, would weaken fear, the foundation for obedience and therefore for peace.

This is true whether he is one man, a few, or many. Rousseau will opt for what Tocqueville called "soft totalitarianism" in his preference for democracy and the infallibility of "the General Will" instead of a single monarch, but we can see the same principle there: that there is no higher law, no "natural law" that can give any meaning to the question of whether the rulers are good or evil. Politics is above morality, not vice versa, for both Hobbes and Rousseau.

We tend to think that democracy and totalitarianism are opposites. They are not. They are answers to two different questions. Democracy is an answer to the question of where the sovereignty lies, how many will share it. Totalitarianism is an answer to the question of how much sovereignty the sovereign has, whether there are any limits to it. Rousseau's infallible "General Will" is an example of a democratic, or soft, totalitarianism. So is *Brave New World*, in contrast to *1984*. Hobbes prefers monarchy, but his principles work, he claims, for all governments, including oligarchies and democracies.

Even though the only things that can make man moral are fear of punishment and rational calculation of self-interest, and even though he will act morally only under compulsion, for Hobbes this does not make man less moral, for egotism is the only basis for morality. In plainer language, what most people call morality—a truly loving, altruistic motive, or even a passion for justice—simply does not exist and cannot exist for Hobbes. We are all devils who can only be forced by a stronger devil to act like angels.

Hobbes vs. Locke

To put Hobbes into the context of "the great conversation" about politics between his main predecessor Machiavelli and his main successor Locke, it is illuminating at this point to quote from Leo Strauss' *What Is Political Philosophy?*:

> Hobbes' teaching was still much too bold to be acceptable. It, too, was in need of mitigation. This mitigation was the work of Locke. Locke took over the fundamental scheme of Hobbes and changed it only in one point. He realized that what man primarily needs for his self-preservation is less a gun than food, or more generally, property. Thus the desire for self-preservation turns into the desire for property, for acquisition, and the right to self-preservation becomes the right to unlimited acquisition. The practical consequences of this small change are enormous. Locke's political teaching is the prosaic version of what in Hobbes still had a poetic quality. It is, precisely on Hobbes' premises, more reasonable than Hobbes' own political teaching. With a view to the resounding success of Locke, as contrasted with the apparent failure of Hobbes, especially in the Anglo-Saxon world, we can say that Machiavelli's discovery or invention of the need for an immoral or amoral substitute for morality became victorious through Locke's discovery or invention that the substitute is acquisitiveness. Here we have an utterly selfish passion whose satisfaction does not require the spilling of any blood and whose effect is the improvement of the lot of all. In other words, the solution to the political problem by economic means is the most elegant solution, once one accepts Machiavelli's premise: economism is Machiavellianism come of age.

Hobbes on Religion and Politics

Hobbes' opinions about religion—which take up the whole second half of *Leviathan*—are always determined by his politics, never vice versa.

He calls Christianity the true religion and calls himself a Christian; but it is a form of Christianity few Christians, and no Christian churches, would recognize. For one thing, the only distinction between religion and superstition is that superstitions are ideas that are not allowed by the public authorities, while religion is what is allowed. Religion and superstition are generically the same: "the fear of power invisible."

Among all opinions, the one that is most harmful to the peace of a Christian nation is any that leads citizens to believe they owe any obedience to anyone else than the political sovereign. They have no king but Caesar. Hobbes speaks of the need to purge from the nation "the poisons of seditious doctrines," and he mentions three that are the most dangerous. They all concern the relation of conscience to politics.

First is the teaching of theologians who say that each man ought to follow his private conscience to judge good and evil. Hobbes says this may be necessary in the state of nature, but in civil society the monarch, not conscience, is the absolute sovereign.

Second, that whatever a man does against his conscience is a sin, even if his sovereign commands it. On the contrary, says Hobbes, it would be a sin for a citizen to disobey his sovereign. (This was the defense the Nazi war criminals used at the Nuremberg trials: we were doing our duty—because our duty was first of all to Hitler, not to our conscience. See the play and the movie *Judgment at Nuremberg*.) If the sovereign commands the citizen to do something sinful, Hobbes assures us, it is not the citizen that God will hold responsible for the sin, but the sovereign. (How does he know this? Did he interview God?)

Third, there is an idea that Hobbes says originates in the fear of the unknown and the fear of spirits: that there should be a division of powers between temporal and eternal, secular and sacred, state and church. This is impossible because, as Christ taught, "no man can serve two masters." (Hobbes, incredibly, interprets Christ here as saying that *Caesar*, not God, is our total master in this life, even of our conscience!) Hobbes was very much against the separation of church and state, not because it deprived the church of the power of the state but because it gave the church some freedom from the state.

Any religious idea that threatens the sovereign's sovereignty, for Hobbes, must be seditious and a threat to peace. If men believe that there is a greater, divine power that gives greater rewards and punishments in the next life than the sovereign can give in this life, they will obey this greater power and weaken the authority of the sovereign. Logically, this ought to mean that all alternatives to atheism should be illegal. But again Hobbes claims to find his opinion in the Bible: he interprets all its references to "the kingdom of God" to mean a political kingdom in this world.

He also says that not the church or the saints or the theologians but only the political sovereign should be the authoritative interpreter of the Bible. He interprets the Bible's term "church" as meaning a Christian *state*, and "eternal life" as a life here on earth when Christ will assume political rule. Heaven and hell are both this-worldly and physical. Satan is any earthly enemy of the earthly church—which, of course, is totally subordinate to the state; thus *Satan = any enemy of the state*, including any Christian church that opposes it. (Linguistic terrorism again.)

Hobbes wanted the sovereign to believe in God—not because he believed it was true, that God really existed, but because only the fear of God could possibly check and tame the sovereign's power. The only other restraint on the sovereign is his own selfishness and self-interest: no one wants to be hated and thought to be wicked, cruel, and unjust by the people. But this assumes that the people still have some moral conscience to criticize the sovereign; but Hobbes says that conscience is to be totally submitted to the sovereign. There seems to be a logical contradiction there.

Hobbes was either (1) an atheist who only pretended to be a Christian, to avoid persecution; or (2) a Christian who only pretended to believe many religiously unorthodox opinions about the subordination of religion to politics, to curry favor with the king; or (3) an honest and sincere but unintelligent Christian who sincerely believed all the many absurd things he said about what the Bible really means. You must decide for yourself whether to question his intelligence or his honesty.

The decision is not difficult. A typical example is Hobbes' interpretation of the biblical passage where Israel complains that, unlike pagan nations, they have no king but God, and God warns them that if they had a king, the king would take their children away from them and slaughter them in battle for his own greedy lust for power. Hobbes interprets this *warning* as a *promise*, this dystopia as a utopia, and this evil as a good, as God's approval of an institution of absolute monarchy. Even a child can see that this is not what the passage means; so if Hobbes is honest and means what he says here, he is not as intelligent as a child.

Hobbes is a valuable and important philosopher, because whether you agree or disagree with him, you can learn much from him. If you agree with him, you can learn some ideas that are so unusual and so radical that very few other philosophers dare to teach them; so Hobbes is precious. And if you disagree, you also learn, for you can often learn more from philosophers you disagree with than from those you agree with. For you understand and appreciate good philosophers most clearly and sharply by contrast with bad ones—especially if the bad ones are as logically consistent as Hobbes is.

71

JEAN-JACQUES ROUSSEAU

AD 1712—1778

Rousseau is one of the most popular and influential philosophers in history. Yet he had nothing significant to say about logic, methodology, metaphysics, cosmology, theology, or epistemology. He was not interested in theory but in practice, especially revolutionary politics. Indeed, he was the main mind behind the archetypal revolution of all time, the French Revolution, though he did not live to see it. Its architects virtually deified him.

He was at once one of the most poetic, passionate, powerful, and provocative writers of all time *and* one of the most consummately hypocritical, untrustworthy, self-indulgent, self-pitying, egotistical, and emotionally pathological minds in the history of philosophy. At least that is the judgment of his friends, and even some of his admirers, almost all of whom were French. (Is the admiration of decadence a uniquely French secret?) He was both appealing and appalling. He was, above all, a sentimentalist, with incredible cunning at conning other sentimentalists, like a televangelist who makes his fortune manipulating the emotions of wealthy middle-aged women (he never had a lasting male friend in his life) with tender hearts and tender brains, weeping all the way to the bank. (Someday I'll tell you what I *really* think of him.)

The historian Paul Johnson calls him the first and most influential of the new class of "intellectuals" (in his book by that title). The modern intellectual, as distinct from the premodern, conceives himself not as an interpreter of an authoritative tradition that preceded him and overarches him, but as the creator of a new world of thought, with himself as the sole authority. He is, therefore, by definition, secular rather than religious, unless he is the inventor of a new religion.

Johnson lists five characteristics of this new breed of intellectuals:

1. They are radicals, freed from all tradition and authority. The revolutionaries guillotined the king, but it was primarily Rousseau who guillotined the whole existing European order, the *ancien régime*.
2. They are supremely confident in their own ability to create a radically new and better order of thought and life, from scratch.
3. They look to politics to incarnate their ideals.
4. They appeal neither to faith nor to reason but to will, instinct, intuition, imagination, sentiment, or feeling. They give readers fire, not light. They are propagandists, masters of the sound bite.
5. They claim to do this out of love for "humanity" but almost always show remarkably little love, interest, or even awareness of actual individual human beings in their lives. It takes only one intellectual to change a light bulb: he just holds it while the whole world turns around him.

In other words, modern intellectuals are typically radicals, utopians, ideologues, irrationalists, and egotists. Rousseau is the archetype of all five of these features.

His Life

The German poet Heine said it was impossible to write the history of the fascinatingly dull life of Kant because he had neither life nor history. Rousseau is the opposite: he had multiple lives, histories, and perhaps personalities.

He was born in Calvinist Geneva. His mother died shortly after childbirth. "My birth was the first of my misfortunes," he wrote. He credits his parents for giving him only one thing: "a sensitive heart. . . . It has been the cause of all the misfortunes of my life." His father left him to an aunt, who raised him. But though he was a precocious child, like almost all philosophers, his formal education ended at twelve. He left Geneva and roamed from place to place like a '60s hippie, meeting many sympathetic benefactors who pitied and supported him.

At fifteen he converted to Catholicism to obtain the protection and money of Baroness Madame de Warens, thirteen years his senior, whom he called his *maman* and who became his off-and-on mistress. She had left her Protestant husband and converted to Catholicism. She was very "pious" but did not believe in sin, judgment, or hell, and like Rousseau believed that it could not possibly be sinful to follow your own personal passions and inclinations. ("It can't be wrong if it feels so right." Sounds familiar.)

Rousseau valued his own family only for their money and did the same to his adopted "maman." She rescued him from poverty repeatedly, and in return he ignored and abandoned her when she aged and needed money and his company; in fact, he let her die, probably of malnutrition.

He lived at her expense for fifteen years, frequently wandering and returning, during which he tried and failed at at least thirteen different jobs. The longest-lasting one was copying music. He later composed some rather third-rate arias and overtures, which, once he had become famous through his political writings, became the most popular music in France with all classes of society, and even the king.

He met many influential French intellectuals, especially Denis Diderot, the editor of the new French *Encyclopedia*, "The Bible of the Enlightenment," which was a summary of all the new learning in the world and an attack on all the old. In 1850, when Diderot was imprisoned for defending atheism in print, Rousseau made a long journey, on foot, to visit him, and while on the road experienced an event that was to change his life and the life of Western civilization forever.

He read an advertisement in the paper from the Dijon Academy of Letters inviting entries for an essay competition on the topic "Whether the Rebirth of the Sciences and the Arts has contributed to the Improvement of Morals." He wrote, "At the moment of that reading, I saw another universe and I became another man. Suddenly I felt my mind dazzled by a thousand lights; crowds of lively ideas presented themselves at once, with a force and confusion that threw me into inexpressible turmoil. . . . I declared to myself: 'Virtue, truth! I will cry increasingly, truth, virtue!' . . . My waistcoat was soaked with tears I had shed without noticing it." It was a moment like Descartes' dream, Augustine's voice in the garden ("Take and read"), or Socrates' message from the Delphic oracle.

Other submissions to the contest, as expected, enumerated and praised the ways the "Enlightenment" had added to human welfare. But Rousseau flatly contradicted the essential creed of modernity and the "Enlightenment" with a scathing criticism of modern science, which he said had contradicted and replaced religion. Reason had been elevated over feeling, sophistication over simplicity, city over country, rich over poor, commerce over virtue, and Athens over Sparta, the city of reason and sophistication and self-indulgence over the city of simple moral virtue (*sic!*). It was like a defense of kosher Judaism on a pig farm. Yet it not only won the prize but made him instantly famous.*

Rousseau had a lifelong mistress, Thérèse Levasseur, whom he refused to marry until late in life. She was a barely literate laundry maid in his residential hotel,

---

* It is difficult to be sure (1) whether Rousseau actually sincerely believed what he wrote, or (2) whether it was a cynical "con job" by a consummate actor to elicit adoration, fame, and financial support from sentimental suckers, or (3) whether it was simply something he happened to feel at the moment, a thought experiment from one part of a split personality.

a sweet, simple, loving soul who adored Rousseau and claimed, after he died, that if he was not a saint then no one ever was. Rousseau did not reciprocate this love. He explicitly said that he "never felt the least glimmering of love for her. . . . The needs I satisfied with her were for me purely sexual and had nothing to do with her as an individual." He never took her out in public, and when he invited people to his house, he would not allow her to sit down with them. He used to make lists of her verbal mistakes and mock them to his friends. He quarreled with her family and publicly accused her brother of theft and her mother of greed.

Each time Thérèse got pregnant, Rousseau insisted, over her tearful objections, on depositing each of their children (there were five) into an orphanage, where he knew that two-thirds of the children died of malnutrition in the first year, only 14 percent survived to the age of seven, and only 5 percent to adulthood, almost all of them becoming beggars. Rousseau never even gave any of his children names, nor made any note of their birthdays. In his *Confessions*, this writer who had glorified the child-centered family defended his hypocrisy: "I said to myself: Since this is the practice of the country, when one lives there one can follow it. I made up my mind cheerfully and without the least scruples. . . . I believed that I was performing an action of a Citizen and father." He rationalized that this was for Thérèse, "to save her honor."

He also explained that children would have been "an inconvenience. . . . How could I achieve the tranquility of mind necessary for my work, my garret filled with domestic cares and the noise of children?" Yet he spoke of abandoning his children as a "sacrifice" in claiming that he had found "compensation for my sacrifice." He argued that

> it would assuredly be the most unbelievable thing in the world if the *Heloise* and the *Emile* [his two popular works of fiction that exalt children] were the work of a man who did not love children. . . . I know full well that no father is more tender than I would have been. . . . My ardent love of the great, the true, the beautiful and the just; my horror of evil of every kind, my utter inability to hate or injure or even to think of it; the sweet and lively emotion which I feel at the sight of all that is virtuous, generous, and amiable; is it possible, I ask, that all these can ever agree in the same heart with the depravity which, without the least scruple, tramples underfoot the sweetest of obligations? No! I feel, and loudly assert—it is impossible! Never, for a single moment in his life, could Jean-Jacques have been a man without feeling, without compassion, or an unnatural father.

He also blamed the godlessness of his intellectual friends for putting the idea of an orphanage into his head.

How did he accomplish his fame? Rousseau had desperately desired to personally impress Parisian high society, but he simply could not, until he became famous with his essay, for he was too awkward socially. So he turned his social defect into a virtue and deliberately offended everyone by ostentatiously rejecting not only civilization but civilized behavior itself, practicing crude buffoonery and insulting his hosts. It was playing a part, the part of Diogenes the Cynic, the antisocial Greek philosopher who lived and acted like a dog. And, of course, French society loved it.

The very proper Kant admired Rousseau so much that his portrait was the only picture on the walls of his home. He called him "a subtle Diogenes." Shelley, Schiller, John Stuart Mill, George Eliot, Victor Hugo, Flaubert, Tolstoy, and Leo Strauss all paid his writings great homage—but none of these had known him personally.

He also had a warm affection for animals (as did many great tyrants in history). He proclaimed himself the greatest lover of "humanity," but he quarreled with every actual human he ever met. He alienated every male friend he ever had, both the famous (Diderot, Voltaire, Hume) and the non-famous, by inventing extravagant and baseless accusations against everyone. Voltaire called him an "arch madman . . . a monster of vanity and vileness" and a hypocrite who "writes against the theater after having written a bad play. . . . He writes against France which nourishes him," as he did against all his friends. Diderot concluded that he was "deceitful, vain as Satan, ungrateful, cruel, hypocritical, and full of malice."

Yet no matter how many friendships he destroyed, he always found new admirers, especially rich old ladies who lavishly supported him. Apparently simple and guileless, he was always setting little traps for people and looking for opportunities to insult them, especially when they helped him. What made this success possible was, at least in part, his ability to exploit the guilt of the rich and sophisticated by being deliberately rude. In return, he was affectionately called "the Bear" and "the Brute of Nature." But it was a pose, an actor's mask. What *was* genuine in him was his self-pity and self-righteousness. He wrote, "My sentiments . . . dispense me from being polite." That was his absolute: his sentimentalism, his own feelings and emotions as the sovereign and infallible justification for everything.

He was absolutely convinced of his superiority to all other men, both in his sufferings and in his virtues. He wrote, "What could your miseries have in common with mine? My situation is unique, unheard of since the beginning of time. The person who can love me as I can love is still to be born. . . . No one ever had more talent for loving. . . . I was born to be the best friend that ever existed. . . . Show me a better man than me, a heart more loving, more tender, more sensitive. . . . I rejoice in myself, my consolation lies in my self-esteem." (A paragon of pop psychology!) He wrote, "My idea of happiness is . . . never to have to do anything I don't wish to do." It is the philosophy of a precocious child, a moral dwarf with gigantic rhetorical skills.

This notoriously crafty liar and grudge-bearer wrote, "I am never crafty and never bear a grudge." This was not inconsistent, for truth was to him not objective, rational, and impersonal (that was the old rationalism that he attacked) but subjective, emotional, and personal. This also explains his inability to make permanent friendships: as the consummate egotist and subjectivist, he equated any hostility to himself with hostility to truth and virtue, so that by definition all his critics were dishonest and vicious men, deserving of nothing less than hell itself.

The philosopher Hume invited him to England when he felt persecuted in France. (He was not really persecuted, of course; he had very little to grumble about. Yet no philosopher who ever lived was a greater grumbler.) The friendship with Hume was a friendship made in hell. Hume was polite, self-controlled, moderate, and rational; Rousseau was passionate, unpredictable, prey to wild mood swings, and continually embarrassing both himself and his host; and they simply could not comprehend each other. Though Hume initially thought very highly of Rousseau; defended, sheltered, and protected him; and introduced him to English intelligentsia, Rousseau came to believe that Hume was his enemy and at the head of a vast international plot to destroy him. His twenty-five-page letter attacking Hume is a treasure trove for any psychiatrist studying acute paranoia, perhaps dementia. Burke considered him literally insane. Hume's conclusion about him was that he was "a monster, who saw himself as the only important being in the universe."

He denounced a family servant and got her fired to hide his own theft, then explained that "affection for her was the cause of what I did." He lied to a gullible priest and to a rich aristocratic lady from whom he stole a silver medallion. He found another such lady to live off and became her lover while her former common-law husband still lived with them as a *ménage à trois*.

In his lifetime, Rousseau's two most popular books were two novels, *Julie, or the New Heloise* and *Emile, or On Education*. *Julie* is a story of seduction followed by repentance and punishment; thus, it was calculated to appeal to both prurient interest and moral conscience—like his life. The Archbishop of Paris accused it of "insinuating the poison of lust while seeming to proscribe it." Its clever preface warned that "chaste girls do not read love stories"—and so of course they did. Women fainted over the book. One reviewer wrote, "One must suffocate, one must abandon the book, one must weep. One must write to you that one is choking with emotion and weeping." Another wrote, "Your divine works, Monsieur, are an all-consuming fire. . . . Feeling has taken over once again: love, pity, virtue, sweet friendship have forever conquered my soul." Rousseau knew and played his audience like a master fisherman plays a fish. How convenient to make virtue a *feeling*!

Emile is an idealized romance of education. It is a program for forming the feelings of the few elite among the young who could return to nature and preserve their innate virtue even while living in corrupt society. Its themes would become the platitudes of Romanticism, in which feeling replaced reason as the holiest human power, and the return to the "noble savage" replaced progress and civilization. *Emile's* definition of freedom was Rousseau's: that one "wants only what he can do, and only does what pleases him." The state of nature is described as the feeling of the sheer sweetness of existence, with no worry about the future or self-preservation—the two motives that later would lead man to found civilization. According to *Emile*, only an elite few are capable of this return to nature (like Rousseau himself, of course), and these "solitary dreamers" will never quite fit into society as good citizens.

But if only a few can return to nature, what hope is there for the many? Rousseau's answer is found later, in *The Social Contract* and its vehicle, "the General Will," a sort of Big Brother, which is "infallible" and "can make all men perfect." More on this book later; it is Rousseau's most important.

In his old age Rousseau gave public readings from the parade of his shamelessness that was his autobiographical *Confessions*. One of these readings lasted seventeen hours—egotism is inexhaustible. After his final reading he said, "If anyone knows some things contrary to what I have just set forth, even if they are proved a thousand times, he knows lies and impostures. . . . He does not love justice or truth. . . . He ought to be choked."

His next to last book was three interior dialogues with himself (a fitting summary of his life) that he titled *Rousseau, Judge of Jean-Jacques*. (Who else could possibly judge him?)

His last book, *Reveries of a Solitary Walker*, confesses that "to act against my inclination was always impossible for me." (This is, in fact, literally true of only animals and God.)

After his death and the posthumous and enormously popular publication of his *Confessions*, he became the object of a fanatical quasi-religious cult, with pilgrimages to his tomb, guidebooks, book-burnings of Diderot's criticisms of him, and séances in which his worshipers would evoke his spirit. Five years after the French Revolution, which everyone felt he had inspired, his body was exhumed and given highest state honors in a three-day-long public procession.

The Connection between His Life (and Character) and His Philosophy

Why have I taken so much more time to detail Rousseau's life and character than those of any other philosopher? Not for prurient, or even psychiatric, interest, but because there is a uniquely close connection between his thought and his life, character, and emotions, which so powerfully moved both him and his admirers. Rousseau neither believed nor lived any separation or independence of objective, rational truth from his own subjective feelings. Most other philosophers, like Buddha, said, "Look not to me, look to my *dharma* [teaching]." But one can no more separate Rousseau's teachings from his person than one can with Nietzsche—or Christ. His philosophy was an exaltation of sentimentalism because he was a sentimentalist in person, not the other way round.

Insisting on a relationship between the philosopher and his philosophy may seem gossipy, intrusive, unfair, and unnecessary—until we come to Martin Heidegger, who was probably the most profound philosopher of modern times, but who was also an enthusiastic Nazi and even called Hitler "the new god"—and never apologized for it! Can this be dismissed as accidental?

With the possible exception of Nietzsche, I cannot point to a more pitiably diseased soul among philosophers than Rousseau. But Nietzsche at least had the integrity, consistency, and courage to be a martyr to his philosophy; Rousseau was a monstrous hypocrite. Also, Nietzsche truly suffered; Rousseau only pretended to. One of his lasting influences concerns educating children for life; and we know how he "educated" his: for death. His writings passionately exalt honor, honesty, altruism, friendship, virtue, women, family, and children—and in his own life he repeatedly maligned or destroyed every one of these things.

But how does this illumine his philosophy of the state and politics? Most directly. All who knew him saw him as a child. At first they naïvely saw him as naïve, as an innocent. They ended by realizing, to their great cost, that he was a brilliant savage. Since Rousseau was himself a child, he could never imagine bringing up children of his own, so he cast his "inconvenience" to the orphanage. *He did the same in his political philosophy, but there the orphanage is called the state.*

Like Plato, he saw education as the key to moral and social progress; and for him, as for Plato, the educator was the state, not the family. The state must educate not only children but also adults (for adults were only larger, cleverer children, like Rousseau himself). Thus the sweet and sentimental Rousseau became the father of modern totalitarianism.

We will summarize Rousseau's philosophy under six main headings:

a. Emotionalism vs. Rationalism
b. Man in the State of Nature
c. Freedom and Revolution
d. The Social Contract
e. The General Will
f. Totalitarianism

(a) Emotionalism vs. Rationalism

The two great sources of Western civilization are the biblical and the classical: Jewish and Christian religion and Greek and Roman philosophy. As to the first, Rousseau either did not understand it or simply did not believe it. (This would account for his four faked conversions.) As to the second, he knew it well enough to see the contrast between it and modern, narrow, scientific "Enlightenment" rationalism, but not well enough to understand its alternative notion of reason, which was far broader than that of either Rousseau or his modern philosophical opponents. So when he attacks modern "reason," he does not return to either the biblical or the classical versions of reason, especially the idea of a "natural moral law" known by reason (in the broader, older sense) rather than by feeling and emotion.

Feeling was where he thought both good morality and good politics resided. This emotionalism has been his most influential legacy, for today the typically modern mind classifies virtues like love, mercy, compassion, sincerity, honesty, and sometimes even truth as feelings, without realizing how radical a departure this is from both biblical and classical thought. Before Rousseau, no one ever wrote "I feel that . . ." instead of "I think that . . ." But now nearly all students write that way. For Rousseau, morality itself is based on neither faith nor reason but on feeling, especially the "natural" feeling of compassion, which he says ruled human life in the "state of nature" before the invention of civil society brought rationalism, artificiality, and individualism. Thus, no self-discipline, effort, courage, or choice is necessary for morality; it is just a spontaneous feeling.

Rousseau distinguishes "the good man" from "the moral man." The good man is superior. The moral man acts from moral duty and keeps his promises to friends, family, and country. The good man simply follows his instincts—and every innate, natural instinct is good, according to Rousseau. The good man is a friend and lover out of sentiment, not principle; he follows his feelings. He is a solitary dreamer, a lover of nature, unsophisticated, and idle. He despises money, science, war, and business. He is the salt of the earth; he is one of the few, not the many; he is not ordinary, but superior. He is Woodstock; he is Hollywood. Rousseau, of course, classified himself as a good man, not a moral man.

Thus, despite his sharp critique of everything modern—rationalism, science, sophistication, city life, the modern state, the arts—he was no traditionalist. In fact, he brought Western civilization much farther away from traditional thought, both classical and biblical, not back to it. He was the first postmodernist. "Postmodernism" is still a vague term that has almost as many meanings as it has defenders or critics; but at its heart is irrationalism, or at least anti-rationalism, and subjectivism, which are essentially Rousseau's reaction against the "Enlightenment."

There are many aspects of this anti-rationalism. One is the exaltation of the simplicity of ignorance. Thus, Rousseau exalted Sparta over Athens. Sparta, he says, was "as famous for the happy ignorance of its inhabitants as for the wisdom of its laws . . . eternal proof of the vanity of sciences," while Athens, he says, was "the seat of politeness and taste, the country of orators and philosophers."

(Actually, Rousseau would not have lasted two days in Sparta, while Athens would have felt like Paris and home to him.)

Another shocking point in Rousseau's anthropology is that man is not by nature rational, or endowed with reason. The "noble savage" is essentially a happy animal.

Still another is that man is not by nature political, or even social, but solitary and self-sufficient. In the "state of nature" man saw his mate as a casual and temporary sexual object, not as a co-founder of a family. (Rousseau's notion of this "natural" state conveniently matched his own behavior—and that of modern Western man.)

Rousseau's views on religion, while claiming to be pious and using some traditional Catholic vocabulary, pretty much matched those of his secular anti-religious friends. He attacked established religion as totally as he attacked established morals and politics. He rejected both reason and divine revelation as sources of religion, substituting a spontaneous religion of heart (i.e., feeling) rather than mind or will. "The essential worship is that of the heart. God does not reject its homage if it is sincere, in whatever form it is offered." (We must remember that for Rousseau sincerity is a *feeling*, not an intellectual or moral virtue of will and choice.)

(b) Man in the State of Nature

Rousseau's most famous idea is the fundamental point of his first publication: that "man is by nature good, and that only our institutions have made him bad." Although they are "our" institutions, we are not to blame for the harm done by them. And therefore, as Marx later argued, all problems are to be solved by changing institutions, by politics, rather than by changing man, by morality or religion. Man is a lettuce, not a potato: the rot comes from without, not from within. And therefore there is no reason to suffer the rot: revolution, not revelation or repentance, is the key to goodness.

This idea underlies everything in Rousseau. As he wrote, "The fundamental principle of all morality about which I have reasoned in all my writings . . . is that man is a naturally good being, loving justice and order; that there is no original perversity in the human heart." In other words, there is no such thing as sin. "All our first [natural] inclinations are legitimate." All wrongdoing is (1) involuntary, (2) forced on man by external causes, and (3) totally curable by our own power. The first of these three points (that vice is only ignorance) is from Plato; the second is from Adam and Eve (who blamed God, each other, and the snake); and the third is from Pelagius, the heretic whom Augustine and the Church condemned most strongly.

Already present in embryonic form in his first essay (conventionally known as the *First Discourse*), Rousseau's account of "the state of nature," and thus of human nature, is further detailed in *The Social Contract*. It is the polar opposite of Hobbes' account: a state of peace, not war; cooperation, not competition; happiness, not misery; free individualism, not tribalism; instinctive tenderness and compassion, not fear. By the fall, which Rousseau interprets as the invention of civil society, human nature itself was radically transformed; we live in an abnormal, fallen state. In that respect Rousseau's account is like that of the Bible's. But it was not rebellion against God that caused human misery, but against nature by the invention of civil society.

Thus, man is not by nature social or political. Nor is he by nature rational, or even capable of speech. Society, speech, and reason all stand or fall together, both for their supporters and for their enemies.

In the state of nature, man had no fear of death, since he had no concept of it. He had no need to fight, only to eat and copulate. He had no foresight and thus did not hoard or store wealth. He was idle and solitary, simply enjoying the bliss of being alive, sensing "the sweetness of his own existence." He had no vices, no pride or greed, but also no virtues; he simply did whatever he pleased. That is, he was "good," not "moral." There was no distinction between "is" and "ought," no law, no duty, and no conscience. There was natural self-love (*amour de soi*) but not vanity (*amour-propre*). Rousseau's "natural man" is, in short, Rousseau himself, as he conceived or fantasized himself.

Family and society stand or fall together, like seed and plant; therefore, in the state of nature there were no private families. Sex was casual, irresponsible, and non-jealous, like a modern college campus' "hookup culture." Mothers (but not fathers) cared for children, by instinct, until they were physically strong enough to be independent. There was no authority or hierarchy, no obedience or disobedience.

In the state of nature everyone was totally free, with "natural liberty" and equality. The noble savage "breathes only peace and liberty."

How did the "fall" into society and misery happen? Through man's free mind and will (as in the biblical account). But the fatal temptation was not sin but private property (as in Marx): "The first man who, having enclosed a piece of ground, bethought himself of saying *This is mine*, and found people simple enough to believe him, was the real founder of civil society. From how many crimes, wars, and murders, from how many horrors and misfortunes might not any one have saved mankind by . . . crying to his fellows, 'Beware of listening to this imposter, you are all undone if you once forget that the fruits of the earth belong to us all, and the earth itself to nobody.'"

Thus arose competitive selfishness, the gap between rich and poor, social inequality, and misery. Man freely gave up his freedom. "All ran headlong to their chains in hopes of securing their liberty."

Rousseau's Big Idea produced enemies both religious and secular. Voltaire wrote to him, "I have received your book against the human race, and thank you for it. Never was such cleverness used in the design of making us all look stupid.

One longs, in reading your book, to walk on all fours. But as I have lost that habit for more than sixty years, I feel unhappily the impossibility of resuming it."

But Rousseau's new anthropology was enormously influential. It was the primary source of nineteenth-century Romanticism. But did he mean his account as historical fact or as mere myth and abstract thought experiment? Evidently the former, but not literally and scientifically. He says at the beginning of his *Discourse on the Origin of Inequality* (the *Second Discourse*) that one must set "aside all the facts" in order to "judge properly" about man's nature and the state of nature by "meditating on the first and most simple operations of the soul" that we can discover, not in the past by science, but in the present by experience. The model and standard is not history but the heart: "Where could the painter and apologist of nature, today so disfigured and slandered, have found the model if not in his own heart?"

For Rousseau, as for Christianity, there was no returning to Eden, since human nature itself had changed. Only the select few, like great saints and mystics, the "solitary dreamers" like Rousseau himself, could even taste that lost paradise anymore—until, perhaps, a great political revolution threw off these chains and restored natural liberty and equality. That cataclysm came to France two decades after his death, and the West today lives amid the world of its constructions and destructions.

(c) Freedom and Revolution

Rousseau's *Discourse on the Origin of Inequality* was also, like the *First Discourse*, occasioned by the Academy of Dijon proposing an essay contest. This one was on the question "What is the origin of inequality among men, and is it authorized by natural law?" Rousseau (who did not win the prize this time) explained how the invention of private property was the culprit. Once all available land was enclosed, some had more than they needed and others had less; thus, envy and competition arose. What is new in Rousseau's account is that this situation is not natural or necessary. Society is to blame—the institution, not other people—for inequality, envy, artificiality, injustice, laws, governments, and force replacing freedom.

A radical corollary of this thesis is that virtually all existing governments are illegitimate: "Man is born free, and everywhere he is in chains." It was left to Marx to draw the conclusion: "Workers of the world, unite. You have only your chains to lose. You have a world to win." Unlike Marx, Rousseau believed in free will, not historical determinism and fatalism, so that our future is in our own hands collectively as well as individually. Implicitly, he called for the storming of the whole old order, for it was as much a prison for all as the Bastille was for a few.

(d) The Social Contract

Rousseau considered *The Social Contract* his most important book, but it was hardly read at all during his lifetime. It focuses on the primary political problem: that all civilized men are in chains, not just the exploited poor. "One thinks himself the master of others, but still remains a greater slave than they."

So the fundamental social and political problem is to unite the private good with the common good, the individual with the community: "The problem is to find a form of association . . . in which each, while uniting himself with all, may still obey himself alone, and remain as free as before." This association must be from the free will of all individuals; thus, it is free in its origin. It must be also free in its end, ensuring that individuals cease selling themselves into slavery as before. Mankind must be "forced to be free." (Sounds suspiciously Orwellian, doesn't it? Give up your rights and you will be free.)

The solution is a "social contract" in which each individual surrenders not just some but *all* his rights and powers to the community, which is a kind of single public person. This seems to create as powerful a public authority as Hobbes' Leviathan, though it is democratic rather than monarchical. But Rousseau conceives it as a new and perfect liberty.

Like most modern thinkers, such as Machiavelli, Hobbes, and Hume, Rousseau believes that morality is not natural but artificial and invented, that there simply is no natural moral law. Society creates morality. The creation of society was also the creation of morality. But amoral man must create society, and thus create moral man. How can morality come from amorality? How can more come from less? Rousseau's reply is that morality is not more but less; that the amoral state of nature is more, not less, than the moral state of civil society. Morality is a fall. Morality is created by something greater, not less, than itself: by freedom. Freedom, which is natural, is not subject to morality, which is artificial.

Morality does not restrict or define freedom. Freedom, since it creates morality, cannot be limited by moral laws. It is absolute. It is the only standard for political revolutions, since neither morality nor society, but only freedom, is natural to man. Man is not directed by his nature to any end. (Rousseau agrees with Hobbes here.) Freedom is not subject to human nature; human nature is subject to freedom. And human nature is malleable; it is changeable by two free choices: the past "fall" from the state of nature into present civil society, and the future redemption of present society by a new "social contract" and "the General Will."

This contract creates not just salvation from servitude but the savior itself, the "public person" whose will is the will of all. We must next consider this savior, which Rousseau calls "the General Will."

(e) The General Will

Unlike Hobbes' Leviathan, Rousseau's "General Will" is not a single concrete individual but a "spirit," a *Zeitgeist*. (It is therefore immortal; it cannot be killed, as a king or tyrant can.) It has no laws, no constitution, nothing to which it is subject. It is a rule of will, not a rule of law. It has no substantive philosophy of man, of good, of life, of meaning; whatever it wills is true, and good, and beautiful, simply because it willed it freely. If it decrees sadomasochism or cannibalism, these things become just, simply because they were decreed by it—that is, by unanimous free consent. It may decree rule by all, by many, by some, by the few, or by one; by a madman or by a philosopher; by a saint or by a sinner; but all must freely consent to the decree, and thus all are subject to it. And it cannot be criticized; there is no higher standard. It is, in fact, Rousseau's own soul writ large.

Since all individuals gave up all their rights to this entity, there can be no appeal against it, for there is no standard above it. It is divine, it is infallible: *vox populi, vox dei* (the voice of the people is the voice of God). It replaces natural law and natural right. It performs all that God and man, faith and reason, tradition and innovation, social institutions and individuals have in the past claimed to perform for man but failed. It brings heaven, or the closest possible approximation to it, to earth. It is the necessary and sufficient condition for human perfection. For, since there is no "original sin," man is perfectible.

The creation of this savior requires a "new man," a messiah who is the first one capable of putting the General Will above his own interests or those of any group, and who can persuade everyone to contract away all their rights. Rousseau calls him "the Legislator."

And since people are formed by laws as well as laws formed by people, Rousseau realizes how great the task of the Legislator must be: "He who dares to undertake the making of a people's laws ought to feel himself capable of changing human nature." He is not just a prophet, like Moses, who gives us a reminder of the law we forgot or disobeyed, but a savior, like Christ, who gives us a new birth, a new nature.

What of nonconformists in such a society? They are by definition wrong. An individual's will is right or correct not morally but politically ("political correctness"); i.e., it is correct when he wills the common interest rather than his own private interest. This is not the majority as opposed to the minority—that very distinction assumes the old regime of individual rights and interests—but the common, universal good as opposed to the individual, private good. (Each individual has given up *all* his rights to the state, remember, just as in Hobbes.) Whoever disagrees with the General Will is by definition wrong and must be compelled to obey it by the whole social body: "This means he will be forced to be free."

How is the common good, or the common interest, to be known? Not by voting, nor by reason, but (surprise!) by feeling, collective feeling. This is Rousseau's new notion of "conscience." It is not individual moral reason, but collective political feeling. He calls it the "infallible judge of good and evil which makes man like to God."

Like a hippie commune, "a State so governed needs very few laws; and, as it becomes necessary to issue new ones, the necessity is universally seen. The first man to propose them merely says what all have already felt."

The General Will is thus a subjective, collective, subconscious, and nonrational God that man created in his own image. It has absolute, total, and infallible authority. Rousseau calls this will "the Sovereign," and it is his radical solution to the fundamental social problem of how to reconcile and unite individuals and society, the private and the common good. The two are not mediated, nor is one preferred to the other, but they are absolutely identified. Whatever is willed by the General Will is willed by each individual will, because each individual freely created the General Will in the first place; therefore each individual, in obeying it, is really only obeying himself. In contrast, Rousseau felt that all obedience to God, to natural law, or to others' authority is incompatible with freedom. (This may be what Kant inherited from Rousseau in his notion of "autonomy.")

(f) Totalitarianism

Only those enraptured by Rousseau's emotional panegyrics to freedom can fail to notice that the regime he proposes as the guarantor of freedom is in fact the most absolute kind of totalitarianism ever invented. One can criticize and even assassinate a Caesar, a Genghis Khan, or a Hitler, but not the General Will. It is a ghost. It is his secular version of the Holy Ghost.

The General Will must order not just behavior *but also thought*. Contending philosophies, religions, moralities, or even sciences would produce disunity and must not be allowed. Philosophy and science both are dangerous because they seek universal objective truth by reason, and such truths could be used to criticize the laws and practices of society, which were arrived at by subjective will and feeling (hooray!).

Pol Pot absorbed a blend of the ideas of Rousseau and Sartre in Paris and applied them to Cambodia, where he became the only ruler in history to murder as many as one-third of his own citizens just to create ideological purity.

Rousseau believed that his new society would be peaceful and contented since everyone would have been educated to love it, by thought control. He wrote, "Those who control a people's opinions control its actions." The key to such control is compulsory public education. From infancy all citizens are taught to "consider themselves only in their relationship to the Body of the State. . . . For being nothing except by it, they will be nothing except for it." This is Mussolini's formula too: "Everything within the State, nothing outside the State, nothing against the State." The State would be the new parent. Thus, politics replaces family, morality, and religion, as in Marxism: "Everything is at root dependent on politics." For politics creates a new humanity, free from all evil. Since the origin of evil is political, therefore the solution is also political: "Vices belong less to man than to man badly governed."

Just as in Hobbes' alternative kind of totalitarianism, the state must also be the judge of religion, not vice versa. Only after we "give to Caesar what belongs to Caesar"—which is everything—can we "give to God what [*Caesar says*] belongs to God." Since most people are religious, the Legislator must learn how to use religious language to "sell" the new politics. The people will be impressed by the language of piety and the appearance of miracles. Once the new state is established, all religious teachings will be judged by the regime, never vice versa.

Not only thought, religion, and education but everything else, including manners, even apparently trivial matters of private enjoyment, of music and the arts, must be controlled by the state, as in Plato's *Republic*.

Private property is one of the most important of these. Rousseau did not quite clearly advocate its total abolition, like Marx, but like Marx, he saw it as the primary cause of all that has gone wrong in human history.

No "partial associations," no trade unions or voluntary neighborhood associations, are to be tolerated, not even a Society of Latin Letter Lovers or chess clubs. Nothing may be allowed to mediate between the individual and the whole, the state; thus nothing can dilute its divine authority. There are no rights reserved to individuals or families; all have been contracted away. It is the classic example of what Tocqueville called "soft totalitarianism." Subtract the hard violence from *1984* and you have Rousseau. It is *Brave New World*.

Every modern totalitarian employed propaganda and promised the people "true freedom." The fact that many scholars deny that Rousseau advocated totalitarianism tells us very little about Rousseau (except that he was a great propagandist) but very much about those scholars.

72

KARL MARX

AD 1818–1883

When Marx died, his collaborator Engels said in his funeral oration, "On the fourteenth day of March at a quarter to three in the afternoon, the greatest living thinker ceased to think." This is not an exaggeration if "greatest" means simply "most influential." The only person in history whose ideas ever conquered more of the world than Marx's was Jesus Christ. No philosopher in the history of the world has ever been more influential than Karl Marx. At one point in the twentieth century almost half of all the people in the world lived under officially Marxist regimes. Like the great religions of the world but like no other philosophy, Marxism captured the minds and lives of billions of human beings.

Marx constitutes and defines one end of the political polarity that dominates the modern world. The more to the "left" you are, the closer you are to Marx. And ever since Marx, the "lean to the left" has been the default position of modern intellectuals. Statistically speaking, the more educated you are, the more likely you are to embrace "leftist" positions on anything.

Yet no philosophy in the history of the world is directly responsible for more mass murders, genocide, terror, tyranny, oppression, and overall human suffering than Marxism. And no other philosophy has ever been proved more conclusively, decisively, and disastrously wrong about nearly everything it claimed to be true, both by philosophical reasoning and by the events of history. No other major philosopher has ever had such a blatant disregard for facts—he even coined the new word "ideology" for the reduction of truth to "political correctness." Rousseau is his only possible rival for personal dishonesty, hypocrisy, arrogance, and divinity complex. Schopenhauer is his only rival for a burning, apocalyptic hatred of everything that exists. One of Marx's favorite quotations is from Mephistopheles (the devil) in Goethe's *Faust*: "Everything that exists deserves to perish."

And *this* is the most well-known and successful philosopher in the history of the world. In 2005, Marx was voted the world's greatest philosopher by a large margin, not in Russia but in England, on BBC Radio 4. There seems to be a wee little puzzle here.

Life

Marx was born in 1818 in Trier, Prussia, to a middle-class Jewish family. Both his parents were children of rabbis and famous Talmudic scholars. Yet Marx was not only an atheist but also an anti-Semite. He received no Jewish education at all. His parents "became" Lutherans and had themselves and their six children baptized when Prussia decreed that no Jew could practice law or medicine.

Marx attended a secularized Jesuit high school, Bonn University, and Berlin University, the most prestigious in the world at the time. He transferred to Jena University, which had much lower standards, to get his degree, but he was never able to get any academic position. So he became a political journalist for various left-wing papers, which were constantly harassed by the conservative Prussian political and educational establishment.

In the universities he studied Hegel, who had just died in 1831 and who was regarded by almost everyone (except Schopenhauer and Kierkegaard) as the greatest philosopher of all time. Hegelians were divided into two camps. The Hegelian "radical" or "progressive" Left emphasized Hegel's historical relativism and the dialectical process, whose principle of growth by negation required all institutions to be dissolved and changed. The Hegelian "conservative" or "establishment" Right emphasized Hegel's worship of the established political order as part of the necessary march of history and as divinely ordained—though to label this state totalitarianism "conservative" today is as grotesque as calling communists "capitalists."

The short, ugly, dirty, arrogant, and angry Marx wooed and married his youthful love, the beautiful, rich, auburn-haired Jenny von Westphalen, daughter of a Scottish baron. (Women also fell for Sartre and Rousseau, but they were French, so they had an excuse.) Marx's money management was so incredibly bad that his parents-in-law refused to support him and Jenny. They lived in desperate, dirty poverty most of their lives and had to frequently move from town to town and country to country (Prussia, Germany, France, Belgium, England) to escape government persecution of communists. They had seven children, four of whom died in infancy of malnutrition. Marx's apartments were dirty. His clothes were dirty. His body was dirty, and full of painful and ugly boils and carbuncles. When his long-suffering Jenny, who loved him to the end, got smallpox, he called *her* "a rhinoceros, a hippopotamus."

They lived the last half of their lives in London, where Marx spent nearly every day for decades in the Reading Room of the British Museum gathering data to support (and ignoring or altering data that did not support) his economic theories, which he finally published in Volume I of *Capital* (*Das Kapital*). (Engels edited and published Volumes II and III after Marx's death, from his thousands of pages of notes.) He thought it his masterpiece, and quite scientific, although it is verbose, pedantic, disorganized, illogical, factually erroneous, and conclusively disproved by the events of history, both before and after Marx. It is a book based entirely on books, not at all on real people, jobs, factories, etc. Marx, the great attacker of factories, never once in his life visited one. And Marx, the great champion of the proletariat, despised them, refused to listen at communist meetings to any real proletarians who had real-world experience, and never had any friends who were not of the bourgeoisie.

Character

Marx was irresponsible, scatterbrained, unpredictable, obsessive-compulsive, and spectacularly inefficient, especially with money: classic symptoms of ADD. But these features often exist in "absentminded professors" who are kindly and benign. Marx, however, (1) was obsessed with violence, (2) was demanding of total power and control, (3) was shamelessly exploitative of all other persons, and (4) had little respect for truth and honesty. He explicitly reduced reason to rationalization and propaganda—even though, ironically, he claimed that his was the world's first "scientific" philosophy of human life and history. As another famous German who spectacularly influenced the twentieth century reminded us, Big Lies work better than little ones; propaganda works best when it is the most shameless.

These character traits exactly describe Marxist regimes in the state as well as in the individual soul, confirming Plato's insight that these two locales for justice or injustice—states and souls—are by nature mirror images of each other.

The most striking example of Marx's exploitation of others is probably "Lenchen" (Helene Demuth), the dwarfish girl who worked as a maid for the Westphalen family, and later for Marx and Jenny. She was never paid a cent. She was the only proletarian Marx ever knew personally—all his communist friends were intellectuals from the bourgeoisie. Marx "knew" her also carnally, but he never acknowledged his proletarian son, Freddy, who never knew who his father was. Freddy was forbidden to use the front door and could see his mother only at the back, in the kitchen. Yet Marxists argue vociferously for "equality" and "justice," and the name of the most famous Marxist newspaper, *Pravda*, means "truth."

Like Rousseau, Marx either subdued and dominated or picked angry quarrels with everyone he ever met, especially those who loved and helped him most. His most typical conversational stance was roaring and bellowing, with dirty hair flying and fists clenched. He had a jarring voice, no manners, a contemptuous tone, and tiny, malicious, suspicious eyes. His most typical expression was "I will annihilate you." Of the three kinds of friendship Aristotle famously distinguished, Marx formed only those of utility, not of pleasure or virtue. And this was almost always *political* utility, except for Jenny. (And even she was useful to him, for she kept his notes legible and in order.)

Marx combined Rousseau's emotionalism, apocalyptic utopianism, and verbal power with Machiavelli's militarism, pragmatism, and willingness to support terrorism and assassination. In one of his poems in *Oulanem* (1839), Marx wrote, "I shall howl gigantic curses at mankind," whom he called "apes of a cold God." In the early work *German Ideology*, admiring the violence and terror of the French Revolution, he looked forward to a day of judgment "when the reflections of burning cities are seen in the heavens . . . when the 'heavenly harmonies' consist of the melodies of the *Marseillaise* and the *Carmagnole*, to the accompaniment of the thundering cannon, while the guillotine beats time and the inflamed masses scream *Ça ira, ça ira*, and self-consciousness is hanged on the lamp-post."

Passages like this probably show more clearly than all his technical historical and economic arguments why Marxism was so feared by ordinary people, who are instinctive "conservatives" (by definition, those who want to *conserve* things)—and so loved by radical intellectuals. Marx called for "a merciless criticism of everything existing . . . a collision with all established powers." For this reason, writing, for him, is not science but propaganda, "not an anatomic knife but a weapon. Its object is its enemy, which it wants not to refute but to destroy." Marx is not a scientist with a theory to test, but an infant in a tantrum, a rhinoceros with lowered horn.

This passionate hate was directed primarily against two virulent scapegoats as its objects. Marx and Hitler shared one of Marx's two hated enemies: the Jews. The other was the bourgeoisie, the middle class, capitalists—which for Marx was almost another way of saying "the Jews." Marx's anti-Semitism, unlike Hitler's, was not racial but economic. He equated the Jews with money and had a burning personal hatred of this mysterious thing that he was remarkably incompetent and irresponsible in making, handling, saving, keeping, or repaying. (So naturally, his philosophy derived everything, even ideas, from economics!) He never even attempted to get a decent-paying job, and the pittance he made from his political journalism kept his family desperately poor all their lives. They lived largely on inheritances from their dead parents and loans from his best friend Engels, with whom he wrote the famous *Communist Manifesto*.

Marx especially hated usury (i.e., interest on loans, which he continually took out and could not repay), and therefore capitalism, and therefore the Jews. In an early essay, "On the Jewish Question" (1844), he wrote: "Money is the jealous god of Israel, beside which no other god may exist. Money abases all the gods of mankind and turns them into commodities. Money is the self-sufficient value of all things. It has deprived the whole world, both of man and of nature, of its own value. Money is the alienated essence of man's work and his being. This alien being rules him and he worships it. The god of the Jews has become secularized and has become the god of the world." When Marx broke his friendship with Lassalle, his former socialist supporter, he called him "a greasy Jew disguised under brilliantine and cheap jewels." He wrote, "The emancipation of Jews is the emancipation of humanity from Judaism . . . from huckstering and money." The communist revolution "would make the Jew impossible."

Marx, like Nietzsche, blamed the Christians even more for exacerbating the evils they inherited from the Jews. Christian society had succumbed to Jewishness. But in later life his scapegoat for all the world's evils largely changed from "the Jews" to "the bourgeoisie," the middle class, as his thought changed to become more abstract and "scientific" rather than concrete and "humanistic." (He was never really either scientific or humanistic.) Whenever he utters the word "bourgeois" in print, you can feel hot spit on it. "That is a bourgeois idea" is his supreme insult that ends all appeal and all argument. His disciple Mao Zedong wrote that the idea of a natural, objective truth before which all were equal was itself "a bourgeois idea."

Epistemology: "Scientific" Philosophy

Epistemology centers on two questions:

1. What *is* human knowledge? How does it work?
2. What *ought* it to be? What is the criterion for truth? *How* do we know?

Marx's answer to both is *ideologism*. Knowledge is not correspondence to reality, by either reason or sense experience, but a reflection of the will to power of the ruling class. (Thus, it is Nietzsche, with his idea of the sovereignty of the "will to power," who reveals the heart of Marxism, rather than Marx.) And once communism is in power, that is also what it *should* be: conformity to the will of the communist party by action, not to the nature of objective reality by reason. He famously wrote that "philosophers have only *interpreted* the world. The thing, however, is to change it."

Marx claimed to be the first to apply science to human history, to do for history what Newton did for physics and Darwin for biology. "Scientific" is the word he uses to distinguish his philosophy from all others.

But central to Marxist philosophy, as a consequence of his materialism, is the idea that ideas as such, and therefore all ideas (logically including scientific ones, and including that idea itself) are merely ideological fabrications, a "superstructure," a kind of icing on the cake. The cake is real, material, and economic; the icing is thought. The cake never rests on the icing, the icing always rests on the cake.

Marx invented the word "ideology" to express this central claim of his philosophy: that not truth or thought but material forces, and in the last analysis economic forces, are the total cause of all ideas and values.

The idea is, of course, immediately self-contradictory; for if *all* ideas are discredited as claims to any objective truth that could be proved by reason and evidence, then that very idea—that all ideas are such—is equally discredited, for it is an *idea*. If all reasoning is ideological rationalization, so is that reasoning. Yet Marx continued to claim that his ideas were "science" (i.e., proved by evidence).

Marx's reduction of ideas to ideologies has proved extremely influential among modern intellectuals, even non-Marxists. The first question typically asked by both academia and media today about any idea is never whether it is true or false but how and where and why it originated, especially what class interests it reflects and promotes.

This has been labeled "a hermeneutic of suspicion." ("Hermeneutics" means "theory of interpretation.") The central idea of the philosophy today called deconstructionism is the idea that ideas (or "text") are not intentional, not signs of any objective reality ("world"), but merely things, forces, or powers that some people use to control other people. This is a sophisticated version of the Marxist "hermeneutic of suspicion." Some deconstructionists have called logic itself a plot by dead white European heterosexual religious male chauvinists.

Marx's claim to be "scientific" is grotesque. In fact, nearly all the "evidence" Marx found for his theories about history, politics, and economics, collected during tens of thousands of hours in the British Museum, was highly selective and deliberately ignored massive counterevidence. (For instance, he claimed that capitalism necessarily worsens both the working conditions and the income level of proletarians; statistically, it almost always does exactly the opposite.) Some of his "evidence" and quotations were deliberately falsified. For Marx began not with data but with dogma—his ideology—and spent all those hours in the British Museum looking for any data he could possibly use as propaganda for it, ignoring any data to the contrary.

It is not certain whether Marx actually believed that his own ideas were objectively true and thus the only exception to his own epistemological rule about all ideas being mere ideologies (that seems unlikely, for that is an obvious self-contradiction), or whether he saw them simply as power plays, propaganda ploys to overpower other minds (that seems much more likely, given his lust for power).

Metaphysics

Marxism is classified as "dialectical materialism," as distinct from Hegel's "dialectical idealism." Thus, Marx is said to have "turned Hegel upside down." According to Marxism, all of human life, history, and culture are determined not at all by ideas but totally and simply by the mode of production of material goods. "The sum total of the relations of production constitutes the economic structure of society, the real foundation on which rise the legal and political superstructures and to which correspond [N.B. *not* "which correspond to"] the definite forms of social consciousness. The mode of production in material life determines the . . . political and spiritual processes of life. . . . It is not the consciousness of men that determines their existence, but on the contrary their social existence determines their consciousness." Consciousness is a passive reflection in a mirror. It does nothing. Invisible things never move visible things, only vice versa. Chesterton calls this the superstition that the trees make the wind, in his classic essay "The Wind and the Trees."

Either Marxist consciousness is the one exception to this rule (Why? Is it alone outside the cycle of history? Is it a divine revelation from above?), or else it, too, is only a passive reflection of Marx's own social existence. But Marx's social existence, both his background and his life, was bourgeois! He says that "the ideas of any era are always those of the ruling class of that era, i.e., . . . nothing more than the idea-expression of the dominant material relationships." But it is not clear how then he can account for nonconformists and radicals in any era, especially the communists themselves. How can he account for himself?

Like Hobbes, Marx never even attempted to give a single reason, premise, proof, or evidence for his materialism. It was his "fundamentalist" dogma, which he considered unquestionable and self-evident to any sane mind: "Does it require deep intuition to comprehend that man's ideas, views, and conceptions, in one word man's consciousness, changes according to every change in the conditions of his material existence?"

This lack of logical justification never troubled him because for him it was only the foolish, non-Machiavellian philosophers who tried to "interpret the world; the thing is to change it." And "the class that has the means of material production at its disposal, has control over the means of mental production." Thoughts are controlled by matter rather than vice versa. Ideas are the products of factories, not vice versa.

What, however, can possibly be meant by either "true" or "false" then? "The question whether objective truth can be attributed to human thinking is not a question of theory, but is a practical question. It is practice that proves the truth." "Praxis" is the Marxist term for this. It means, quite bluntly, that truth is whatever works to move the masses to revolt and embrace communism. Truth is whatever changes society in that direction. That was the philosophy of *Pravda*, the Russian communist newspaper whose title meant "Truth": that ideas are not labels to describe what is; they are little dynamite sticks to destroy what is and to bring into existence what isn't.

Simple and absolute materialism simply denies the existence of immaterial ideas. This is immediately self-contradictory, like a man saying, "I do not exist," since materialism is an idea, an "ism." Most materialists, therefore, like Marx, are modified materialists, or epiphenomenalists. This means that thought exists, but only as epiphenomena. ("Epi" means "on top of," like a flea on a horse or like icing on a cake—or, more aptly, like a label on a package.)

Epiphenomenalists admit that ideas exist but deny that they have any causal power; they are only effects. They are passive, like images in a mirror. They are like the heat generated by electricity running along a wire: it does not do any work, as the electricity does, but simply dissipates into the air, like the puff of smoke that comes from the tailpipe of a car—or like a fart. "The fart theory of thought" is the most memorable way to remember this idea, and I think a very just and appropriate one.

There is, of course, a blatant contradiction between saying that ideas are only passive effects and saying that they are powerful little dynamite sticks of propaganda. But that is itself only a logical, theoretical difficulty, and Marx simply did not care about logic, truth, or theory, but only about practical political power. Marx habitually does not *deduce* conclusions or give *proofs*, but *announces*, like a prophet.

Anthropology

Marx's materialism naturally and instinctively leads him to deny the existence of (1) any soul, mind, or spirit; (2) especially God, or divine spirit; (3) any otherworldly or after-death reality, so that all human hopes reside in this world's future; (4) free will (Marx's version of determinism is historical and economic determinism); (5) any universal, unchanging human nature (human nature itself changes when economic systems change); and even (6) individuality or personality. He is a collectivist, since the collective whole is larger, stronger, and lives longer than the mere individual, and because individual personality, or "I"-ness, is not a material object and does not fit into the metaphysics of materialism. As the communist tells Dr. Zhivago in the movie, under communism, "the personal life is dead."

Philosophy of History

The central feature of Marx's philosophy of history is that history's essence is oppression and conflict between economic classes. Until communism abolishes all classes, the fundamental relationship between them must be rivalry. For money cannot be shared without loss to the sharers; only spiritual goods can do that. Matter, unlike spirit, is essentially competitive. Two chunks of matter cannot occupy the same space at the same time, and a few loaves and fishes cannot feed five thousand people without a miracle. But if materialism can be transcended, two persons can enrich rather than impoverish each other with knowledge, love, joy, humor, beauty, or any other spiritual goods. The essence of Marxist metaphysics is the denial of everything spiritual.

History, like all matter, must be deterministic, not free; for Marx, there is no room for freedom of choice in materialism. The stages of history are fated. It moves through five dialectical stages: (1) primitive communism, (2) slave societies, (3) medieval feudalism, (4) capitalism, and (5) communism. Stage 5 can emerge only from capitalism, because capitalism reduces the classes to two, thus making possible a classless society through the elimination of the bourgeoisie. Feudalism had too many classes to allow any one of them to eliminate all the others.

Thus, Marx has an ambivalent attitude toward capitalism: it is his hated enemy, but it has performed the valuable service of destroying the previous order. Marx calls this precapitalist order "romantic" and "idyllic"—but this is meant as an insult to precapitalist society, not a compliment! Marx has even less sympathy for medieval feudalism than for modern capitalism, and he praises capitalism's ruthless destruction of "idyllic" feudalism because "the enemy of my enemy is my friend."

The final, communist consummation of history, according to Marx, will put an end to the dialectic and to historical change itself, because there will be no classes left, and thus no class conflict, and class conflict is the agent of all historical change. The final stage of history will presumably last forever.

This last stage will be preceded by a transitional stage that Marx calls "raw communism," or "crude communism," which will abolish private property but not greed. In fact, it will universalize greed and envy and use these motives to cut down the rich and reduce everything to an absolutely equal level. The communist will simply be the universal capitalist. Culture, freedom, humanism, art, religion, law, politics, the family, morality, and human rights will all be ruthlessly suppressed, by force, by this "dictatorship of the proletariat." For all these things, according to Marx, are children of capitalism and enslave man to money. Dictatorial power will be needed to exterminate all vestiges of capitalism.

Then, magically, the oppressive proletarian government will voluntarily "wither away." Heaven on earth will emerge, a world without greed, envy, or oppression. The formula for this utopian social order will be "from each according to his ability, to each according to his need." In other words, selfish, greedy, materialistic tyrants and dictators will create a society of perfect, unselfish Christian saints. (You may wonder: How could anyone believe this? Remember the "Big Lie" theory!)

The first communist stage will be what Tocqueville called a "hard totalitarianism," but the second, final stage will be what he called a "soft totalitarianism," eerily similar to Rousseau's General Will. Individuality and specialization, having been suppressed by force in the first stage, will not return in the second. The will of "society" will replace the will of individuals. "We" will replace "I." Society will not contain the *specialization* that was the root of the *competition* that was the root of *class conflict*. There will be no "alienation" (a key but vague Marxist concept) of man from himself, his fellow workers, or his work. There will be no division of labor and thus no capitalist-style individualism. In this utopia, not individuals or groups but "society" will regulate everything: "Society regulates the general production and thus makes it possible for me to do one thing today and another tomorrow, to hunt in the morning, to fish in the afternoon, raise cattle in the evening, criticize after dinner, just as I have a mind, without becoming a hunter, a fisherman, a shepherd, or a critic." Imagine the Harvard philosophy department running the Pentagon, or the Dallas Cowboys teaching nuclear physics. And this will work and last forever.

If you believe that, you have probably already bought the Brooklyn Bridge.

Ethics

Marx simply has no ethics. The only salient point he makes about morality is that it changes as economic society changes, so that there is no common, universal, unchangeable morality. Communist ethics has a radically and totally different set of values than capitalist ethics. For communism changes human nature itself.

Theology

Marx is not just an atheist but a "secular humanist atheist." In his earlier, more Hegelian phase, he was intoxicated with the idea that man is God—an idea he derived from the insight that in Hegel's philosophy God is not independent of man, that everything Hegel says about God, or "the Absolute," is really meant about man. This is a genuine insight on Marx's part: that Hegel probably was, indeed, an atheist, if judged by the standard of traditional Judaism or Christianity.

The "Young Hegelians" or "Hegelians of the Left," who formed Marx's early philosophical development, were closer to Nietzsche than to Democritus or Hobbes: man without God is not a mere bug but a superman. For if (1) there is no transcendence and independence of the Absolute in Hegel, but (2) there is an Absolute, and its development is within the human sphere, then (3) man is the true God. But history and society had not yet realized this, and the Hegelian Left saw it as their high and holy destiny to prophetically announce to man his own divinity, not just by argument but by world revolution. Though Marx abandoned the Hegelian language later, he never abandoned this messianic and apocalyptic spirit.

Objections

Marx answers various objections to communism in the *Manifesto*. Each objection takes the same form: that communism abolishes something good (private property, individuality, motivation for work, culture, the family, private education, private marriage, nations, religion, morality, and all eternal truths). His answer to each is the same: capitalism has already abolished these things and subjected them all to money. There is nothing common to (1) precapitalist, (2) capitalist, and (3) communist versions of them; all of these concepts are equivocal.

Thus, logically, it is the last objection, the one Marx himself regarded as the *least* important, that is the key to all the others: if there are no unchangeable and universal "eternal truths," it is impossible to compare capitalist and communist versions of any of these things by any common universal standard. Logically, it is nominalism that is the culprit again, as so often before in modern philosophy (Hobbes, Locke, Berkeley, Hume).

We can summarize the specific objections to Marxism as follows, in random order.

1. It is based on deliberate lies. Just to quote one of many: when Marx wrote in the preface to the *Manifesto* that "communists of various nationalities have assembled in London and sketched the following Manifesto," there was no meeting in London and the only communists Marx knew were his little circle of friends.
2. This is not accidental, because "truth" is reduced to "ideology." Truth is what works, not what is real. So, logically, if that idea does not work, it is not "true"! We can prove communism *false* simply by not *believing* it.
3. This ideologism, in turn, logically follows from Marx's materialism. Psychologically, the causality was clearly the opposite: the motivation of power came first, and the materialism was a convenient rationalization for it. A rationalization is the opposite of a reason, as propaganda is the opposite of honest search for truth.
4. Marxism's claim to be "scientific" is absurd, for three reasons. First, Marxism is a praxis, *not* a theory, by his own admission. Second, it is not based on data and evidence. Third, it is not refutable, not testable or falsifiable, even in principle. Any theory immune from possible refutation is a religious dogma, not a scientific hypothesis. It is based on faith, not reason.
5. It may not be falsifiable in principle, but it has been falsified in fear. It is contradicted by the facts of history. Every major prediction Marx made was falsified by history: capitalism worked; workers liked it; factories were improved; communism took hold only in developing places like Russia and China, not

industrialized places like Germany and England. It did not eliminate classes and institute equality. It did not last forever but collapsed from within in 1989.

6. Even the technical apparatus of *Capital* is almost universally rejected by all economists outside Marxist circles, especially its "labor theory of value."
7. Marx's historical determinism contradicts his appeal to workers to freely choose to unite to create the revolution. Why fight for the inevitable? Why risk and sacrifice for something as necessary as tomorrow's sunrise?
8. If all ideas are products of the economics of the society out of which they came, then Marxism is 100 percent bourgeois, because Marx and all his friends were not members of the proletariat but of the bourgeoisie. So according to communist theory, communism is thoroughly bourgeois! Marx kicked out of his party all proletarians who had actual work experience and practical workplace goals.
9. Communism did not arise from history but from pure theory, from books. Everything Marx knew about the real world he knew from books, not real people, real factories, real experience, or real money management.
10. All of history, for Marx, is class conflict and exploitation. Yet very few people before Marxism felt it. They felt cooperative at least as often as they felt competitive. Marx tells all previous human beings that they were really full of envy, hate, and greed even during the times when they felt and acted cooperatively. Like Machiavelli, Marx ignores half of human experience. It is a one-sided and squint-eyed anthropology that reveals little about *anthropos* but much about the anthropologist.
11. And then, in his utopianism, he ignores the other half. Total selfishness will suddenly turn into total unselfishness. What will motivate the dictatorial communist state to "wither away"? What will infallibly turn sinners into saints? Even God can't solve that problem. Neither Jesus, Buddha, Muhammad, Confucius, Moses, Socrates, nor Lao Tzu created a utopia on earth. Is it likely a dirty, selfish, lying, violent, hate-filled, power-hungry, apocalyptic poet will?

    Human nature is obviously neither totally selfish nor totally unselfish. Marx's account of past history (totally selfish) and future utopia (totally unselfish) are equally unrealistic.
12. Marx's purely empiricist and materialist epistemology is self-contradictory, for we do not see, as empirical data, the truth of this theory (or of any other, for that matter). Mere empiricism is not itself empirical. It is an idea.
13. Another, similar contradiction inherent in materialist epistemology is this: If all thoughts are merely material forces, they are simply things, like pistons in an engine. But thoughts are thoughts *of* things, not just more things. How can one of the pistons be either true or false about the other ones?
14. What material criterion distinguishes true ideas from false ones? Are true thoughts brown, or square?

15. Marx's nominalism and his notion that human nature itself is malleable disallows any appeal to human nature as the standard for preferring communism, and disallows any comparison between capitalist man and communist man, for there is no common essence, as Marx himself insists (no "species-being," is his technical term for it); therefore, it is logically meaningless to call one superior to the other, since there is no common standard to measure both.
16. Social nonconformity is impossible by Marxist theory, since it is social determinism. The consequence of determinism is conservatism, not radicalism. Social radicalism, whether of a communist revolutionary or a Christian saint, is a form of nonconformity. It is countercultural thinking and behaving. So communist theory makes communist practice logically impossible.
17. If there is no free will, Marx's thoughts are no freer than those of a drunk with delirium or brain damage. Why should we listen to people whose tongue cannot choose how to wag?
18. How can there be a moral appeal to justice if everything is simply matter? If there is no "ought"-reality superior to the "is"-reality, why transform the "is" into what "ought" to be? Why is anything, even oppression of workers, "wrong"?
19. Epiphenomenalism contradicts experience. We directly and indubitably experience the thought to move our lips not just as the effect but as the cause of moving our lips.
20. The abolition of private property, which is the first and most important change Marx lists in his *Manifesto*, always has and always will produce laziness. No one keeps public toilets as clean as his own.
21. The abolition of families, which Marxism called for but never succeeded in implementing anywhere, even when it ruled half the world, would be the abolition of the only place we are loved not for our workplace performance or utility but for our very person. Thus, love would disappear from the world, and selfish greed, far from being abolished, would conquer.
22. All Marxist "utopias" in history have proved to be exactly the opposite of their promises of happiness, prosperity, peace, and freedom. Marx appealed to history to verify communism. That is the most damaging appeal he could possibly make.
23. To create his beloved utopian future, Marx wanted to destroy everything everyone (except Marxists) loves in the present. That is like producing pacifism by violence, or cooling by fire. As a means to creating perpetual peace, Marx would be willing to murder all non-Marxists.

Communism's Appeal

Twenty-three is a pretty large number of basic objections. What accounts for the popularity of Marxism? There is no mystery about the cause of its seventy years in power—it is the lust for power among dictators. And there is no mystery about its decline—it is that only the dictators loved it. But what accounts for its continual appeal, in modified and "humanized" form, among modern intellectuals? Of all the philosophies in history, Marxism has more unanswered questions than any other. Yet of all philosophies in history, it has captured the lives of more of the world's peoples, and the minds of more of the world's most famous intellectuals, than any other. How can this astonishing paradox be understood?

I believe it is Nietzsche rather than Marx who can answer that question. It is the "will to power," not the will to truth, that is the attraction of Marxism, and it is this will, this new *summum bonum*, that, ever since Bacon, has dominated modern man, both rich and poor, both capitalist and communist, both philosopher and non-philosopher. Marxism is a nuclear weapon. Every nation wants it, even though it is the most dangerous and destructive invention in the history of mankind. To have undermined this force, to have defused this weapon, to have won the "cold war," to have passed through 1989, is to have saved the world—unless the victors, too, succumb to it.

It is fitting to finish this volume with Marx. For he is not only radical but apocalyptic. Also, though there are significant political philosophers after Marx (Mill, Niebuhr, Rawls), none have anything like the influence of Marx. He remains a pole of the "left-right" dialectic that defines modern political thought.

It will be very obvious to the reader that I find the ideas of Hobbes, Rousseau, and Marx both philosophically shallow and practically destructive. By comparison, Machiavelli seems almost harmless, honest, and refreshingly innocent.

There are no personal political agendas or hidden assumptions behind this evaluation. The evidence, both logical and experiential, for these unfashionably negative opinions about these fashionable thinkers is laid out in detail in the above chapters.

Conclusion

Unlike ancient philosophy, and unlike medieval philosophy, modern philosophy has no conclusion. It goes on.

It also turns into its opposite, postmodernism—a catch-all term with almost as many meanings as you want it to have (which in a way is almost the very meaning of "postmodernism").

It also bifurcates in the twentieth century even more severely than it did between the seventeenth and nineteenth centuries (think of Pascal vs. Descartes and Kierkegaard vs. Hegel) into two very different kinds of things, both of which call themselves by the same name, "philosophy"—i.e., two different concepts of what philosophy itself is, viz., the English "analytic" and the "continental" (existentialist, phenomenological, and humanistic).

These two "philosophies" resemble each other about as much as a sparrow and a locomotive (which is what they often sound like, respectively). The two streams have become less severely critical of each other and have stopped ignoring each other, but there is no identifiable contemporary philosophical school that even attempts to do the kind of philosophy done by Plato, Aristotle, Augustine, Aquinas, Descartes, or Kant—namely, to combine clarity and profundity, logic and life. Some representatives of both the analytic and continental traditions have even suggested that philosophy is dying. Most of the early analytic philosophers thought they had effectively and definitively refuted and destroyed the very enterprise of traditional philosophy, especially metaphysics. Heidegger saw Nietzsche as philosophy's undertaker.

But, as Étienne Gilson noted, "Philosophy always buries its undertakers."